Leadership Development

*Paths to Self-Insight
and Professional Growth*

SERIES IN APPLIED PSYCHOLOGY

Edwin A. Fleishman, George Mason University,
Jeanette N. Cleveland, Pennsylvania State University
Series Editors

Manuel London
How People Evaluate Others in Organizations

Manuel London
Leadership Development: Paths to Self-Insight and Professional Growth

Robert F. Morrison and Jerome Adams
Contemporary Career Development Issues

Michael D. Mumford, Garnett Stokes, and William A. Owens
Patterns of Life History: The Ecology of Human Individuality

Kevin R. Murphy and Frank E. Saal
Psychology in Organizations: Integrating Science and Practice

Ned Rosen
Teamwork and the Bottom Line: Groups Make a Difference

Heinz Schuler, James L. Farr, and Mike Smith
Personnel Selection and Assessment: Individual and Organizational Perspectives

John W. Senders and Neville P. Moray
Human Error: Cause, Prediction, and Reduction

Leadership Development

Paths to Self-Insight
and Professional Growth

Manuel London
State University of New York at Stony Brook

Psychology Press
Taylor & Francis Group

New York   London

Cover design by Kathryn Houghtaling Lacey

Library of Congress Cataloging-in-Publication Data

London, Manuel.
Leadership development : paths to self-insight and professional growth /
Manuel London.
    p. cm.
    Includes bibliographical references and index.
    ISBN 0-8058-3851-1 (cloth : alk. paper) — ISBN
    0-8058-3852-X (pbk. : alk. Paper)
    1. Leadership. 2. Executives–Training of. I. Title.
    HD57.7.L663 2001
    658.4'07124–dc21   2001023024

Books published by Lawrence Erlbaum Associates are printed on acid-free
paper, and their bindings are chosen for strength and durability.

Printed in the United States of America

10 9 8 7 6 5 4 3

For my wife, Marilyn,
and my sons, David and Jared

About the Author

Manuel London is professor and director of the Center for Human Resource Management in the Harriman School for Management at the State University of New York at Stony Brook. He is also associate provost for Enrollment and Retention Management at Stony Brook. He received his A.B. degree from Case Western Reserve University in philosophy and psychology and his M.A. and Ph.D. from the Ohio State University in industrial and organizational psychology. He taught at the University of Illinois at Champaign for 3 years. He was then a researcher and human resource manager at AT&T for 12 years, before moving to Stony Brook. His books include *Self and Interpersonal Insight: How People Learn About Themselves and Others in Organizations* (Oxford University Press, 1995), *Job Feedback: Giving, Seeking, and Using Feedback for Performance Improvement* (Lawrence Erlbaum Associates, 1997), and *360 Degree Feedback: A Tool and Process for Continuous, Self-Directed Management Development* (co-edited with Walter Tornow; Jossey-Bass, 1998). London is a consultant to business and government on areas of competency modeling, performance evaluation and management, and employee attitude surveys, including 360-degree feedback, coaching, and career development programs.

Contents

SERIES FOREWORD

Edwin A. Fleishman
George Mason University

There is a compelling need for innovative approaches to the solution of many pressing problems involving human relationships in today's society. Such approaches are more likely to be successful when they are based on sound research and applications. This Series in Applied Psychology offers publications which emphasize state-of-the-art research and its application to important issues of human behavior in a variety of societal settings. The objective is to bridge both academic and applied interests.

This book, "Leadership Development: Paths to self-insight and professional growth," by Manny London, presents a view of leadership that is solidly grounded in psychological theory and research and recognizes the centrality of self and interpersonal judgment to effective leadership. Unlike other leadership books that take a "how to" approach, this book recognizes that there is no simple formula for effective leadership. Leaders discover this for themselves. To do so, they need an accurate view of their strengths and weaknesses, organizational requirements and situational conditions, and others' capabilities. Self-insight is the key to this process, because leaders need to understand themselves—their own motivations, interests, and abilities—before they can assess others and make sound judgments.

Dr. London is especially qualified to write this book. His research and practice focus on how managers and leaders see themselves, how they evaluate and make decisions about others, and how they enhance their own and their subordinates' career growth. His work on feedback processes, career development, and continuous learning come together here to explain how leaders develop self-insight and use this insight to improve their own performance and build effective teams. London's focus on leadership competencies in high technology and emerging businesses makes this book all the more timely as leaders struggle with understanding what it takes to be successful in a highly competitive and changing economic climate.

London begins the book by defining the meaning of effective leadership in today's organizations and explaining why self-insight is important to leadership effectiveness. Self-insight helps leaders regulate their behavior, maintain their motivation, and overcome barriers to job performance and career growth. Self-insight and self-regulation are the foundation for establishing a meaningful career identity as a leader and developer of people and organizations. This identity is likely to change as the leader moves into different roles and life stages.

Leadership development is a systematic process that begins with assessment of organizational needs, leadership capabilities, and developmental gaps. London shows how leaders can use this evaluation to formulate development plans and identify needed support programs. Meaningful feedback is important for these development plans to work. Readers will learn how to give feedback that is constructive, behaviorally focused, and non-threatening. This will help leaders not only to seek, but actually welcome feedback. It will also help them provide constructive feedback to their subordinate managers.

The book describes popular techniques such as 360-degree feedback, executive coaching, and a variety of training programs that support leadership development. In addition, the book helps leaders consider ways to overcome career barriers, become continuous learners, and, more broadly, be diplomatic leaders grounded in a sound set of management and personal values.

The book is for individuals in leadership positions, human resource managers, management training and development professionals, organizational researchers, and students. It can be used as a supplementary text in courses on leadership, organizational behavior, training, career development, and human resources management. It should interest anyone who wants to better understand the factors that are critical to effective leadership.

PREFACE

Self-awareness is key to being a responsive and effective leader. Effective leadership requires that leaders know how others react to them, what others expect from them, whether others believe they are doing a good job, and what they can do to improve. Leaders' learning about themselves and their environment is a continuous process that is largely under their control. This book explores the ways leaders gain and use self-knowledge for continuous improvement and career development. As such, it explains how leaders can help themselves and their coworkers understand themselves and become more self-determined, continuous learners, and make the most of resources (e.g., feedback and coaching) to foster their own continuous learning and development.

The book addresses questions, such as:

- What are the distinguishing characteristics of an effective leader?
- Do leaders see themselves as others see them?
- Do leaders welcome and seek information about themselves?
- Do leaders vary their behavior depending on the situation? Are they responsive to others' needs and expectations?
- Do leaders understand what the organization and their coworkers expect of them?
- Are leaders clear about what they expect from the people who report to them?
- When do leaders have self-control; under what conditions are they self-motivated?
- Are leaders motivated to learn more about themselves?
- When leaders receive information about themselves, do they put it to good use or ignore it?
- How do leaders react when the going gets tough, that is, when things are stressful or they do not get the job or promotion they expected?

Self-awareness is seeing yourself in an objective way. It is an important basis for being a self-confident and sensitive leader, on the one hand, or an egotistical and manipulative one, on the other. This, in turn, influences the way others see you—as responsive, energetic, self-motivated, and visionary; or as self-serving, Machiavellian, demanding, and confused (or confusing).

As leaders gain information about themselves, they attend to it, interpret it, absorb it in their self-concepts, and then apply it to change their behavior appropriately. Often, however, leaders are overly defensive, resistant, or too shy to even listen to feedback about themselves, let alone understand and use it.

Learning to use feedback puts leaders on track to become continuous learners. Using feedback and becoming a continuous learner allows leaders to benefit from their leadership experiences, transfer this learning to new situations, and improve their leadership effectiveness. The key to this process is self-understanding.

This book explains how leaders take advantage of the resources, such as feedback and coaching, to gain and use self-knowledge. Most organizations have a variety of means to give feedback and provide support for continuous learning and career development. Managers evaluate their subordinates' performance and meet with them for formal performance reviews about important aspects of jobs. Others' opinions may be available from employee attitude surveys or 360-degree feedback surveys in which subordinates, peers, and customers provide ratings. Also, a leader may be expected be a coach as well as an evaluator of performance. As a coach, the leader tries to guide direct reports through constructive suggestions and by acting as a sounding board for new ideas.

The book draws on my research, practice, and writings concerned with the ways leaders learn about themselves and others in organizations. Consideration is given to how leaders' self-insight, resilience in overcoming barriers, and sense of identity are keys to career motivation. The book examines ways leaders can enhance the value of 360-degree feedback. It also covers ways to coach leaders to become self-directed and continuous learners, as well as how leaders can increase their employees' welcoming and seeking feedback. Directions for principled, diplomatic leadership as a model of responsive management and self-regulation are also provided. Finally, cases of leaders' experiences are included throughout.

This book differs from my earlier Erlbaum books in several ways. My book, *Job Feedback* (1997), examines the psychological, methodological, and procedural aspects of giving and receiving feedback, including survey feedback instruments like 360-degree feedback. That book is intended for industrial and organizational psychologists and their students. My book, *Career Barriers* (1998), has its foundation in counseling psychology and centers on the ways people in a variety of occupations, organizational levels, and career stages deal with a host of career discontinuities. It was written for people facing potential or actual barriers, as well as professionals and students in career planning and development. The current book on leadership development is aimed at leaders, human resource managers, management training and development professionals, organizational researchers, and students. It could be used as a supplementary text in courses on leadership, organizational behavior, training, career development, and human resources management.

The material here focuses on leaders and leadership competencies in high-tech and emerging businesses (e.g., dot com enterprises and global firms). The book has a solid foundation in recent research and practice in the area of feedback and other "paths to self-insight." The attention is on developing leaders and the leader's role as coach and developer. The book's contribution is to highlight the importance of feedback and coaching in developing self-insight and recognition of changing organizational expectations. Providing a solid foundation for coaching is especially important. Although very popular, the existing coaching literature is of a simplistic "how to" nature. This book draws on research, theory, and data to explain why coaching works and how it can be made more effective.

This book complements my edited Erlbaum book, *How People Evaluate Others in Organizations: Person Perception and Interpersonal Judgment in I/O Psychology* (London, 2001). This work draws on social cognition and person perception from social psychology to examine how people perceive and make decisions about each other. The current book on leadership development calls attention to self-insight—that is, how people perceive and make decisions about themselves to foster their development.

This book begins by explaining why leaders need support for self-insight and professional growth in today's environment. The introductory chapter explores dimensions of effective leadership given business, technological, and economic trends. With this description of leadership demands as a foundation, the book then moves to psychological processes that underlie leadership development. From chapter 2 on, the book is divided into three sections. The first section focuses on leaders' self-concept. The three chapters in this section define self-insight, examine the meaning of internal strength and resilience for self-regulation, and consider how leaders attain a sense of identity. The second section demonstrates how organizations establish development programs to support these psychological processes. The five chapters in this section outline leadership development as a comprehensive, continuous process, including evaluating organizational needs and individual competencies, setting goals for career development and performance improvement, offering needed training and growth experiences, providing feedback, and tracking change in behavior and performance over time. Other chapters focus on elements of this process: how people react to feedback, the 360-degree feedback survey method, coaching, and programs that put these support elements together in a formal way for leadership development. The third section considers challenges and opportunities for leadership development. These include types of career barriers and ways to overcome them, what it means to be a continuous learner, and a leadership model for contemporary society: the principled, diplomatic leader.

I would like to express my appreciation to Jan Cleveland, professor of psychology at Pennsylvania State University, for her thoughtful and constructive comments on an earlier draft of this book. Also, I want to thank my colleagues Edward Mone at Cablevision, Valerie Sessa at the Center for Creative Leadership, James Smither at LaSalle University, and Gerrit Wolf at the State University of New York at Stony Brook for their insights and inspiration for exploring leadership development in a changing world. Finally, I am grateful to my wife, Marilyn, and sons, David and Jared, for their steadfast love and encouragement.

—Manuel London

1

Introduction: Dimensions of Effective Leadership

Pick up a newspaper most any day, or go to the news section of any popular internet platform or search engine, and there will be stories about major organizational changes. It is not even necessary to go to the business section. Leadership challenges are front page news. These range from e-commerce start-ups to expanding competition in industries that had been monopolies. This chapter sets the stage for the book by examining business trends, and the implications of these trends for needed leadership skills. Transformational, adaptive, and enabling leadership are emphasized as keys to effective leadership in the changing business environment. The chapter also considers the implications of these trends and key leadership dimensions for state-of-the-art leadership development programs. It then highlights the themes of the book, in particular, the focus on the importance of leaders' insight into themselves and their environment and how leaders need to take responsibility for their own development and support the development of the people who work for and with them.

BUSINESS TRENDS

The Evolving World Order

Most individuals in the business professions, as well as those in other lines of work, are aware of, and keenly feel, the increased pressure of the rapid pace of change. Consider the following trends: Many businesses are multinational. They have operations that produce and sell products and services around the world. They own foreign subsidiaries and form joint ventures with companies in a variety of nations. This poses challenges for the leaders of these firms to under-

1

stand negotiations and partnership relations that cut across cultures. Leaders need to be sensitive to cultural differences in ways of doing business and, more simply, interacting with others. Moreover, they need to manage this diversity in a way that creates value for their companies and profit for their shareholders.

Populations within countries are becoming more diverse. This is true in the United States, Canada, Germany, and the United Kingdom, as well as Denmark and other Scandinavian nations that tended to have a homogeneous population. As the population in a country becomes increasingly diverse, the diversity of employees as well as customers and suppliers increases. The cultural sensitivity that contributes to good business practice around the world also applies at home—wherever that is. Moreover, leaders themselves are more diverse because they come from diverse backgrounds. This suggests the need for leadership development that recognizes these different backgrounds. For instance, special programs and support may be needed for leaders (and leaders-to-be) who are women or people of color. What unique challenges do they face as a result of cultural stereotypes and biases? What support do they need to overcome these barriers and meet the challenges of leading dynamic businesses?

Most everyone is aware of the challenges of rapidly advancing technology. The internet, although still in its infancy, has blossomed as a source of information and a channel of commerce. E-commerce will evolve as technologies develop and become more integrated. Already, video, audio, and graphic applications have been merged as computer power grows. The internet brings self-service applications to the desk top without having to purchase and install separate software. This offers more vibrant avenues for conveying ideas and delivering all sorts of products, including education and leadership development, to everyone's interactive computer or television.

Leadership of e-businesses and dot.com companies requires dynamic new vision, communication, and decision-making capabilities to establish initiatives and respond to dynamic environments—including the ups and downs of the stock market and a highly competitive marketplace, all of which add up to a vibrant economy. It also requires excellence in tried-and-true business and management skills that are taxed more than ever to cope with information overload and other stresses and demands brought about by new technology. For instance, the various dot.com businesses may no longer need the traditional bricks and mortar to do business. However, leaders of these firms are often surprised to face some of the same strains that confronted their ancestors in the early 20th century. For instance, online superstores or specialty shops may need large warehouses and inventories, real people to answer customers' questions and handle their problems, and access to traditional delivery mechanisms. Also, these companies have to compete in a highly competitive marketplace, where customers can compare prices in an instant no matter how remote their location.

Global business, new technologies, and the competitive marketplace demand high quality, flexible, integrated operations. New organizational structures have evolved. They are less hierarchical and functionally split than the traditional bureaucratic organization. Work gets done where it is needed. People are assigned to work teams where their skills and experience can be of most value, regardless of their current organizational level. Consultants are brought in when required. Organizations seek continuous improvement, and they form teams to bring about change and monitor improvement. Considerable work gets done in teams. Sometimes these are virtual teams, in that the members are geographically dispersed. Members communicate via technology, rather than in-person, although they may meet occasionally.

New work structures impose new directions for leadership. Leaders must know how to create new organizational designs to match their goals. They need to oversee the evolution of these business structures as market, economic, and technological conditions change. Whereas some organizations may have stable structures, or perhaps a core structure that is relatively static, they may also have a more fluid support structure, drawing on resources within and outside the firm as needed. This requires new management systems to chart progress, manage performance, and enhance motivation of employees, many of whom may be temporary and have more allegiance to their own careers and disciplines than they do to the organization employing them at the moment.

Implementation of new technology is also a challenge. For example, consider what it takes to implement a new integrated data system to replace a myriad of separate data systems that have developed independently over a number of years. An organization may have separate systems for placing customer orders, ordering from suppliers, tracking operations, and managing human resources. New distributed computer technology and web access provide the opportunity for self-service so that customers, suppliers, and employees can get the information they need and use this information by interacting with the system directly. Designing such an integrated, enterprise-wide data system requires input from functional experts in all departments of the organization as well as technical expertise from systems managers. Developing the new system may be a top priority for the leadership of the business, but the organization still needs to keep the old, "legacy" systems operating as the firm continues to do business. More staff may be needed, but labor markets are likely to be tight, especially for talented individuals with the needed knowledge and experience. Even if they can be found, there is the challenge of integrating new, perhaps temporary, people into the organization and getting them up to speed. Although the new system may have many benefits, hoped-for cost savings and fewer employees may never be realized. Moreover, the strains of technology implementation may continue because the systems continue to evolve with technology. So the implementation is never fully complete. Leaders have to recognize the value of new technologies, communicate why they are needed, and convey enthusiasm for the initiatives while employees are asked to do more work with fewer resources.

Leaders need to ensure that sufficient resources are devoted to educating employees about the new systems. This means more than simply training employees on how to perform their specific functions using the new technology, but on the ways their jobs and the technology fit within the overall flow of work throughout the organization and between the organization and suppliers and customers. This education is needed so that employees understand the implications of their performance for the business, and how their actions affect everything else. Otherwise, they may not be bothered if they make a small mistake or delay their own work (Wheatley, 2000). Such an attitude can be the downfall of the entire work process, and indeed, organization mission and bottom line. Leaders need to be able to communicate this enterprise-wide perspective and have the patience and resources to ensure that employees have this comprehensive understanding.

Summary

Business challenges have implications for leadership behavior and leadership development. These challenges include the following: The world economy and diversity at home requiring skill to conduct business in a multicultural environment; new technology and its effects on business channels; and new, flexible organizational structures, including geographically dispersed, virtual teams striving for continuous quality improvement. In addition, leaders need to value continuous learning for themselves and their people. Next, consider in more detail how these changes and new demands on leaders influence skill and knowledge requirements and opportunities for leadership development.

TRENDS IN LEADERSHIP SKILL AND KNOWLEDGE REQUIREMENTS

A recent job ad for a leader of a consulting firm specializing in helping e-commerce companies integrate management and technology stated that the firm was looking for someone with the following personal strengths: "relentless commitment to client satisfaction, drive, professional integrity, skills and experience in project management and business process re-engineering, openness to change and experimentation and not blinded by his or her expertise and particular discipline, strong communication skills (written and verbal), exceptional analytical skills, interpersonal effectiveness in all business environments and at all organizational levels." Clearly, leadership is much more than setting direction and organizing and monitoring work. It is a direct product of the development of new technologies, shifting market demands, and the anticipation of continuous change.

Transactional Leadership Skills

This section establishes a comprehensive picture of the actions leaders must take and the corresponding skills they require to meet the challenges of today's complex organizations. The discussion samples the contemporary literature written by experts in leadership and management development.

E. C. Murphy (1996) reported the results of a study of more than 18,000 managers at 562 large and small organizations in a variety of industries in the United States and around the world. The research identified 1,000 respondents who showed exceptional leadership abilities, and then evaluated the qualities that distinguished them from others who were not as successful. Key leadership skills included identifying and selecting talent, networking, solving problems, being able to evaluate people and programs fairly and accurately, negotiating, resolving conflict and healing hurt feelings, guarding and enhancing resources, and promoting synergistic working relationships.

Napolitano and Henderson (1997) outlined the leadership skills needed to deal effectively with an ever-changing business environment. They included self-leadership (exploring values and perspectives), adhering to a set of business values such as integrity and honesty, facilitating individual and team performance, managing across departmental and organizational boundaries, creating a corporate culture, anticipating the future, and taking responsibility for their own development and learning how to learn.

Yukl (1997) presented a broad survey of theory and research on managerial leadership. He discussed leading teams, leading change, and developing leaders. Leadership, according to Yukl, involves formulating strategies, delegating (participative leadership), developing effective relationships with subordinates, acquiring and using power and influence, and being flexible as the situation changes (knowing how to vary behavior to meet the needs of the moment).

Hirshhorn (1997) proposed the need to rework leadership in the postmodern organization marked by turbulence and redefinition. The way people work, the skills they need, and the kinds of careers they expect are changing. For instance, people are expected to dedicate more of themselves to their jobs—that is, to do whatever is needed, often at the expense of family. Hirshhorn's new culture of authority is one in which leaders recognize their dependence on their employees, and indeed, employees can challenge their authority. Leaders need to create a culture of openness as they gain a better understanding of how their own identities and those of their employees are tied to work. Also, leaders need to be tolerant of individual differences, learn from failure, and give employees who fail second chances.

Hitt (2000), writing about managerial challenges in the new millennium, suggested that unprecedented and continuous change, driven by globalization and the rapid development and diffusion of new technology, requires a new leadership mind-set. Executives need to harness advances in e-commerce, artificial intelligence, and knowledge management. Also, they need to hire and develop people who can think creatively as they generate and apply new knowledge and develop global perspectives.

Characteristics of Successful Leaders. In trying to predict leadership success, some research has considered variables that contribute to early career success. McCall (1998) identified five background characteristics that distinguished successful from failed executives:

1. *Track record:* Most people who were promoted to the executive suite had a strong record of success, at least a consistent record of positive bottom-line results.
2. *Brilliance:* Successful executives were perceived to be uncommonly bright in a technical or functional specialty or in a general skill such as the ability to solve difficult problems or analyze complex situations.
3. *Commitment/Sacrifice:* Successful executives were seen as loyal to their company. This is evident in a willingness to work long hours and accept whatever assignments come along.
4. *Charisma:* Successful executives were likely to be highly affable. Often, this is especially evident in their behavior with people at higher levels in the organization.
5. *Ambition:* Successful executives showed hard driving ambition. They wanted to be an executive, and they were willing to do whatever it took to make it happen.

Hernez-Broome, Beatty, Nilsen, Scott, and Steed (2000) identified dimensions of leadership success by asking how top leaders see themselves and other executives. Using data from top executives who participated in the "Leadership at the Peak" development workshop sponsored by the Center for Creative Leadership at the Colorado Springs training institute, participants were asked to describe critical incidents of effective and ineffective leadership, including what led up to the situation, what the leaders did in the situation, and the outcomes. They collected 256 incidents. Expert readers identified the key dimensions of performance evident in the incidents. These were primarily other-focused. Three of the most important dimensions of effective leadership were "motivating," "problem solving," and "planning and organizing." These were fairly observable aspects of leadership. Other dimensions that emerged as important were "ethical behavior and decisions," "risk taking," and "interpersonal skills." Less important dimensions were "clarifying roles," "informing," "monitoring," "recognizing," and "mentoring."

The research also showed that leadership is not just top-down behavior. Leadership dimensions generally focus on what leaders do in managing others, but leadership also includes self-management (e.g., managing one's emotions) and managing the climate in and outside the organization (e.g., managing customers).

An example of a effective, ethical action reported by Hernez-Broome et al. (2000) detailed a chief executive officer (CEO) who was building a firm's operations in the Middle East, where corporate bribes are a common way of doing business. The CEO informed the foreign business partners that such payments or gifts were explicitly against the policies of the company. Instead of losing business, the CEO actually expanded the company's contracts and profitability in the Middle Eastern countries. This demonstrated to executives in the corporation that clear communication and recognition of shared values resulted in positive gain for the firm.

An example of effective risk taking involved a CEO who saw an opportunity for business expansion but recognized that resources were insufficient to make the required investment. Undaunted, the executive took the risk of building a product prototype and establishing a delivery schedule to suit a client's needs. The order was placed, and the CEO was able to borrow the money to achieve the promised delivery date.

An example of negative interpersonal skills was a CEO who reprimanded employees in front of others. An example of positive interpersonal skills was a CEO who respected others' needs, was aware of the effect he had on others by virtue of his position, and created a climate for open communication by prompting open discussion of how people in different departments saw each other.

Transformational Leadership Skills

Tichy and Devanna (1997) described how companies—such as Chase, General Electric, and Chrysler—revitalized their corporations into peak performers. These researchers viewed the leader as a social architect who makes bureaucracy behave and motivates people. These leaders transformed their large, lumbering corporations by overcoming resistance to change, creating a new vision, diagnosing and defining problems, creating a motivating vision, and mobilizing commitment to the change and new mission.

Bass and his colleagues (Bass, 1999; Bass & Avolio, 1994) distinguished between *transactional* leadership (i.e., the effective use of management systems and practices, such as goal setting, performance review, and feedback) and *transformational* leadership (i.e., engaging employees as partners in the design and implementation of a new vision for the organization). Transactional leadership works well when the organization needs clarity, structure, communication, and focus on bottom-line performance, whereas transformational leadership works well when the organization needs major change in response to rapidly evolving markets and technologies. Transformational leaders develop people through delegation and empowerment. They make them responsible and accountable for corporate goals, and then get out of their way. They may introduce processes, such as total quality management as a vehicle for encouraging employees at all levels and functions of the organization to spearhead and/or participate in identifying and implementing improvements for enhanced organizational outcomes.

During the 1980s and 1990s, the focus of leadership moved from maintenance of the status quo to generating change. Kotter (1996) argued that the pressures for change will only increase in the next decade. However, popular management methods (e.g., quality management, reengineering, right sizing, restructuring, cultural change, and turnarounds) fall short because they do not change behavior, at least not enough (or fast enough) to keep up with technological, global, political, economic, and competitive forces. Kotter related corporate experiences and role models of leaders who brought about needed change in their organization. Personality flaws, such as big egos, can undermine successful change. Kotter emphasized the importance of teams to organizational change, and the importance of lifelong learning for individual leaders. He outlined eight key elements of leadership: establishing a sense of urgency; creating a guiding coalition or team; developing a vision and strategy to get there; communicating the vision; empowering employees for action across the organization; generating short-term wins that can be celebrated; recognizing and benefiting from gains (e.g., importing knowledge learned in one part of the organization to other parts) and producing more change; making new approaches, and the concept of continuous change and improvement, part of the organization culture.

Transformational Leaders as Developers.   Whereas transactional leaders produce results by setting goals, clarifying expected outcomes, giving feedback, and rewarding successes, transformational leaders produce results by arousing inspirational motivation, providing intellectual stimulation, showing consideration for individuals, and helping people achieve their potential and reach higher levels of accomplishment (Dvir, 2000). This last element of transactional leadership focuses on developing others (Avolio & Bass, 1988). Transformational leaders evaluate employees' potential, and envision what needs to happen to expand their responsibilities. Instead of setting goals to achieve (the transactional approach), the focus is on supporting a developmental process to help individuals achieve higher levels of responsibility and favorable outcomes (the transformational approach).

Transformational leaders develop people by motivating them, appealing to their sense of morality, and empowering them to make decisions (Dvir, 2000). They arouse needs for self-actualization by presenting challenges, not resolving problems. They demonstrate the organization's moral values and encourage people to transcend their own self-interest for the sake of the organization (e.g., moving people's focus and attitudes from an individualistic to a collectivistic orientation). In addition, they promote people's active engagement in the task by giving people a chance to exert initiative and by rewarding self-starters.

Building Partnerships with Employees

Moxley (2000), argued persuasively that passion and drive are crucial to livening the spirit of the workplace. Leadership drives employees' spirit—the life force or vital energy that excites employees and helps them maintain enthusiasm for their life's work. Lack of energy causes many employees to loathe their jobs and find their lives lacking in spirit. Leaders have the power to set the tone for the entire organization. Relying on coercive power and expecting others to do nothing but follow, leaders can sap the life energy out of their organization, controlling by reward or punishment. However, in today's competitive environment, organizations cannot afford beleaguered workers. Instead, leaders can offer workers partnerships, sharing leadership throughout the organization. As mutual partners with the people they lead, executives share the power and, along with it, their goals. Purpose, responsibility, and respect are shared at all levels. Some leaders fear the loss of control, but they should recognize that their power is only as good as the employees who are willing to abide by it. Partnerships work by sharing ownership, authority, and accountability. Employees in partnership with executives feel energized and inspired by their organizations.

Consider the Silicon Valley company, Calico Commerce, which lost 80% of its stock value in less than 6 months (Berenson, 2000). Turnover at other high-tech firms was high given the free-agent culture of the Valley in which people look out for themselves. But at this company, only 15 of the 330 employees left. The firm's stability, despite the stock meltdown, was a result of the company's understanding and respect for employees that went far beyond promises of riches. Employees, from Alan Naumann, the CEO, to administrative assistants, believed in the company and were willing to stick with it through thick and thin. Despite losing hundreds or thousands of dollars, at least on paper, employees were confident that the organization, a maker of software that helps companies sell products over the internet, would succeed in the long run. Their confidence rested in their feeling of being part of a management team that understood the business and respected employees. This respect was shown by realizing that employees had lives outside of work. The company recruited college graduates who fit with the culture. Management did not confuse loyalty with obedience or fear.

Leadership is tested at the edge, sometimes as a result of disastrous situations. For instance, Malden Mills suffered a devastating fire in December 1995. Aaron Feuerstein, head of the company, vowed at age 70 to rebuild the mill in order to save employees' jobs rather than to retire on the insurance proceeds (Andrews, 2000b).

Consider, too, the story of the 1914 British Imperial Trans-Antarctic Expedition led by Ernest Shackleton. The group expected to cross Antarctica on foot in 3 months. But, Shackleton and 27 crew members spent 600 grueling days in endless cold, near starvation, and with almost no shelter before returning to the island in the Southern Ocean from which they originally set sail. Writing about this expedition and the lessons that can be gleaned from Shackleton's leadership, Perkins, Holtman, and McCarthy (2000, described in Andrews, 2000b) portrayed a leader obsessed with the welfare of his crew. Shackleton maintained equity and mutual respect, saving the most difficult tasks for himself.

The actions of today's executive heroes may not be as dramatic, but they are still meaningful and effective. For instance, in turning around AT&T's Global Business Communications Systems, Pat Russo gave subordinates her home telephone number as an effective symbol of her personal commitment, trust, and need for communication with the rank and file (Andrews, 2000b).

Adaptive Leadership

Another approach to leadership that is closely tied to a transformational approach stems from the idea that leaders need to be flexible in the styles of behavior they adopt. The complexity of organizations and differences between people with whom the leader interacts and depends necessitate behaving differently in different situations. This is *contingency management*, or *adaptive leadership*.

Albano (2000), a leadership trainer and consultant, argued that adaptive leadership is an active form of leadership based on mutual influence, growth, and learning. Organizations are adaptive systems in complex environments, rather than mechanistic, standardized systems that operate by fixed rules and predictable situations. Whereas mechanistic organizational structures are bureaucratic and functionally structured, adaptive organizational structures are fluid, temporary, and change in design depending on need.

Albano (2000) contrasted mechanistic with adaptive leaders. *Mechanistic* leaders focus their attention on activities. Job descriptions are long and detailed. Role expectations are narrow and rigid. *Adaptive* leaders concentrate on adding value and producing outcomes, not doing activities. Adaptive leaders have intentionally broad-based job descriptions to allow them flexibility. Also, adaptive leaders recognize that one activity may substitute for another. Adaptive leaders are proactive, envisioning opportunities and finding resources and then taking advantage of them. They collect differing views before making important decisions. They study their environments, generate alternatives for action, and experiment with them, often taking reasonable risks. They are open to new ideas and are lifetime learners. They are innovative and entrepreneurial. In general, they develop their organization's capacities to learn and evolve.

New leadership strategies and modes of operating are needed to respond to shifts in societies, markets, and technologies. Unfortunately, many leaders have trouble because they are used to solving problems alone, and, in general, they find change stressful. Heifetz and Lauder (1997) explained that adaptive leaders do things differently. Instead of providing answers, they ask difficult questions. Instead of protecting people from outside threats, they allow employees to feel the stress of reality as a way of prompting them to change. Instead of educating employees in current roles, adaptive leaders disorient them so that they form new relationships. Instead of limiting conflict, they draw issues out. Instead of maintaining norms, they challenge the way they do business and help employees understand the difference between values that are immutable and historical practices.

Heifetz and Lauder (1997) offered six *principles for adaptive leadership:* (a) Work hard while maintaining a perspective on the whole situation. Do not get swept up in the press of daily work. Be able to identify conflicts about values and power. Recognize procrastination and work avoidance. Look for other positive and negative reactions to change. (b) Identify the adaptive challenge, that is, what needs to be changed. (c) Regulate distress. Do not let it get out of hand. Yet let people feel stress. One way to achieve this balance is to place people in a "holding environment"—a temporary place, such as an off-site workshop, where managers with different views can discuss real problems and develop ideas for strategic and operational change. (d) Maintain disciplined focus to the challenges at hand. Counteract distractions that arise because people resist change (e.g., finger pointing about who's to blame or arguments over who should do what). (e) Delegate the work back to the people who know how to do it. Involve them in the process of change. Trust them to respond appropriately. Make them a part of the transformation. (f) Allow adaptive leaders to emerge from lower levels in the organization. Ensure they have a voice that is not squelched because they are suggesting doing things differently and raising a need that others, especially those at higher levels of the organization, may not see.

Adaptive leadership is not like solving a technical problem by driving to a solution and convincing others to get on board (Heifetz & Lauder, 1997). Adaptive leaders do not provide the solutions. They engage others in the process of learning and allow others to take responsibility for solving problems. They recognize that adaptive change is distressing and this distress needs to be experienced and managed. Adaptive leaders give others credit for being emotionally mature and able to step up to the plate when it comes to ambiguity, conflict, and responding to a shifting environment.

Forceful and Enabling Leadership Styles

Similar to the concept of adaptive leadership, Kaiser and Kaplan (2000) viewed leadership as a function of versatility—the ability to adapt to competing demands. Effective leaders need to be able to apply at least two types of leadership: Sometimes they need to be assertive and forceful. Other times, they need to be supportive and enabling. The need to adapt leadership style to changing demands is all the more important in a constantly changing business environment (e.g., a shifting global economy, rapid technological innovation, and demographic diversity). This requires leaders to be behaviorally complex. However, executives tend to be aggressive and self-assertive or relational and enabling.

That is, they tend to be "lopsided" in their leadership style, and even find the opposite style aversive. Those who are enabling shy away from assertiveness, and those who are assertive believe that a relationship orientation is ineffective and a waste of time (Kaplan, 1998).

Kaiser and Kaplan (2000) characterized the personalities of forceful leaders as aggressive, competitive, critical, dominant, intense, outspoken, and self-assertive. They described enabling leaders as appreciative, cautious, caring, compassionate, gentle, mildly responsive to others, and understanding. Leaders tend to be one or the other, but those who are strong in one of these styles to the exclusion of the other are less likely to be effective than those who can use both styles, that is, those who have the behavioral complexity to balance competing demands of these different styles. Similarly, leaders who disengage (i.e., shy away from building relationships and forcing behavior) are not likely to be effective, especially in demanding situations.

Using a 360-degree feedback survey (ratings from the superior, peers, subordinates, and managers themselves), Kaiser and Kaplan (2000) asked employees to indicate whether their managers had "too little," "the right amount," or "too much" of characteristics associated with enabling and forceful behavior. Forceful leaders were those who were evaluated as having too many (i.e., "too much") forceful characteristics (e.g., leading visibly, making touch calls, pushing people hard, and forcing issues) and too few (i.e., "too little") enabling characteristics (e.g., receptiveness, compassionate, understanding, and fostering harmony). Enabling leaders were just the opposite—they had too many enabling characteristics and too few forceful characteristics. Versatile leaders had the right amount of both enabling and forceful characteristics.

Kaiser and Kaplan's (2000) survey results showed that forceful leaders were not likely to be enabling leaders, and vice versa (i.e., there was a negative relation between forceful and enabling behaviors). Also, more executives were overly forceful than overly enabling (i.e., forcefulness was the dominant style among executives). A minority of executives were versatile—able to balance forceful and enabling leadership. In addition, leaders who lacked versatility on forceful and enabling behavior were less likely to be effective than those who were versatile.

Inspirational Leadership

Another approach to leadership is based on the leader's charismatic personality. Patricia Wallington, former chief information officer of Xerox Corp., captured this idea in the concept of inspirational leadership (Wallington, 2000). She described a leader she remembered as inspirational as a person who always made time for her, never solved her problems but provided guidance in the form of principles that could be used in different situation (e.g., "Kill your enemy with kindness"), and encouraged her by praising her strengths. He made her feel she could accomplish anything, and to her, that was inspiration. More generally, she outlined the following eight characteristics that draw people to a leader and a project, inspiring energy and involvement:

1. *Passion and vision*: Inspirational leaders have a deep interest in their work, and they find the words to capture others' imagination.
2. *Will and determination*: They are intent on accomplishing their goals.
3. *Courage*: They take on the "big idea" without worrying "what's in it for me."
4. *Confidence*: They welcome reasonable risks and learn from failure.
5. *Caring*: They empathize with others, understand their motivations, and meet their needs.
6. *Charisma*: They are social, extroverted personalities who draw people to them, or they have low key personalities that build rapport and inspire devotion.
7. *Authenticity*: They mean what they say.
8. *Connectedness with people*: They listen intently with open minds and learn from everyone.

Inspirational leaders take on risky projects because they are passionate about the possibilities and the potential positive outcomes. They create a mystique around the project, helping others to see it as a chance of a lifetime. As a result, people stand in line to volunteer and participate actively with real commitment (Wallington, 2000).

A Situation Ripe for Inspiration.   When is inspirational leadership needed? Consider a rather mundane situation begging for inspirational leadership but that did not get it. Actually, this situation is fairly typical of many organizations engaged in implementing enterprise-wide data systems. A university was implementing a new, comprehensive, integrated student data system. This was to replace separate data systems for admissions, financial aid, billing, registration, and advising/degree audit. The old systems operated on the school's mainframe computer. They were designed at different times with different software, and they did not interface well with each other. The new data system would be based on a single, Windows-design, run on servers, and accessible through the internet for most applications. Also, it would connect with other new systems being implemented to run other parts of the enterprise, in particular, finance and human resources.

The university staff was faced with several difficult problems in fitting the software to the school's policies and procedures: (a) The software was new and had a lot of bugs to be worked out. (b) The administrative departments did not have many professionals to spare to work on the system as functional specialists. The budgets were lean and mean, and there was little slack in operations. The departments had all they could do to keep regular operations in production, let alone design a new system. Although a few technical consultants were brought in as needed, the professionals' knowledge of the school's policies was needed to retrofit the new system to the university. (c) The administrative areas did not feel that the university's information systems department was providing sufficient support to the project. Also, the administrative areas worried that the technical support would not be sufficient once the new systems were in operation. They feared they would be left high and dry by the technical wizards when problems occurred. (d) The administrative staff also worried that the university would not spend the money to hire the staff needed to operate the new system, which required more time for data entry than did the old systems. (e) Some administrative staff had been working part time on the new software for several years, and they had not seen the fruit of their labors. They were already burned out and other administrative departments were just beginning their work under tight time pressures. (f) The logical person to lead at least one major part of the effort had serious doubts about whether the new system would work and was very reluctant to take the initiative to move the process forward. He had the knowledge and the role, but not the motivation. Letting him know that the project depended on him was not enough to inspire him, let alone get him to inspire others. He had the ability, but he did not have the interest or energy. Moreover, he did not believe in the system and the possibilities. The likely result: The university would continue to muddle through the project development without this inspiration. This would take more time, and entail more psychological pain and aggravation than necessary. Eventually, the system would be fully installed, but without the seize-the-opportunity excitement and energy that could suggest new applications and efficiencies.

Principled Leadership:
A Style that Transcends Situation

Maxwell (1999) distinguished between understanding leadership and actually leading. These are two different but—of course—related things. Character is the key quality that distinguishes effective leadership from merely understanding leadership. Aspects of a person's character activate and empower leadership ability, or, conversely, prevent leadership success when they are not present. Other key attributes of leadership are charisma, courage, problem solving, teachability (the ability and willingness to keep learning), and vision.

The leadership challenge in this rough and fast-paced world is to get things done expeditiously and profitably, and to do so in a way that shows high integrity, trust, and honesty. These values are "morally right" in terms of Western thinking, and can be good business practice regardless of culture. Being good, doing good, and increasing profitability require a principled, diplomatic style of management. Principled leadership was defined as the application of ethical business values, including honesty, fairness, mutual respect, kindness, and do-ing good (London, 1999a, 1999b). This happens through business diplomacy, which is treating people with respect, being honest, recognizing and valuing dif-ferences, voicing agreement when appropriate, and accomplishing goals. Diplo-macy is the use of tact and understanding to build trust and develop relationships. Principled leadership and business diplomacy, as management styles and strategies, are mutually supportive ways that work especially well in making tough decisions, resolving emotional conflicts, and negotiating sensi-tive issues.

Principled, diplomatic leadership is the ideal, yet practical, leadership style. It extends the transformational, adaptive, enabling leadership styles, recogniz-ing the realities of today's world combined with the need for treating people sen-sitively and behaving ethically as the foundation for effective leaderships. This theme is revisited in the last chapter as a goal for leadership development built on self-insight and professional growth.

Summary

Complex environments and resulting organizational change demand transformational and inspirational leadership that creates and communicates a clear vision, engenders commitment, and empowers participation. Today's leaders create and lead new, adaptive organizational structures that rely on teams and have a global, multicultural perspective. Moreover, leaders need to maintain a principled, diplomatic stance, particularly in dealing with difficult situations.

Before going on, consider the extent to which you, and the leaders you know, are transformational, adaptive, inspirational, and principled. Consider the characteristics in Table 1.1, and indicate the extent to which they apply to you, your boss, and senior executives in your organization. Also, consider the char-acteristics you and the others you rated need to develop most.

TRENDS IN LEADERSHIP
DEVELOPMENT PROGRAMS

So far, this chapter has outlined a variety of leadership skills that respond to changing business environments. Organizations need to decide what skills they want their leaders to have and then establish training, support, and evaluation methods to help leaders learn and enhance these skills. This section considers how organizations design comprehensive development programs to meet their specific objectives. Leadership development then becomes a key strategy for ac-complishing organizational goals.

TABLE 1.1
Evaluating Leadership Style

Think about each of the following characteristics. To what extent do they apply to you? To what extent do they apply to your supervisor and to senior executives in your organization? Select the five areas you need to develop most? Considering leaders throughout your organization, what five areas need to be developed most? Ask a coworker to evaluate you on these characteristics. Do you agree with your coworker's assessment? If not, why don't you see yourself in the same way as your coworker sees you? Does this suggest directions for development? Ask coworkers to assess your boss and the top executives you rated. Do you agree with them? If not, what does this say about your coworkers' insight? What does this say about your own insight and the leadership style you value? As you address these questions, feel free to add other characteristics that you believe should be on this list:

- Seeks feedback
- Sets direction for change
- Communicates a clear vision for the organization or department
- Helps diagnose and define problems
- Mobilizes commitment
- Forms coalitions for support
- Empowers employees
- Holds employees accountable
- Is sensitive to others' feelings
- Is tactful
- Has unshakable moral principles
- Is passionate about business goals
- Is driven
- Inspires others' imaginations
- Always has time for others
- Makes people feel there is nothing they can't do
- Identifies what needs to be changed
- Holds self accountable
- Holds others accountable
- Asks tough questions
- Does not have all the answers, and knows it
- Seeks feedback
- Desires a balanced set of outcomes around profit, people, self
- Values learning
- Develops self and others

A Goals-Based Approach to Identifying Leadership Needs

Business environments differ in the leadership skills required today. They also differ in the leadership skills they need to develop to prepare leaders for the future. One way to determine leadership requirements for today and the future is to analyze the organization's goals. The idea is to determine the organization's financial goals, customer needs, business processes, and employee requirements. These have implications for the support needed by employees to be prepared for today and the future. As such, the resulting leadership competencies are not abstract or generic, but rather are based on specific multidimensional business goals (financial, customer, business process, employee development, and individual leadership development), or what Kaplan and Norton (1996) called a "balanced scorecard" for evaluating performance.

So, for instance, executives may decide their corporate goal is to increase return on equity from 12% to 20% per year and to maintain that level for at least the next 5 years. Regarding customers, they may set the objective to become the market leader in sales in four major products and to expand to three new global markets. They may establish a team philosophy to promote collaborative work relationships across units, and they may implement a continuous quality improvement program to reengineer key work processes and drive unnecessary expenses out of the business. They may establish a fast track manager development program to ensure that the business has the global executives it needs given its financial and market goals. In addition, they may charge themselves and other managers to take responsibility for their own development as well as become coaches and developers to the people who work for them. These goals, which of course would be even more specific to a given business, would then drive the objectives and behaviors of business unit leaders and their direct reports who manage individual departments. Each department contributes to the business unit and corporate objectives in different ways depending on its function, and the objectives drive the leadership behaviors needed at all levels of the organization.

Experts in leadership development have argued that traditional leadership development programs fall short of today's corporate needs because most programs start by identifying appropriate competencies (Zenger, Ulrich, & Smallwood, 2000). Instead, Zenger et al. believed that companies should begin with business-related results and work backward to attributes. This follows from the Balanced Scorecard approach that organization should establish objectives and measures from multiple perspectives.

Zenger et al. (2000) proposed a multistep process for organizations to achieve a better return on their investment in leadership development. In particular, they recommended the following:

1. Clarify and communicate desired business outcomes and tracking data so that all employees understand organizational goals and accomplishments and can consider their role.
2. Put leadership development into the organization's current context (i.e., the organization's strategic objectives).
3. Start at the top of the organizational hierarchy to be sure that developmental experiences follow from executive's plans and that all executives have the same experience and convey the same message in their business units.
4. Build scorecards for results starting with financial, customer, business process, and employee development indicators (as described earlier and in chap. 5, this volume).
5. Identify the competencies that are needed to achieve the scorecard indicators.
6. Change the learning methods to fit the competencies and individual learning styles.
7. Create accountability so that individuals are responsible for their own learning, as well as achieving the financial, customer, business process, and employee development goals.
8. Recognize that development does not happen in a single event (e.g., a week-long training class or a boss-subordinate performance appraisal discussion), but is a long-term, ongoing process of goal setting, training, feedback/performance review, and behavior change).
9. Simplify the complexity—make the reasons and methods for development clear and easy to understand.
10. Educate everyone to lead—that is, to take responsibility for contributing to organizational change and goal accomplishment.

As suggested earlier, the complexities of business today (i.e., globalization, sustaining corporate growth, new technologies, and e-business, to name key trends) require a new set of leadership skills. Recognizing this, Yearout, Miles, and Koonce (2000) outlined seven challenges based on their knowledge of companies like Shell and Bank One that have done a good job of developing leaders to meet these challenges. Leaders in such companies communicate a strong vision of the future. They ensure that the company's executives are in sync with each other—that their behaviors are consistent. They emphasize continuous development and replenish their leadership talent pool. (See the discussion of forming pools of managers with executive potential, investing in their development, and tracking their accomplishments and readiness for increased responsibility and new job experiences in chap. 9, this volume.) They identify specific leadership competencies to support the organization's strategy. They maintain tight strategic alignment among the organization's departments, business units, and business partners. They maintain unity of purpose and action among the executive team—ensuring that the top team not only understands corporate goals but also agrees about how to accomplish them. In addition, they demonstrate commitment to continuous organizational renewal, always trying to do better and experimenting with marketing new products and services.

Hillenbrand Industries, a global firm in healthcare services headquartered in Batesville, Indiana, is a good example of a firm that developed a leadership development and performance management strategy to meet its specific needs ("Assessing and developing top leaders," 2000). First, the company conducted a study to determine executive-level competencies for use in their leadership selection, development, and succession planning processes. The results also served as a foundation for performance management and appraisal, including a 360-degree feedback survey. The company wanted to determine what its executives needed to know to accelerate the growth of the business, and what processes and systems should be introduced to support the development of leaders who were ready now to help the business grow. The company's human resource staff, working with an external consultant, identified competencies critical to top leaders' performance. The competencies focused on the three areas of change, business, and people. The competencies indicated behaviors with a significant effect on performance. Moreover, they allowed the firm to focus leadership development on areas that are important to the company. This custom-made, performance model was used by the company to guide selection, assessment, and promotions throughout its worldwide operations.

In 1999, the firm assessed its top 50 executives to determine their current strengths and weaknesses and areas for development. To communicate the model, Hillenbrand sponsored a leadership summit for its top 200 executives in spring 2000. The meeting raised participants' consciousness of the importance of executive selection, assessment, performance management and development, and each leader's responsibility for making them happen. Leaders began to implement the competency model as they selected areas for their own development and that of their subordinates, and as criteria in hiring decisions. As Steve McMillen, the company's director of executive development and performance improvement, said, "In today's 'grow or die' business environment, we need more and better leaders in order to accelerate our organizational growth, and we need the processes, systems and tools to select, develop and deploy leaders in our organization" ("Assesing and developing top leaders," 2000, p. 3).

Feedback-Based, Relationship-Oriented Development

Once organizations establish needed leadership skills based on corporate objectives, they need to design and implement development methods to ensure that their current leaders are prepared to meet these objectives. Consider six proven methods of leadership development: 360-degree feedback, feedback intensive leadership training exercises, skill-based training, on-the-job experiences, developmental relationships such as mentoring and role models, and experiencing and overcoming hardships. These are used by the Center for Creative Leadership in their highly regarded executive training programs (McCauley, Van Velsor, & Moxley, 1998). These methods can be incorporated into a leadership development process that is essentially a continuous, input–throughput–outcome system. The methods recognize that people can learn from experience. Organizations should assess the impact of development experiences, especially training programs and workshops, so that the organizations know what methods are most effective and which ones need to be recalibrated to enhance their value for the individuals participating in them and for the organization as a whole. In addition, development programs should address emerging issues in leadership, including leadership growth for women and people of color, cross-cultural leadership development, and the development of global leaders (McCauley et al., 1998). Examples of programs that do this are provided in chapter 9 in this volume.

Rothwell and Kazanas (1999) argued that leadership development begins with recruitment and selection. Starting this way ensures that managers entering the business have a strong foundation of skills and abilities needed to achieve the organization's objectives. Development, then, tries to maximize their value to the organization and enhance opportunities for career development.

Leadership Development for Organizational Renewal

Vicere and Fulmer (1998) argued that leadership development in large corporations should focus less on developing a few chosen successors than on an organizational development strategy that promotes the flexibility, commitment, and competitiveness of the entire enterprise. As such, methods of leadership that benefit only a few individuals are less valuable than change methods that affect the organization as a whole. Traditional executive development methods follow the life cycle of managers from the time they enter the organization, first learning the ropes, perhaps being part of an entry-level leadership development program that tests potential for promotion to higher levels. This includes rotation between staff and line jobs, supervisory experiences, coaching, and attendance at various leadership development short courses. Rotational assignments continue as the successful individual moves up the organizational hierarchy, eventually becoming a general manager in midcareer. Job rotation may continue as the individual moves to senior management and develops an overall CEO perspective. Finally, the senior individual becomes a mentor to others, thereby ensuring executive succession in a common mold.

The strategic leadership development model promulgated by Vicere and Fulmer (1998) argues that successful leadership behavior and style varies with the stage of organizational development and growth. Companies in the early stage of development (or established enterprises undergoing major renewal) require an inspirational and visionary leader, in other words, someone who has a prophet and crusader mentality. Examples include Ray Kroc of McDonald's, Jack Welch of GE, and Stephen Jobs of Apple Computer. These leaders had an outsider's openness to new ideas and an insider's power base. They saw and communicated the need for change, and quickly established a group of motivated believers. They adapted to change by moving their organizations into new products and markets, sometimes by forming partnerships or alliances with other organizations.

Executive development programs, such as the approach used at Westinghouse, recognize these new roles for leaders. Designing these programs to meet the organization's needs begins by identifying corporate strategies and identifying the competencies required to achieve these strategies. Such competencies may be the ability to focus on results, enhance a customer-focused mind-set, form and lead geographically dispersed teams, be a model for business ethics, develop people, and work effectively in a multicultural, global setting. The next element in establishing an executive development program is to assess current managers and search for new managers outside the firm who are potential leaders. Methods of development include movement across functions and business units, external educational programs, participation on task forces, and receiving feedback (often using a 360-degree feedback survey). Progress is measured and rewarded through the annual incentives and rewards (including stock options), additional responsibility, and movement to more challenging key positions.

Summary

Leadership development strategies and programs follow from the changing needs of the business and the environment in which it operates. Development is not a one-time event, but a comprehensive approach to individual and organizational growth and renewal. This requires tremendous insight into business needs, associated leadership requirements, and methods to hire and prepare leaders, communicate and refine the vision for the organization (a vision that, itself, is likely to be dynamic), and meet the emerging challenges faced by the organization.

CONCLUSIONS

Seven trends emerge from the previous discussion of organizational change and directions and methods for leadership development:

1. Skill needs follow from business goals. The trend in leadership development methods is to ensure that there is a clear understanding of needed leadership skills that follow from the directions and strategies of the business.

Organizations need to ensure they will have the leadership talent required to accomplish their goals today and in the future. As such, they combine education and development with individual career planning and organizational succession planning. They identify a group of managers who have the potential to advance now and in the future. Then they use career planning to channel development resources to these individuals. The success of these managers needs to be evaluated frequently. New managers should be assessed, and those with leadership potential should be afforded opportunities for development in line with the organization's vision for the future.

2. Leaders' individual differences (e.g., learning style, openness to feedback, self-esteem, and other characteristics) influence how they engage in the development process. Organizational conditions, (e.g., resource availability, external and internal pressures, rewards for development, opportunities for growth, and human resource expertise) influence the development programs offered and their likely success in the short and long term.

3. Leadership skills include envisioning the future, establishing goals, communicating and rallying support for the vision, planning for its implementation, and putting the plans in place. However, activities do not always go so smoothly. Unforeseen events alter the vision or goals or present barriers to achieving them. Also, leaders are not so omniscient that they can always create a clear, understandable, valued, and achievable vision. Transformational leaders involve others in the process, seek and value others' input and participation, and delegate responsibility as they facilitate change. Adaptive leaders recognize that different behaviors work best under different conditions. They are adept at diagnosing situations using different information from diverse perspectives. They are sensitive to others' opinions, needs, motives, and abilities. Moreover, they are flexible, changing their style of behavior to match the situation. Principled leaders are adaptive and diplomatic when necessary, but they adhere to a set of values (e.g., integrity, trust, honesty, and mutual respect) that transcend situations and cultures.

4. Leaders are expected to take responsibility for their own career development while the organization provides the enabling resources. Development is a continuous, long-term process, not a one-time event. Feedback is central to development because it promotes self-insight and sensitivity to others. A variety of vehicles may be used to provide this feedback (e.g., 360-degree surveys, performance in experiential exercises, and assessment centers). The leader's role is to establish and work toward developmental goals based on insight into self and job/career demands while the organization provides supporting resources, such as feedback and coaching.

5. Leaders need a repertoire of behaviors in order to apply appropriate behaviors (or at least try different techniques or approaches) in different situations. This means they also need to be flexible. Leadership development can help executives collect information to understand their situation and learn different behaviors and when to apply them.

6. Leaders need insight into their environments and themselves. One aspect of environmental insight is a matter of perceiving and comprehending changes in technology, economic conditions, and competitive forces. Another aspect of environmental insight is interpersonal and social. It entails perceiving, comprehending, and being sensitive to other people's motives, needs, and reasons for acting as they do. Sensitivity means caring about others feelings and attitudes and recognizing how they perceive and react to you. Self-insight is important to both aspects of environmental insight. People who understand their own strengths and weaknesses, motives, and attitudes are likely to be better at understanding their own behavior and why people react to them as they do. Another aspect of self-insight is recognizing how one learns as well as what there is to learn. Knowing how to learn is critical to being able to acquire new skills and benefit from positive and negative experiences. Self-insight is the foundation for environmental insight and leadership that is adaptive, transformational, and principled.

7. In order to build self, interpersonal, and, more generally, environmental insight and encourage adaptive, transformational, and principled leadership, leadership development experiences will encourage the manager/executive to analyze the situation with various lenses. This means filtering information from multiple perspectives, diagnosing conditions, and considering different approaches. Learning experiences may arise from critical events on the job, working on real problems with colleagues in concentrated workshop settings, participating in business simulations, obtaining feedback from colleagues and executive coaches and human resource professionals at work and in training, as well as involvement in more didactic experiences such as attending lectures, reading, and courses that may be self-paced or instructor-led.

These trends reflect new directions in leadership development, but there are still some basic principles that underlie professional learning and growth. They focus on the importance of self-insight and self-regulation in establishing and recalibrating a meaningful career direction and sense of identity and capability, and on the way they perceive and make decisions about each other and themselves. They deal with the way people react to feedback and incorporate performance information into their planning and self-concepts, sometimes as they respond to and learn from failure, but always as they engage in continuous learning.

This book covers the trends in leadership development as well as the mainstays of person perception, self-regulation, and learning that are the foundation for leadership development, even in this rapidly changing business environment. The flow of the book is outlined in Fig. 1.1. The figure suggests that leadership styles required to meet changing organizational demands, described in this chapter, affect the psychological processes needed to produce the desired leadership behaviors. These processes include the development of self-insight

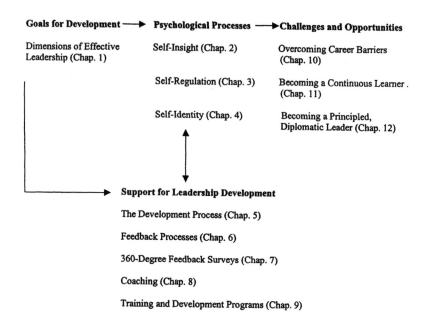

FIG. 1.1. Organization of the book.

(chap. 2, this volume), self-regulation (chap. 3, this volume), and self-identity (chap. 4, this volume). These processes suggest elements for the design of comprehensive, systematic leadership development programs that include career planning, training, job rotation, and career paths as a new manager rises to executive leadership positions (chap. 5, this volume). Given the importance of self-insight to effective leadership, feedback is a key element of leadership development programs (chap. 6, this volume). Organizations often facilitate feedback by the use of 360-degree feedback surveys (chap. 7, this volume). Another important vehicle for feedback and development is coaching (chap. 8, this volume). In addition, a variety of leadership training methods are available (chap. 9, this volume). Once implemented, leadership development programs affect the strength of the psychological processes, which in turn ultimately affect career challenges and opportunities, such as dealing with career barriers (chap. 10, this volume), becoming a continuous learner (chap. 11, this volume), and finally practicing principled, diplomatic leadership (chap.12, this volume).

I

Psychological Processes Underlying Leadership Behavior

2

Self-Insight: Prerequisite for Understanding Others and the Environment

Insight is the foundation for development. People have to know themselves and understand their environments in order to adapt and learn. Transformational, adaptive, and principled leaders need to understand themselves and those with whom they work. Authoritarian leaders who rule by fiat do not need accurate self or interpersonal insight. Their power resides in force or resource control. They may acquire new skills and knowledge, however they will not fully understand how to apply them in relation to other individuals' abilities and attitudes. In contrast, leaders who recognize that they cannot get anything done without cooperation value insight into their own and others' goals and motives. They may use transactional strategies to set standards and goals that can be understood and valued. In addition, they may use transformational strategies to engage others in the change process. They work with others to establish, refine, and create their vision for the future.

This chapter is about self-insight. Leaders who do not understand themselves are unlikely to have an accurate view of others or be sensitive to others' feelings, needs, and attitudes. Self-insight is the bedrock of meaningful personal growth and development. The chapter begins by examining the meaning of self-insight and its relation to other forms of self-understanding. The way people acquire self-insight and measures of self-insight are presented. Next, the meaning of self–other agreement (and disagreement) is explored as an indicator of self-assessment and self-awareness. Finally, guidelines outlining ways for leaders to enhance their self-insight are included.

SOME DEFINITIONS

Self-insight is a multidimensional concept that boils down to recognizing personal strengths and weaknesses. This includes knowing that in cases where strengths are overused, they can become liabilities. Self-insight leads to self-identity. Ross (1992) and McCauley (2000b) presented some definitions of the elements of self-insight. These may be thought of as a continuum that ranges from being aware of oneself to recognizing what one can accomplish and feeling good about it:

Self-awareness: Self-awareness is being aware of how one typically behaves or is perceived by others. The extent to which we are aware of ourselves may depend on the situation. For instance in uncomfortable or new situations, we may be more aware of ourselves than in routine, common experiences. Since self-awareness is situational, it may be more dependent on how we are feeling at the time (out state of mind) than permanent characteristics (traits).

Self-understanding: This is a clear recognition of one's strengths, weaknesses, needs, emotions, and drives. It also refers to recognizing how one's past experiences and current situation influence how one views oneself.

Self-consciousness: Unlike self-awareness, which is situational, self-consciousness is dispositional. Being self-conscious is more like a fixed trait. One meaning of self-consciousness is feeling uncomfortable, for instance, the feeling of being observed. It also means being conscious of oneself as an individual. Self-conscious people are aware that their behaviors and feelings are part of themselves and originate with them.

Self-assessment: This occurs when people determine the capabilities and abilities they possess.

Self-evaluation: This is the judgment people make of their capabilities and abilities.

Self-monitoring: This is the process of comparing one's behavior to a standard and adjusting one's behavior to meet that standard. The standard may be imposed externally (as when a boss establishes a certain level of expectations), or internally (as when people set goals and expectations for themselves).

Self-esteem: This is how people feel about themselves, based on their self-assessment and evaluation.

Self-confidence/self-control: This is the belief people have about their ability to bring about positive outcomes.

These are different ways of interpreting self-insight. A person who has high self-insight can be thought of as someone who is high on each of these elements. They are aware of, and understand the reason for, their strengths and weaknesses. They assess their own capabilities and recognize the judgments that others make of them. In addition, they monitor their behavior and capabilities in relation to a standard. The feeling they derive from this, good or bad, is their level of self-esteem. Insightful people are keenly aware of this feeling. Those who are high in self-esteem are likely to develop the confidence in their ability to be effective.

Leaders' Need for Self-Insight and Interpersonal Sensitivity

To be effective, leaders need insight into their skills and capabilities and how others react to them. To not have this insight is to be oblivious to the world—that is, to go about trying to make things happen without regard for anyone else's needs or concern as to whether the particular behaviors and decisions are having the desired effect. Everyone knows people like this. We have been frustrated by them, and they have been frustrated by the barriers they have encountered as a result of their unrealistic behavior. However, sometimes being oblivious to the world seems to be a benefit in that it does not hamper people from overcoming tough barriers and threats to their self-esteem. So a balance seems desirable. A person needs enough insight to make good decisions, but not so much as to see every barrier and impossibility, which might be crippling.

There is a difference between self-awareness and self-understanding. Self-awareness usually means "aware of how one typically behaves" or "how one is perceived by others." Self-understanding refers to a deep understanding of one's strengths, weaknesses, needs, emotions, and drives. It also refers to recognizing how one's past experiences and current situation influence how one views oneself (McCauley, 2000b).

Acting in Self-Interest

The concept of self-interest may underlie the idea of self-insight. There is an assumption that people recognize their needs and then act in their self-interest. Acting in one's self-interest is a societal norm in Western culture. Indeed, this is the basis for reward systems—that this, the notion that people will behave in ways that produce a positive outcome for themselves.

Norms of self-interest are "shared perceptions of appropriate behavior that possess the power to induce people to act publicly in ways that … maximize their material interests, whether or not they are so inclined privately" (Miller, 1999, p. 1056). People pursue self-interest because they fear that to do otherwise would cause them to be exploited. They also fear that, because of this norm, deviating from their own material self-interest will provoke dismay, suspicion, or derogation from others. People believe that acting in their self-interest is a natural law (Kagan, 1989). Because they believe they should obey natural laws, they try to do so, and it thus becomes a self-fulfilling prophesy. The power of self-interest may be due more to the power of social norms than to the power of innate proclivities (Miller, 1999). People interpret self-interest as inevitable and universal rather than cultural or historical, and therefore this strengthens their belief that pursuing self-interest is appropriate, rational, and sensible. This, in turn, further increases and strengthens acting in one's own self-interest.

So self-interest cannot be ignored as an outcome of increasing self-insight. This explains why people may be inclined to clarify and enhance their self-insight—because, ultimately, it leads to a better, more fulfilling and rewarding (or rewarded) life. Consequently, acting in one's self-interest is not necessarily bad. It is simply using the information embedded in self-insight, such as filling the gaps in one's skills and knowledge and/or meeting one's needs and desires.

Some Examples of Self-Insight and Self-Direction

Some people seem to know themselves very well. They understand their abilities and desires, and they go about using their abilities to set and achieve their goals. The watch phrase here is "Know yourself, and do what works for you."

Self-Confidence. Here's an example of someone who appears to be a highly self-confident executive and newly appointed CEO. Betsy Holden became CEO of Kraft Foods in May 2000 after 16 years with the company and as a rising star in the industry. Kraft is the nation's largest food packager, with more than $18 billion in revenue. Holden was concerned that her company sometimes placed more emphasis on her being a woman than on the results she produced (Barboza, 2000). Nevertheless, her leadership strategy was to continue to deliver impressive financial results while making the workplace friendlier for other women. She was known for her teamwork, competitive drive, and inventiveness. Trained as a teacher, she applied ingenuity that worked in the classroom to engage students to management. For example, at one point, she invented cheers for her team at Kraft. Overall, she set priorities and organized her activities at home, in volunteer work, and in business.

Entrepreneurial Initiative. Next is an example of a person who had a vision, flexibility, a recognition of his own tolerance, and sensitivity to others. Some may call this an example of bravado or chuztpa. Certainly this was someone who was self-directed, self-confident, and able to make things happen. Seth Kaplan moved to Shanghai in 1996 with a 20-year plan (Kaplan & Smith, 2000). His goal was to create a business running schools. After writing a thesis at the University of Pennsylvania's Wharton School of Business on how to manage not-for-profit schools, he decided to found a chain of schools in China.

Seth quickly discovered that doing business in China was handled in a completely different manner than it would be in the United States. For instance, the formal opening ceremony of his first school was scheduled for a Sunday. All the details were arranged; a special location was secured and invitations were dispensed to students and their parents, the press, and dignitaries. Two days before the opening, Kaplan received a call indicating that a top Chinese official wanted to attend the event, but could be there only on Saturday. Saturday, however, turned out to be a special day in the Chinese calendar for weddings, and every hotel in the city was booked. After hours on the phone, Kaplan received permission to use a government guesthouse. At 7 pm on the evening before, he and his staff began calling all the students and their families. Because the Chinese are used to making adjustments for government officials, they were not upset by the change.

In another incident, Kaplan was stuck on a train that was stopped by protestors farther down the tracks. After waiting 2 hours without moving, he suggested to fellow passengers that they abandon the train. Twenty people followed him, setting out on foot with no paved road in sight. Finally, they waived down a car. Kaplan was able to get to his appointment on time.

A Corporate Executive Who Learns From Others. Carly Fiorina, who assumed the position of CEO at Hewlett-Packard in 1999, seeks tough situations to manage (Fiorina, 1999). She recalled that in 1984, when she was 30 years old, she was working for AT&T at the time of the company's divestiture that split the Bell Operating Companies and formed a separate AT&T for long-distance service ("The boss: Making the best of a mess," 1999). A problematic area was access management, the division responsible for connecting long distance calls to the local phone company, which is where Fiorina chose to work. Although the systems were a mess and the function and department were brand new, she felt this was the place where she could have a real impact. Working with a team of engineers, she discovered that the local company's charges were AT&T's biggest cost, and AT&T had no idea whether they were being charged an accurate amount. The team spent months reviewing each of the bills manually, and found substantial overcharges. Eventually, they created a bill verification system that was implemented across the country and saved the company hundreds of millions of dollars. They accomplished something nobody thought was possible.

From such experiences, Fiorina formed seven principles for personal and business growth and success:

1. Find difficult challenges—they're more fun and present a chance to make a difference.
2. Develop a clear vision of the goal, with clarity, realism, and objectivity about the resources and commitment necessary to accomplish it.
3. Avoid self-imposed limits. People can generally accomplish more than they realize, and they are often their own worst enemy in slowing themselves and their company down.

4. Value the team. Major goals are not accomplished single-handedly.
5. Don't give in or give up, no matter how bleak things get. It takes time and pain to make a difference.
6. Balance confidence and humility. Be confident, but know when to request help.
7. Have a passion for what you do.

The True Self

R. T. Hogan and J. C. Hogan (2000) considered some limiting factors in prior approaches to leadership. Leadership theories focus on leadership behaviors. Leaders seem to depend on the situation in which they find themselves. However, he argued that more attention should be placed on who leaders are as people, in other words, their character and ability to understand and relate to others. One reason why psychologists and other researchers have focused on leader behaviors and situations, Hogan suggested, is because psychologists tend to be analytic and precise, and they do not like ambiguity and risk. However, executives are enterprising risk takers. They do not necessarily act systematically or consistently.

R. T. Hogan and J. C. Hogan (2000) argued that the key to effective leadership is the ability to care, and make accurate judgments about how others react to you. He called this the sociopolitical intelligence quotient (SPIQ). People who are high in SPIQ are socially perceptive of a wide range of interpersonal cues; are aware of the impression they make on others; have skill in social techniques, such as humor; have insight into their own motives and behaviors; and evaluate others' motives and behaviors, and do so accurately.

R. T. Hogan and J. C. Hogan (2000) distinguished between executives and entrepreneurs. Effective executives in large organizations have political skills. They are self-confident and charming. This is just the type of behavior that helps people do well in management assessment centers and interviews. Interviews and assessment centers capture what people do. Personality measures evaluate why they do it. They may be insensitive to others. Executives who fail are usually those who ignore negative feedback and make decisions they believe are politically correct. Entrepreneurs, on the other hand, have the ability to get things done. They may not be likable, but they are high in ambition and very smart. They are driven, but a bit raw in how they behave toward others.

A Buddhist View of Insight

The concept of insight may be understood better by comparing different cultural and philosophical perspectives. Western psychology emphasizes the importance of building a strong ego structure and healthy sense of self. This is key to basic well-being. People who have a misperceived or underdeveloped self-image will not operate effectively in the world or feel happy. In Eastern psychology, Buddhism in particular, reality is absent of self (Goldstein, 1994). That is, the self as an unchanging entity is a fiction. Experience is constantly in flux and does not have to refer back to a single identity. In Buddhism, self is an illusory mental structure. In the Eastern tradition, "Insight is seeing clearly and deeply that everything in the mind and the body is a changing process, and that there is no one behind it to whom it is happening.... There is no thinker apart from the thought itself.... Everything is just what it is, and only what it is" (Goldstein, 1994, pp. 93–94).

The Western goal of building a strong ego structure and the Eastern goal of seeing the selfless nature of experience actually are complementary, according to Goldstein (1994): "A healthy sense of self develops through learning to see clearly and accepting all the different parts of who we are; realizing the emptiness of self comes from not adding the burden of identification with those parts" (p. 94). In Western psychology, insight is blocked because people do not want to accept negative feedback and the negative feelings that accompany it. Eastern psychology teaches acceptance of the fullness of the feedback experience. By developing mindfulness, self-acceptance becomes possible: "Based on this acceptance, we can then bring a very focused awareness to seeing the impermanent, momentary nature of all these parts of ourselves" (p. 94). All thoughts and feelings are momentary and constantly changing. Individuals can experience, appreciate, and learn from them without worrying about what they mean to their self-identity. This is where Eastern and Western philosophies come together.

Individuals need a strong sense of personal concept and understanding before they can accept that there is no self. Once they have that understanding, they can be mindful of thoughts and feelings. These things come and go. Individuals break down, accept, and learn from their experiences. They discover insight through a process of opening and accepting all the parts of themselves without judgment. From a Buddhist point of view, this allows people to see the transient and impermanent nature of phenomena. Doing so comes from experience—watching through one's own mind. This is not knowledge, per se; it is wisdom that stems from meditation. (I learned this from my son, David, a blackbelt in Kempo Karate, a senior in college majoring in religious studies, and a practitioner of meditation.) Leadership development is usually based on cognitive methods, not meditation. Nevertheless, the idea of accepting and learning from experiences is similar.

In a search for self-understanding, Charles Segal, the late artist and magazine publisher, painted his own self-portrait over and over for about 60 years (Lewis, 2000). "When one is still and listens, one begins to be in touch with a mysterious element that is within each of us, which can transform and shape us and help to transform the world" (Lewis, 2000, p. B7). Consistent with Zen Buddhist meditation, people should practice silence, stillness, and contemplation to discover the secret spiritual forces within themselves. People learn about themselves, not by focusing on the self as a permanent entity, but in understanding their experiences and feelings in the moment.

An intriguing question is whether our current pace of life (the complexities of organizational and family life) is consistent with developing insight. Practicing silence is not easy, and meditation takes time away from other things. Of course, the basic idea of self-insight through contemplation is that this approach can enrich rather than detract from daily life and can help people cope with rather than ignore pressures. Self-insight may emerge in many different ways, but a key to self-insight is understanding one's experiences and feelings. Organizations hope to support this by providing information. This is discussed next.

Summary

Self-insight is a complicated construct. The foundation of self-insight is being aware of one's strengths and weaknesses. Carrying this further, self-insight requires individuals to recognize how others react to them and the effect they have on others. People who use this information to change their behavior and achieve positive outcomes feel good about themselves and have positive outlooks about what they can accomplish. That is, they are likely to be high in self-esteem and self-efficacy. Some people know themselves well, set realistic although maybe ambitious, goals and set out to achieve them. Others go further to seek experiences and challenges as learning opportunities and value others as role models and sources of feedback. This raises the question of the ways people use information about themselves and their environments to form self-insight. This is the topic of the next section.

INSIGHT THROUGH FEEDBACK

A key question involves figuring out how to self-insight. The current pace of organizational life, not to mention many people's personal lives, is the context in which self-insight develops. Some people are readily open to information about themselves. They go out of their way to find it. Moreover, they welcome both unfavorable and favorable information. They use the feedback to alter their behavior and their views of themselves. Other people do everything in their power to avoid such feedback. They prefer the risk of no information at all rather than the possibility of hearing something negative about themselves. Most people are probably somewhere in between these two extremes. They are uncomfortable with feedback. They feel threatened by negative feedback, but they are willing to accept it, especially if it helps them to identify specific behaviors they can change to be more effective. They like the feedback much less if it reflects generally on themselves as people, unless, of course, the comments are highly favorable. Even then, they may view effusive praise with suspicion, wondering if the person who gave the praise wants something in return.

Public Feedback

Sometimes feedback is very public. This happens to politicians and actors who are subject to public scrutiny and criticism, but it also happens to executives. For instance, Anne Mulcahy, head of Xerox's general markets organization, was named president and chief operating officer of the firm in 2000. This put her in line to succeed G. Richard Thoman, the ousted CEO. In the *New York Times* article announcing Thoman's removal, Mulcahy, age 47 and a 24-year career veteran with Xerox, was featured as Thoman's possible successor (Deutsch, 2000). The article noted that Mulcahy would not be the first woman in her industry to achieve CEO status. That would be Carly Fiorina at Hewlett-Packard. In the article, Mulcahy's career history was reviewed: her success in running the New York City and Boston sales territories (previously male bastions), her job as director of the human resources department, and her position as leader of Xerox's first internet offerings. As head of general markets, she led the fastest growing division and $6 billion in sales to small businesses and consumers, selling copiers through channels (e.g., CompUSA) that had long been Hewlett's market domain. Mulcahy organized Xerox's $1 billion purchase of Tektronix, giving Xerox a line of color printers. The article noted that whereas many who knew Mulcahy lauded her numerous positive qualities, some questioned whether or not her experience was broad enough to run Xerox. David Nadler, management consultant, was quoted in the article as saying, "Anne is incredibly open and honest. But she's not a technologist, and she's never been heavily into product development" (Deutsch, 2000, p. C19). Another consultant noted that Mulcahy had leadership and motivational skills, but her long tenure at Xerox did not give her an outside perspective. Leaders need to learn how to reconcile such feedback with what they know about themselves and what they know about the source. Mulcahy herself expressed self-confidence: "I know the Xerox team well. I know how to get things done."

Using Information to Enhance Self-Insight

An earlier work detailed a model of how people glean and apply information to alter their self-concepts (London, 1994, 1995). The following is an outline of this model.

Forming insight is a multistage sequential process. It consists of (a) receiving information, (b) categorizing the information (i.e., integrating and reconciling it with other information), (c) deciphering the reason for the information (attributing some cause, such as one's own ability or luck), and (d) changing one's self-concept as a result of the information, if appropriate. The first stage (receiving information) may be preceded by seeking information. Characteristics of the information, such as its favorability and specificity, may determine one's initial reaction to it. Favorable information is accepted readily. Specific information (e.g., information about behaviors rather than general personality characteristics) is more useful. General information that deals with an individual's overall characteristics may be hard to take if it is negative (e.g., attacking the individual's personality). The data itself may be observing others' reactions—for instance, what people say or do in response to others' behavior. Alternatively, the information may be quite direct and specific, such as a formal performance appraisal from a supervisor. The perceived accuracy and realism of the information affect the extent to which people take it to heart and change their behavior and self-concept as a result.

Individuals' preexisting images of themselves and others filter information about themselves. They test to see if it fits with preestablished views. Information that is consistent with their self-image is accepted readily. Actually, people are prone to interpret information as consistent with their current beliefs to the extent that they may ignore or discount information that is inconsistent. Once they recognize information that contradicts any preexisting views, they are likely to take notice, determine the cause as accurately as possible, and use the information to reevaluate their self-concept and make changes in their behavior. This is more likely to happen if the information cannot be ignored or denied and if the most likely feasible explanation is that they were to blame. In this situation, they could not attribute the information to factors beyond their control, even if they would like to be able to say they were not the cause. Most people are likely to attribute positive feedback to themselves and negative feedback to factors beyond their control, so information really needs to stand out to be accepted and processed accurately so that it is useful.

These ideas about ways people process information about themselves stem from *image theory* (Beach, 1990; Mitchell & Beach, 1990). These processes are outlined in Table 2.1. The theory holds that when people receive information, they test whether it fits preexisting categories of the way they think about themselves. They process this information unconsciously (automatically) if it easily fits an existing category (e.g., feedback about a presentation they just gave fits their self-conception as a good public speaker). The information is processed mindlessly with little awareness. Mindful or controlled processing occurs when there is a problem with the information. It is ambiguous, inconsistent, unique, counterintuitive, or unexpected and, as a result, it cannot be categorized easily. In this case, individuals may seek new information for clarification and in hopes of confirming preexisting impressions. Once the information has to be confronted, the individuals next seek reasons for it, attributing the information to an internal or external cause. Internal causes are their own behavior, skills, and knowledge. External causes are luck, the situation, and unreliability of the information source. Self-insight occurs when the information cannot be readily

TABLE 2.1

Image Theory: How People Process Information About Themselves and Develop Self-Insight

Characteristics of Information Received:

• Favorable information that is consistent with other information and preexisting self-schemas (categories) is processed unconsciously (automatically).

• Unfavorable, inconsistent, unexpected, unclear, counterintuitive information is processed mindfully.

Information Categorization:

• Automatically processed information that fits existing categories confirms or reinforces self-image.

• Information that fails a category test (does not fit existing self-schema) is processed mindfully.

• Mindfully processed negative information is likely given an external attribution whenever possible (i.e., blamed on others' behavior or situational conditions).

• For negative information, when an external attribution is not possible or information cannot be ignored or denied, the individual is forced to make an internal attribution.

Change of Behavior and Self-Insight:

• Internal attributions (recognizing "I am the cause") change behavior and eventually self-image.

Characteristics of the Individual and Situation:

• Feedback is sought and welcomed by individuals who are high in self-esteem and/or when the situational demands and stakes are high.

---

categorized, and internal attributions are made. That is, people are forced to draw a conclusion about themselves, for instance, about their ability to be effective in certain situations. People tend to be more open to information about themselves when they are high in self-esteem. They are also likely to be open to information about themselves when the situation is pressing—that is, when so much is at stake that they cannot afford not to pay attention to the information, no matter how difficult it is to hear and respond to.

Unconscious Insights

The concept of insight implies consciousness—and, by definition, an insight is a familiar idea. The term also implies a new idea, often one that occurred suddenly. People use expressions such as, "Ah ha! Now I see," or "Eureka, I've got it!" to express the emergence of the insight. However, insights may arise unconsciously before they arise consciously. Although seemingly contradictory to the definition of self-insight, some insights arise gradually in the unconscious, even though their conscious realization makes them seem sudden (Siegler, 2000).

People may discover and use ideas unconsciously before they are able to express them. So, for example, leaders who receive unfavorable feedback about the high employee turnover in their department and low employee morale from attitude survey results may not admit that their own lack of consideration for employees' needs and interests is to blame. They may deride the employees' abilities and motivation and lament how the work ethic has declined. However, they may begin to use more considerate management strategies. As the situation turns around, they become able to study the attitude survey and turnover data in depth and recognize their own learning and need for further development. Research is needed to test this idea of unconscious self-insights and behavior change preceding the insight and shift in self-concept and lasting behavior change.

Some Examples of Insight Emergence

As an example, consider a CEO who just gave an important presentation to a group of stockholders. She generally feels confident in such situations and enjoys giving public presentations. One stockholder in the audience kept pressing for clarification on an issue. The stockholder was not belligerent, but was relentless in asking for more details. The CEO initially attributed this to the stockholder's desire to keep attention on the topic. Later in the evening, it dawned on the CEO that maybe she had not been clear, and indeed, perhaps she really did not have a good understanding of the issue herself. She wondered if she had a tendency to avoid complex issues in public situations. She thought that maybe she should spend more time preparing, anticipating tough questions that might arise and making sure she has a clear explanation before exposing her thinking in a public setting.

As another example, consider the executive who was stunned when his boss called him into her office to tell him that he was being removed from his position immediately and would receive outplacement assistance to find another job. When the executive asked why, he was bewildered to discover that the boss felt she had no choice at this point: There were many complaints from his staff, peers, and some customers labeling him as an autocrat who felt he always had the best answer and did not listen to the wants or recommendations of others. His ouster took several weeks and some coaching from an outplacement counselor before reality set in. The executive always viewed negative comments as complaints from disgruntled people, never thinking that he actually needed to change. He was beginning to realize that indeed he could do things differently, and if he had been more sensitive and open to others' ideas, things might have turned out differently. He began to wonder if this same behavior carried over to his home life. His grown children rarely called, and his wife had become increasingly career oriented. He began to realize that during the last few years his family let him have his way and avoided in-depth communication with him.

WAYS TO ASSESS SELF-INSIGHT

Self-insight may stem from a number of reliable, authoritative sources. Consider a few possibilities:

- *An insight assessment center.* AT&T uses an assessment center for high potential managers called "Insight." Participants take part in a number of business simulations, interviews, and psychological tests. The results are used solely to give them feedback and help them set goals for development.
- *360-degree survey feedback.* This is a process that collects ratings from a manager's subordinates, peers, and supervisor, as well as self-ratings. Such information may be used to supplement performance feedback from participation in organizational simulations and games, an additional source of self-insight. This is the subject of chapter 7 in this volume.
- *Sharing ideas and self-disclosure.* People may learn about themselves by talking about their feelings and ideas to others. They glean insight as they put their thoughts into words and as others react. Self-disclosure is a way to seek feedback without asking for it directly.
- *Self-monitoring.* Observing the environment is another way to gain insight. Some people are very sensitive to norms, roles, and other features of a social situation. These people are called high self-monitors. They vary their attitudes and values in relation to the needs of the specific situation. Other people care more about their own internal, dispositional features, such as their attitudes, values, and personality traits. These individuals are low self-monitors. They do not vary their attitudes or values according to the situation, but rather are consistent in their views regardless of others' feelings or who is observing them (Anderson, 1987; Snyder, 1974, 1987).
- *Frame-breaking change.* Challenging work assignments provide individuals with an opportunity to learn about themselves as well as develop new skills. Frame-breaking change is major change that creates new, unexpected, and different situations than experienced by the individual in the past. Examples would be moving to another country or managing a different type of department (e.g., switching from staff to a line assignment with major supervisory responsibility). Because the individuals do not have a fixed frame of reference for evaluating the situation or a fixed set of behaviors to meet new work demands, these individuals are likely to be open to new ideas and to learning about what others' expect and how others react to them.

Interventions to Enhance Self-Insight

Leadership development programs may include many methods to deliberately try to enhance self-insight.

Self-Assessments.   Leadership development programs often ask participants to evaluate themselves. For instance, they may complete a personality measure or a rating form asking them to evaluate their performance and behaviors.
They may get comparative information from similar ratings made by their supervisor, peers, or subordinates. Also, they may receive information about how others,
on the average, evaluated themselves. The survey cues respondents to the behaviors and aspects of their performance that are important to the organization. The
process causes respondents to think about their actions and compare themselves to
others. Supervisors, coaches, or trainers may encourage the leader to discuss the results. Having comparative data and sharing results to get others' comments are important because people often do not have an accurate view of themselves. Poor
performers tend to overestimate their performance. They may recognize that they
did not do very well, but they usually do not recognize how badly they actually did in
comparison to others. Excellent performers tend to underestimate their performance. They may recognize that they are high performers, but they believe that
others must have done about as well (Kruger & Dunning, 1999).

Feedback.   Sources of feedback may include developmental assessment
centers (such as the AT&T insight assessment center already mentioned),
360-degree or upward (subordinate) feedback, performance appraisals from the
supervisor (ratings and feedback discussion), and regular reports (e.g., weekly
sales reports). These may be designed with the express purpose of providing
leaders with information about themselves and encouraging them to seek avenues for performance improvement. Organizations that do this promote feedback cultures. Feedback becomes ingrained in the way the organization does
business. Leaders learn to seek and welcome feedback, to analyze it purposefully, and to use the information to set or revise goals for the future, rather than
to discount or rationalize it away. Chapter 6 in this volume examines how feedback works and why it is important.

Coaching.   Coaching is becoming increasingly popular as a method to
support leader development. External consultants who coach executives usually have a background in business, human resources management, or psychology. Their role is to help the executive process feedback and use it to set
development goals. Coaches may also help executives analyze their current
work challenges, including the characteristics of the people with whom they
deal. The coaches do this by helping the executives understand themselves, as
well as the individuals on whom they depend. Coaching is discussed in chapter
8 in this volume.

Group Facilitation Methods.   Leaders can learn a lot about themselves by observing their performance in group settings. They can discover how
they communicate their point of view, influence others, and participate as a

member or leader of a team. Some groups hire facilitators to help the group do its work. The facilitator focuses on the group process, for instance, the clarity of communication and the extent to which all members have a chance to participate. Also, the facilitator may implement various methods to enhance the group's work, such as brainstorming (going around the room to get input from all members), flow-charting (examining the elements of whatever is being developed and outlining how they fit together or flow in a logical sequence), and designing measures to collect data from outside the group. (These are methods commonly used in quality improvement teams.) The facilitator may also stop the group's work occasionally to elicit discussion of the group process so members can examine how they work together, and sometimes, if the members are very comfortable with each other, consider how the members view each other. In any case, this focus on process helps participants consider how they contribute to the group and the ways their behavior affects others on the team.

Role Playing Exercises and Simulations. Leadership development workshops use various exercises that help participants become more aware of their strengths and weaknesses. These exercises are also a way for participants to test new behaviors in a relatively nonthreatening setting. While their fellow participants will observe them, at least the exercises have no impact on actual job performance. Methods might include role reversals placing individuals in a new setting and forcing recognition of roles and relationships. For instance, executives may be asked to take the role of their subordinates, and in the process may see job demands and stresses and their own behavior from a different perspective.

SEEING WHAT OTHERS SEE

One way individuals can view self-insight is by being aware of how others view them. On the one hand, building their self-views based on how they believe others see them may be a faulty foundation. Individuals may not accurately interpret others' views, especially if they are not told directly, but rather glean their impressions from the way people behave toward them. On the other hand, individuals can compare views of themselves with others' ratings in order to gain some key information about self-insight. When individuals' self-ratings are higher or lower than others' ratings of them, the obvious question is, why? People may be quick to discredit the data (e.g., "they don't know what they're talking about" or "they have an axe to grind"). However, the information can be valuable in helping people think about directions for change. This section considers the value of self–other comparisons.

Self–Other Comparisons Do Matter

L. E. Atwater, Ostroff, Yammarino, and Fleenor (1998) argued that both self-ratings and ratings by others are related to organizational outcomes. That is, the way people see themselves affects their performance. Also, their performance is related to the way others see them. Others generally have a reasonably accurate view of a person's performance. Considerable literature has shown that others' ratings of performance (e.g., ratings by peers and subordinates) tend to be reliable and valid (L. E. Atwater et al., 1998). People tend to agree about their ratings and can accurately judge the performance of others.

Self-ratings tend to be overly positive because of a self-enhancement bias (L. E. Atwater et al., 1998). People want to think highly of themselves. This, of course, may be true as long as people have a reasonably high self-esteem—a high sense of being able to control their behavior and effect positive outcomes. However, people who overestimate their performance tend to have fewer negative thoughts and higher expectations of success in new endeavors. Unfortunately, those who are more extreme in overestimating their performance are likely to ignore criticism and discount failure, which in turn results in lower future performance. They may pursue tasks for which they are not suited and take unnecessary risks. They misdiagnose their strengths and weaknesses and have negative attitudes because they believe they deserve more credit for their accomplishments than they have received. People who do not think highly of themselves may keep themselves from trying initiatives for which they are indeed qualified. They try harder to compensate because they overestimate their weaknesses, and this leads them to do better than they think they are doing.

L. E. Atwater et al. (1998) suggested that in the optimal situation, where self-ratings agree with other ratings and the ratings are favorable, individuals rated have an accurate view of how they are perceived by others, receive positive feedback, have realistic expectations for reward and recognition, and, because of these factors, should achieve very positive results. In the case where self-ratings and other ratings are in agreement but the ratings are poor, individuals also have an accurate view of how they are perceived by others. These individuals receive negative feedback and, as a result, develop a sense of negative self-worth and low expectations for improving.

L. E. Atwater et al. (1998) studied 1,460 managers who participated in leadership development programs. These programs included a multirater feedback survey completed by the manager, peers, and subordinates. Also, the direct supervisor rated the manager's effectiveness, and this was used in the study as the measure of effectiveness. The results showed that effectiveness ratings were higher when both self and other (peer or subordinate) ratings were high and when self-ratings were substantially lower than other ratings (severe underestimation). Overestimators with moderate self-ratings and low subordinate ratings received the lowest effectiveness ratings from their supervisors. In general, underestimators (those whose self-ratings were lower than peer or subordinate ratings) received higher supervisor ratings than overestimators.

The researchers conjectured that managers who received high ratings from others but rated themselves still higher were effective because their weaknesses had a limited effect on their performance, whether or not they recognized it. Those who were rated low by others but higher by themselves may not have recognized they had critical weaknesses that negatively affected their performance. Underestimators may have been more effective because they were continually trying to do better and were not overconfident or complacent.

Types of Disagreements

Cheung (1999) outlined the sources of mistakes and errors people make in evaluating themselves and others. These explain why individuals rate themselves differently than others rate them. These differences may cause people to react to the results in different ways than were intended by the raters. Cheung (1999) identified seven such disagreements—two arising for conceptual reasons and five arising for measurement (psychometric) reasons.

Conceptual disagreements occur when people have different frames of reference for evaluating performance. This may be manifest in two ways.

Differences in Performance Dimensions. Raters think about performance as a set of dimensions that consist of multiple components. They may differ in the dimensions that compose performance. This may happen for a variety of reasons. They may misunderstand the job because it was never fully explained to them. They may not receive adequate feedback about their performance, and so do not understand the full range of performance that the organization expects of them. They may have different implicit views of the job and performance requirements, maybe because of a difference in their training or prior experiences.

Differences in the Components of Performance Dimensions. Even if people agree on the dimensions, they may define the dimensions in different ways—that is, differ in the components that represent a given dimension. Then, too, even if they use the same components to define a dimension, they may differ in the importance (weights) they give to the components in each dimension. These differences could be a result of the same reasons why there might be disagreements in performance dimensions. In addition, people may have different self-interests, for instance, emphasizing one performance dimension or component of a performance dimension over another because they have higher ability in one area and so view that area as more important.

These two differences are evident by analyzing performance ratings on items. The items represent the components of performance. Factor analysis examines the relations between the items and separates the items into groups, called factors. The items in a given factor are highly interrelated and have lower relations to items in other factors. Differences in factors indicate differences in performance dimensions. Differences in the items in a factor represent different ways of defining performance. Differences in the weights of the items in a factor represent disagreements in the importance given to different components of performance. Analyses can be conducted to determine if self-ratings from a group of managers differ systematically in the dimensions and item loadings from their supervisors, subordinates, or peers.

Studying a group of 332 midlevel managers in a public service agency, Cheung (1999) compared their self-ratings with their supervisor evaluations. He found no significant difference in factor form or factor loadings across the self-ratings and supervisor ratings. Both the managers and their supervisors conceptualized behaviors in the same way (a set of internal and external roles) and agreed on which components belonged to each set of performance dimensions (e.g., internal roles consisting of leader, resource allocator, and disseminator of performance, and external roles consisting of negotiator, liaison, spokesperson, and entrepreneur; a model of performance developed by Mintzberg, 1973). This does not mean that other groups of managers and their supervisors would agree. The focal managers (those who rated themselves and were rated by their supervisor) were highly experienced. They had an average of 2 years experience in their current jobs, 16 years of supervisory experience, and 21 years in their organization. People with less work experience or less experience in evaluating themselves may differ from their supervisors.

In addition to differences in dimensions and their components, Cheung (1999) considered additional measurement problems that might contribute to disagreements. These are *psychological disagreements* as opposed to conceptual disagreements. Consider each and the reasons why they might occur.

Random Differences in Measurement Errors.   These may occur simply because raters are unfamiliar with the rating scales and scoring formats. Also, they may happen because raters differed in their opportunities to observe the ratee. Alternatively, the raters may vary in their ability to absorb, or concentrate on, different information.

Differences in the Variability or Range Raters Use to Evaluate Dimensions.   Raters may restrict the range they use to evaluate others or themselves. They may be more lenient, which is common for self-ratings. There may be some implicit norms of responding—the belief that no one should be rated poorly (a phenomenon that occurs in the armed forces). Raters may not feel comfortable differentiating among raters (a phenomenon that occurs in companies that have been downsized and, supposedly, only the best managers have survived). Raters may be unwilling to explain high or low ratings. They may disagree on the standards of effective or ineffective performance. Alternatively, they may disagree on the meaning of the differences between scale intervals (some raters' feel there really is not a substantial difference between a rating of "good," a 4 on a 5-point scale, and "very good," a 5, whereas others see a marked difference between these categories and are more discriminating in their use of the "very good" category).

Differences in the Favorability of the Evaluation. Some groups of raters may be more lenient or more severe than others. This would be evident by comparing mean differences between rater groups. A leniency bias may emerge because the raters are unwilling to give negative feedback, maybe because they want to be liked. Self-ratings are generally marked by leniency. This occurs because people inflate their view of their own performance and because people generally attribute positive outcomes to themselves and negative outcomes to others.

Differences in the Correlations Among the Factors. These differences may arise because one factor affects another. One dimension of performance becomes so predominant in the rater's mind that the rater sees the individual the same way on the other dimensions. The rater may generalize from the dominant factor and essentially assume the person rated must be the same way in other respects. Or, the rater may allow the perception of the individual on the dominant factor or overall impression to color the way the rater sees the person in other ways—a concept called "halo." In this case, the rater cannot get beyond viewing the person on the dominant factor to see the person in other ways. The rater simply discounts any inconsistent information, denying its importance or credibility. Another reason for this error is that, to some degree, different performance dimensions are, in fact, due to an underlying ability. For instance, communication skills may be important to a number of aspects of performance, such as influencing others, negotiating, resolving conflict, and friendliness. Individuals may be rated similarly on all these aspects of performance simply because they are vocal and outgoing.

Differences in Agreement Among the Raters. This is evident from differences in how raters rank order the ratees on a given performance dimension. This may be low because the raters disagree in their evaluations and/or have a self-serving bias that causes them to see themselves more positively than they see others (which was also a possible reason for differences in the favorability of the evaluation). This would not be unusual because raters often observe different aspects of an individual's performance. Inaccurate self-perceptions alone may be the reason why self-ratings do not correlate highly with ratings from other groups (subordinates, supervisors, or peers). This may be why people are likely to believe they are being treated unfairly, if, for instance, pay decisions are based on the supervisor's ranking of subordinates (cf. Yammarino & L. E. Atwater, 1997).

Continuing the results of Cheung's (1999) study, self-ratings showed lower measurement errors than supervisor ratings. This indicated that self-appraisal can, indeed, be a supplement to traditional performance appraisals usually conducted by supervisors alone, although research is needed to determine the conditions under which self-ratings are preferable to supervisor ratings and how self and supervisor ratings can be used together. Differences between groups in measurement errors can cause inaccurate results when studying variables related to performance.

Cheung (1999) also found smaller variability in self-ratings than supervisor ratings, perhaps because the managers did not want to explain extreme ratings (very high or low) to their supervisors. Regarding the favorability of the ratings, self-ratings were higher for the internal roles than supervisor ratings, but there were no mean differences for the external roles. The data do not tell us whether the managers were more lenient in rating themselves on the internal roles or whether the supervisors were more stringent. Nor do the results reveal why there were differences on the internal and not the external roles. Possibly, the internal roles are viewed as more visible to supervisors, and so managers are more lenient in rating themselves on these aspects of performance or supervisors are more discerning in evaluating these roles.

The correlations among the factors were rather high overall and not significantly different between self- and supervisor ratings. This may be due to response biases or underlying performance factors that pervade the ratings of items for both groups. Finally, the rank order of managers based on self-ratings did not correlate highly with the rank order based on supervisor ratings. This showed that the rater groups did not agree in their evaluations.

Of course, different results may emerge for other samples. However, these results illustrate the different reasons that may explain rater disagreements. They show the importance of exploring more than just mean differences to understand fully the underlying differences in perceptions. These differences may have conceptual causes (i.e., differences in factor structure or composition in the minds of the raters) or psychometric causes (i.e., differences in the way the scales are used).

Reasons for, and Effects of, Self–Other Disagreements

L. E. Atwater and Yammarino (1997) proposed reasons why self-ratings differ from other ratings and what the implications of these differences are for individual and organizational outcomes. Their review of the literature shows that self-ratings tend to be inflated, unreliable, invalid, and biased compared to ratings of others, such as supervisors, subordinates, and peers. One reason for this is self-enhancement bias, or people putting the best light on their own behavior. This tendency has some key psychological benefits in that it allows individuals to ignore minor criticism, feel good about themselves, and have optimistic expectations about what they are able to accomplish.

Observer ratings are not necessarily accurate and can be biased by a number of factors, including limited opportunities to observe the person rated, poor judgment, wrong information about standards for performance, and self-serving tendencies to make themselves look better than others. However, observer ratings are more valid than self-ratings when skills, abilities, performance, and leadership are being evaluated (cf. L. E. Atwater & Yammarino, 1997; Harris & Schaubroeck, 1988).

Despite these problems, self-perceptions and individuals' comparisons of their self-evaluations to how others see them are potentially important for organizational and individual outcomes. Others' perceptions influence people's reactions and motivation. Work group members are influenced by what their supervisor thinks of them. Their teamwork may be affected by what their co-workers think of them. Salespeople's performance may be influenced by information about what customers think of them. Self-perceptions stimulate a self-regulatory process in that people's self-perceptions of their strengths and weaknesses influence how intensely they work (cf. Ashford, 1989; L. E. Atwater & Yammarino, 1997).

L. E. Atwater and Yammarino (1997) developed a model to predict self–other agreement. In their model, based on a review of extant literature, self–other agreement is a function of individual and personality characteristics, biographical characteristics, cognitive processes, context, such as pressures and comparative information, and job experiences, including past feedback. The research results were sometimes mixed, however, they found evidence for the way a variety of characteristics affect self–other agreement, listed in Table 2.2 and described here:

- *Gender:* Women see more value and detail in others' evaluations than men, and so are more likely to use that information to evaluate their own performance. They have more accurate ratings than men because they incorporate more self-relevant information in their self-perceptions.
- *Age and tenure:* Older, more experienced people are less likely to seek performance feedback because they do not want to convey a negative impression that requesting feedback might convey. Alternatively, they may be complacent or more confident about their performance than younger and less experienced employees. As a result, older and longer tenured employees tend to inflate their self-ratings.
- *Leadership role:* Leaders whose behaviors are highly observable are likely to be evaluated more accurately than nonleaders who are not constantly being watched. Because leaders interact with people more, they are likely to receive more feedback than nonleaders. These factors contribute to leaders' self-assessments agreeing with ratings made by others about them.

TABLE 2.2
Variables Affecting Self–Other Agreement

Self–other agreement is likely to be higher for those who are ...

- women
- younger
- less tenured
- leaders
- majority group members rated by other majority group members
- intelligent
- able
- high in internal locus of control
- high and stable in self-esteem
- introverts
- not depressed
- self-aware
- high in private self-conscious (in touch with their inner thoughts and feelings)
- high in interpersonal sensitivity and feelings
- low self-monitors—those who don't vary their behavior to match the situation
- high in expecting a lot from themselves
- seekers of feedback
- less likely to feel pressure about being evaluated
- high in receiving feedback, including comparative information
- focused on their behaviors, not themselves
- experienced in rating others

Note. Based on the literature review by Atwater and Yammarino (1997).

• *Minority group status:* Ratings of minority group members by those with majority status are likely to be inaccurate because of stereotypes, or maybe because there are too few minority group members to recognize that stereotypes really do not hold true. Other factors, such as the exaggeration of differences between members of minority and majority groups, may also contribute to inaccurate and generally lower ratings of minority group members by majority group members. As such, self–other ratings are likely to be lower when the person rated is a minority and the person doing the rating has majority status than when both rater and ratee are from the majority group. This may change over time as the rater gains more experience working with minority group members.

• *Intelligence:* Because people with higher intelligence are better able to process information than those with lower intelligence, raters with higher intelligence will have more accurate self-perceptions.

- *Abilities*: Raters with higher ability (including the analytic/cognitive ability to distinguish differences in their own and others' performance) and those who achieve at a higher level will be more concerned about evaluating themselves accurately than those with low ability or low achievement. Those who are uncertain about their ability will seek more information about themselves and will develop a more accurate self-understanding over time.

- *Locus of control*: Those who believe they influence what happens to them (high locus of control) are more interested in realistic self-evaluations and so have more accurate ratings than those who believe there is little they can do to affect the events and consequences in their lives.

- *Self-esteem*: People who have high self-esteem that is stable, founded on positive feedback, and are likely to change their behavior in response to feedback are likely to evaluate themselves accurately. However, those who have a consistently high self-esteem that may not be backed up by positive feedback and generally high performance are people who are insensitive to cues and feedback. These individuals will have less accurate self-ratings than those whose self-esteem rests on performance feedback.

- *Introversion*: People who are inner directed spend more time reflecting on their behavior and performance and know themselves better, and so will have high self–other agreement.

- *Depression*: Depressed individuals are likely to rate themselves more harshly, perhaps as a way to avoid criticism or as a way of seeking praise. In any case, they are likely to have lower self-ratings as compared to those who are not depressed.

- *Self-awareness*: People who tend to compare their own behavior against standards or new information are able to incorporate this information into their self-evaluations. That is, people who are more self-aware are more likely to have higher self–other agreement than those who misread comparative information and performance feedback.

- *Self-consciousness*: On the one hand, people who worry about others' impressions of them (those who are high in "public" self-consciousness) are likely to believe they are being monitored by others even when they are not. They misread cues perceiving information as relevant and directed at them when it is not. On the other hand, people who attend to their inner thoughts and feelings and their positive and negative attributes (those who are high in "private" self-consciousness) are likely to have more reliable self-reports and higher agreement with others' perceptions of them than those who are high in public self-consciousness.

- *Interpersonal orientation*: Those who are "feeling" types of people are more sensitive to interpersonal aspects of their jobs, and so are likely to have more accurate self-ratings, as compared to those who pay more attention to technical aspects of their jobs (i.e., "thinking" types of people).

- *Self-monitoring*: People who behave differently with others depending on the situation (high in the concept called self-monitoring) are likely to have lower self–other agreement. They tend to evaluate themselves more highly than others evaluate them and have larger differences between self-ratings and ratings from others as compared to those who are low in self-monitoring. Low self-monitors are more consistent in their behavior and so are better able to describe themselves and to see themselves in the same way others see them.

• *Past experiences and current expectations*: People who performed poorly and have low expectations for future performance are likely to underrate themselves (e.g., women who received poor performance on traditionally masculine tasks). They attribute their poor performance to themselves and have low expectations for the future. However, those who have accurate expectations based on accurate attributions for the reasons for their performance are likely to have self–other agreement.

• *Feedback experiences*: People who pay attention to feedback and find that the feedback is specific, consistent, and thought to be accurate (regardless of whether it is positive or negative) will develop more accurate self-perceptions and have higher self–other agreement than those who receive feedback that they ignore or that is general, inconsistent, or perceived to be inaccurate.

• *Pressures from evaluation*: When ratings are used to make decisions about employees (e.g., determine their pay or whether they are eligible for promotion), people will inflate their self-ratings. However, if people are held accountable for the accuracy of their ratings (e.g., they will be asked to justify their ratings of themselves), then they will be more likely to provide more accurate ratings.

• *Availability of comparative information*: When information about how others did (e.g., average ratings) is available, people will tend to evaluate themselves more accurately. The comparative information provides standards others use to make their ratings and against which people can judge themselves.

• *Specificity of information requested*: The more specific the behavior being evaluated, the more individuals are likely to rate themselves in the same way others see them.

• *Experience rating*: Raters who have had more experience rating themselves and comparing their self-evaluations to how others see them are likely to agree more highly with others' ratings of them as compared to those who have had little experience. As a consequence, self–other agreement is likely to be low the first time self and other ratings are collected in an organization.

Overestimation:
Why Poor Performers Don't Get It

In general, people overestimate their performance in many intellectual and social situations. This is particularly true for people who do not, in fact, perform well on a task or in a social environment where they expect they should be able to do as well—at least as well as the next person (Kruger & Dunning, 1999).

These are people who lack the skill needed to perform better, and this absence of skill not only hurts their performance, but also prevents them from being able to recognize their poor performance. That is, they cannot distinguish accuracy from error. They suffer from the dual burden of not having the skills needed to do well and not having the ability to recognize their limitations: "The same knowledge that underlies the ability to produce correct judgment is also the knowledge that underlies the ability to recognize correct judgment. To lack the former is to be deficient in the latter" (Kruger & Dunning, 1999, pp. 1121–1122). Because they cannot recognize their poor performance, they assume they have done well. Indeed, they tend to grossly overestimate their performance. As a result, lacking the ability to assess themselves accurately, incompetent people do not know enough, or even feel a need, to seek the training or practice they need to correct or avoid errors. When they do receive training to improve their skills, this allows them not only to perform better, but also to recognize their limitations. Essentially, they learn what they do not know, and they are better able to evaluate their improving performance more correctly.

To summarize, the link between competence, the ability to judge one's performance accurately, and inflated self-assessment occurs because of several reasons:

- Incompetent people overestimate their ability and performance.
- Incompetent people are less able than their competent coworkers to recognize competence when they see it in themselves or anyone else.
- Incompetent people have trouble using information about others' performance to judge their own (i.e., when told about how well others do, they assume they did as well).
- Training to make people more competent improves both their performance and their self-insight in being able to judge their own limitations and recognize the quality of their performance.

These points were made by Kruger and Dunning (1999) in a series of social psychological experiments. College students were given various tasks, such as a 20-item logical reasoning exam taken from a Law School Admissions Test (LSAT) preparation guide. After taking the test, they were asked to rate their general logical reasoning ability as compared to their classmates, to estimate how their score on the exam would compare to their classmates, and finally to estimate their test score. The students overestimated their general ability and their predicted performance relative to their peers. The students who did most poorly on the test overestimated their logical reasoning ability and test performance to the greatest extent. Whereas they scored in the 12th percentile on average, they believed that their general ability fell at the 68th percentile and their score fell at the 62nd percentile, on average. The poorest performers believed they were above average! Those who did better on the task did not misjudge their performance as much. Indeed, those in the top quartile of performance tended to underestimate their ability. They estimated that their test performance would be at the 68th percentile and their logical reasoning ability was at the 74th percentile, and their actual performance was at the 86th percentile.

Kruger and Dunning (1999) found similar results for other types of tasks as well, such as grammar and humor. In a subsequent study, the researchers followed the logical reasoning test with a training packet or a filler task prior to asking participants to estimate their performance. Participants who received the training packet evaluated their own tests more accurately than those who did not receive the training. This was especially pronounced for those who scored in the bottom quartile. These individuals were just as accurate as those who initially scored in the top quartile. The incompetents had become expert enough to recognize their own deficiencies.

Kruger and Dunning (1999) offered some possible reasons why overestimators do not perceive their own incompetence:

1. They do not receive negative feedback about their skills and abilities from others because people shy away from giving negative feedback.
2. Some task settings preclude workers from receiving self-correcting information that would show them their suboptimal performance. That is, the setting does not provide any feedback. The task is done, but the results are not available, comparative results are not provided, or the individual leaves the job without feedback.
3. Even if negative feedback is given, performers may not accurately understand why they failed. They may attribute their lack of success to situational factors beyond their own ability. In general, the cause of failure is likely to be ambiguous, and it can be attributed to a number of factors other than oneself. Success is less ambiguous. Luck and support help, but success generally also requires knowledge, ability, and effort. People who are incompetent may have trouble taking advantage of social comparison data. Although people generally gain insight into their own abilities by observing others (this is the foundation of social comparison theory; Festinger, 1954), incompetent individuals do not have the cognitive skills to understand their own deficiencies.
4. Motivation makes a difference as well as ability. People naturally want to attribute failure to factors beyond their control instead of admitting they are to blame. Also, people naturally want to believe they are the cause of their own success.
5. Other factors causing people to overestimate their ability include selective recall of past performance and the tendency to ignore others' proficiencies (Kruger & Dunning, 1999).

People can become more accurate self-evaluators by acquiring some knowledge about a subject or skill. This will not necessarily make them more proficient, but rather will help them understand their deficiencies better. They become aware of the limits of their abilities. For instance, people taking up bowling by practicing alone may feel pretty good about their improvement until they watch others who are more talented and experienced.

Underestimators Suffer from the False-Consensus Effect. Whereas people who perform poorly may overestimate their performance, people who perform well may underestimate their performance relative to others (or, more precisely, they overestimate others' performance). This has been called the false-consensus effect (Kruger & Dunning, 1999; L. Ross, Greene, & House, 1977). These individuals assume that because they did so well, their coworkers must have done at least as well. They tend to recognize their own absolute abilities accurately, but they assume others have equal or better abilities. Kruger and Dunning (1999) discovered that once these underestimators learned how poorly their coworkers had done, they raised their self-assessments to more accurate levels. So, just as overestimators lack both ability to perform and ability to discern their poor performance, underestimators perform competently but fail to recognize that their ability is not shared by others.

Presumably, people who need to improve most as a result of 360-degree feedback are overraters, that is, those who give themselves higher evaluations than others feel they deserve. Performance dimensions for which self-ratings are higher than other ratings are the areas that ratees look for to pinpoint development needs. However, it could be that ratees ignore this information in favor of areas of agreement, particularly when these areas are rated favorably. Ferstl and Bruskiewicz (2000) studied 84 executives after they had received 360-degree feedback. The feedback report consisted of a competency summary, results by item, a gap analysis (differences between self-ratings and others' ratings), rating distributions (degree of agreement or disagreement among others' ratings), a top five list of development needs, and a bottom five list. Also, anonymous narrative comments were available on effective areas and potential growth areas. The raters and ratees were told that the results were for feedback only—results would not be used to make administrative decisions. The feedback process called for working with supervisors who were responsible for ensuring that the ratees actually established a development plan as a result of the feedback and for overseeing the ratee's progress on that plan. The postfeedback survey asked raters to indicate the extent to which they paid attention to each element of the feedback report and the extent to which they found the element useful for creating their development plan.

Ferstl and Bruskiewicz (2000) found that, as expected, overraters agreed more strongly than did others that they learned something from their feedback and intended to use it to improve their performance. Thus, overraters, at least based on their self-reports of reactions to the feedback, seemed to be more likely to benefit from the feedback than underraters or those who agree with other raters' assessments of them. In addition, the ratees said that they attended to narrative comments more than they did to the ratings in the feedback reports. This indicates that managers perceived that they found the narrative descriptions and examples of their behavior cited by the raters to be more valuable than the average numerical ratings. The narratives were more specific and conveyed more substance, although they were less systematic and comprehensive than the ratings themselves. Also, because the narratives were comments volunteered by the raters about areas the raters felt were most important, the ratees may have given the comments more weight. This does not mean that the information was necessarily more reliable, and it certainly was not more comprehensive. This suggests that supervisors who are asked to coach their subordinate managers in using feedback and setting development goals should be trained to help their charges use all the information—the ratings and the narratives—and to guard against giving limited information more weight than it deserves.

CONCLUSIONS:
GUIDELINES TO ENHANCE SELF-INSIGHT

This chapter examined the meaning of self-insight, how self-insight forms (i.e., how people integrate information about themselves into their self-concept), how feedback is acquired and measured, and the value of seeing yourself as others see you. Methods for increasing insight through feedback were cited, including assessment centers, employee attitudes (e.g., 360-degree survey feedback), and coaching. The following section concludes the chapter by outlining methods for inducing self-insight by leveraging different elements of the insight formation process. In particular, leaders' self-insight can be enhanced by focusing on sources of feedback, encouraging mindful processing (i.e., avoiding automatic categorization of information, especially discounting or ignoring negative feedback), facilitating accurate internal attributions (i.e., leaders recognizing when the feedback results are a direct reflection of their behavior), and helping leaders reevaluate their self-concept and formulate plans for development.

1. *Sources of Feedback*
   A. Train leaders in self-observation skills, such as paying attention to verbal and nonverbal behaviors, experimenting with how others react to various modes of behavior, thinking about an interaction from the viewpoint of the other person, and stepping back as if a third-party observer.
   B. Encourage self-assessment. Provide opportunities for leaders to evaluate and interpret their own behavior and results. Give time for leaders to reflect on their behavior in a structured way. For instance, in a workshop setting, explain a theory of leadership and ask participants to

evaluate themselves using a survey designed for the purpose. Have them score themselves and discuss the implications of their score.

C. Encourage leaders to seek feedback. Educate leaders concerning how to ask for feedback in a way that is sincere so that it results in a range of useful information (i.e., says something about behaviors that can be changed). Leaders need to understand, first of all, that it is okay to ask others how they are doing and to probe respondents to find out more about what they mean. Leaders need to do this in a way that is not threatening to the parties asked. An executive coach who is external to the organization can be helpful in collecting input from others and presenting it in an objective way that protects the sources' anonymity and protects the receiver's confidentiality.

D. Collect feedback from multiple sources and perspectives. A leader is seen in different ways by people in different positions. Subordinates may vary in how they perceive a leader because the leader may behave differently with different subordinates depending on the situation, their capabilities, and the relationship the leader has with the subordinate. People in different roles (peers, customer, supervisor) will see the leader in different ways because their role in relation to the leader determines the expectations and demands placed on the leader. In the context of a 360-degree survey, responses from people in the same role (e.g., all the peers) will be averaged, assuming that variation of responses from people within a role is not that helpful. This may not be the case because differences may accurately reflect different ways that the leader interacts with each rater. However, these differences may be a function of the individual rater's rating errors, and averaging across raters within the same role may more accurately reflect the rater's performance from the viewpoint of people in the particular role. The important point here is that different perspectives be represented in the evaluations collected, whether they are collected by means of a survey, interview, focus group, or some other means.

2. Mindful Processing

A. Provide positive and negative feedback. It is easier to tell people what they are doing well than what they are not doing or what they are doing poorly. Providing comprehensive information, however, is a way to encourage leaders to focus on all important aspects of their performance.

B. Focus feedback on behaviors, not personal characteristics that threaten a person's self-image. Leaders need to recognize their dominant behavioral tendencies, and change them if they are not effective. Behaviors are easier to change than personality characteristics, which are thought to be relatively enduring and that translate into behaviors anyway. Feedback on personal characteristics (e.g., "you are divisive"

or "argumentative") puts people on their guard and causes them to discredit the information if they can.

C. Present new frames of reference, such as clear descriptions of organizational changes and their implications for performance expectations
and career opportunities. Information about what is happening in the
firm, especially when major changes are occurring, provides a new context for evaluating performance feedback, and causes people to pay
more attention and take feedback less for granted. They may realize,
more than usual, that their jobs are at stake, and may take time to think
about the match between their capabilities and changing organizational needs.

D. Communicate explicit definitions of performance dimensions, expectations, and rewards. The more the organization is clear about what behaviors and outcomes are valued and rewarded, the more those
behaviors and outcomes (and feedback about them) are salient to individuals.

3. *Internal Attributions*

A. Show leaders how to avoid defensiveness and denial as initial reactions
to negative feedback. People do not learn when they deny the importance or accuracy of information or are defensive about it and blame
the information on factors beyond their control. Avoiding defensiveness and denial is easier said than done, especially for people who have
favorable opinions of themselves. Coaches can help leaders avoid discounting information by asking them to consider several reasons why
the feedback was negative, not just one reason. Cases and workshop
exercises might be used to demonstrate the different impact of ignoring
feedback versus determining and evaluating different reasons for it,
and how the feedback could be attributed to themselves or to other
factors.

B. Provide comparative performance information. Information about
how others performed is useful, especially because poor performers are
likely to overevaluate their performance, and top performers are likely
to underevaluate their performance relative to others. Comparative
data (e.g., norms based on average ratings received across other managers at the same organizational level) help recipients calibrate their
results—that is, judge its meaning and put it in perspective.

C. Focus feedback on behaviors to avoid the threatening nature of feedback (as stated in 2A).

D. Give feedback frequently, not just once a year. Give in-the-moment
feedback. This means providing feedback immediately after the behavior has occurred, for instance, as soon as a meeting or presentation
is over. It is easier to discuss behaviors and to remember details of per-

formance at that point than it is at a later, formal performance feed-back discussion. The immediate feedback discussion can focus on how things went, the effects of the feedback recipient's behavior on others, and what the feedback recipient could have done differently. The feedback recipient may focus attention on others (e.g., "Do you believe what so-and-so did?"). However, the provider of feedback can turn the attention back to the feedback recipient (e.g., "I think the group's re-action might have been different if you had not said such-and-such.").

4. *Re-evaluating Self-Concept*
   A. Use feedback in the process of setting performance and development goals (integrate feedback into the firm's performance management sys-tem). Setting development goals forces a relation between the feed-back and ways the individual should change. Leaders who use feedback to set development goals begin to rethink their self-concepts in the process. Their revised self-image motivates development to make the image a reality.
   B. Require goal setting and development planning at least annually. Planning should be an ongoing process, and feedback should be an ex-pected part of the planning process. When this occurs regularly, feed-back becomes less threatening and more a regular part of doing business. Moreover, attention is on accomplishments and ways to im-prove, not just on what went wrong.
   C. Tie together business goals and individual leadership development goals. Leaders' development needs follow from their own career ambi-tions and the needs of the business for certain levels of expertise and performance. Development is needed to do better in the job today, im-prove in the job tomorrow, and be ready to meet future needs of the business in this job or in other assignments. As such, development does not occur in a vacuum, but has a direct effect on career opportunities. This prompts leaders to consider their skills and abilities in relation to business needs, and to reevaluate their self-concept as they set goals for development and their career.
   D. Offer leadership development resources. Development planning and implementation is primarily the responsibility of the leader. The orga-nization provides the resources to support the planning. This begins with advice and assistance of the leader's management, often with a mind to the organization's succession plans. It also includes the avail-ability of executive coaches and leadership training courses (i.e., work-shops and classes as well as computer-based, self-paced learning).
   E. Reward managers for their development as leaders. Executives should put their money where their mouth is. If they say that leadership devel-opment is important to the firm, they should show they mean it by not

only providing the enabling resources, but rewarding positive outcomes. Leaders should be rewarded for implementing their development plans, showing improvement, and demonstrating that they are ready for increased responsibility and advancement. This will make feedback more potent, and make it more likely that leaders will take feedback to heart and use it to change the way they think of themselves and provide direction for change (perhaps so that the leaders can become the type of manager they want to be or thought they were already).

F. Reward executives for contributing to the leadership development of the people who report to them. If executives want leaders to take feedback and development seriously, then they too should be rewarded for providing feedback, providing time and resources for development, and coaching leaders in their organization. This will show the leaders that the organization takes feedback, development, and change seriously. This, in turn, will cause them to pay more attention to what feedback and opportunities for development really mean to them.

3

Self-Regulation: Processes for Maintaining Motivation and Resilience

One important facet of gaining self-insight is being able to incorporate new information about themselves and make changes in their behavior and performance. Leaders need to be able to regulate their behavior effectively and respond appropriately in different situations and under different conditions. They need to understand their capabilities in relation to the changing demands of the business. As they get feedback about what is and is not working, they may need to alter their views of themselves. This requires recognizing that the information disconfirms what they already thought about themselves (an uncomfortable position to be in) and then using the information to revise their self-concept and change their behavior. This is the process of self-regulation. Self-regulation allows people to maintain their motivation and have the resilience they need to overcome barriers to goal accomplishment.

This chapter examines how leaders and people, in general, regulate their behavior. The chapter considers conditions that foster self-regulation and what happens when leaders fail to regulate their actions and change their self-concepts. The discussion begins with a general explanation of self-regulation.

THE MEANING AND VALUE OF SELF-REGULATION

Self-regulation, or self-control, is any effort to alter one's own responses, whether these responses are thoughts, actions, feelings, desires, or performances (Baumeister, Heatherton, & Tice, 1994). Without self-regulation, people would respond to a situation on the basis of merely habit, inclination, or innate tendencies. Self-regulation prevents this natural response and substitutes another, or there may be a lack of response altogether.

Self-regulation involves a hierarchy of processes. Lower processes are immediate reactions that are generally gratifying. Higher order processes entail longer time spans, such as postponing or foregoing gratification. When giving in to instant or rapid gratification overrides a resolution to abstain, the individual has failed in self-regulation. This implies a competition between responses. Higher processes suggest standards individuals would like to attain. However, this requires the strength to overcome natural tendencies and achieve a higher order response, which may be equally or more rewarding, but the rewards may be longer in coming. Not succumbing to natural or habitual tendencies requires strength (or willpower). It also requires a supportive environment. Few people can resist a rich chocolate cake if it is shoved in front of them for desert or is readily available every time they open the refrigerator door. However, if the environment limits temptation and provides support for control (the Weight Watcher's concept), then people are more able to resist.

Self-Regulatory Behaviors and Attitudes

Table 3.1 lists attitudes and behaviors that are typical of someone who is good at self-management. These were developed by De Waele, Morval, and Sheitoyan (1993). People who are good at self-regulation, or self-management, to use De Waele et al.'s term, take care of themselves, know their limitations, are able to delay gratification, and recognize how changes around them affect their lives. They do not wait for others to establish the rule or for things to happen. They set their own standards and create their own opportunities. In short, they have insight and willpower, and they are proactive.

Self-management is very much embedded in Western individualistic culture. Self-managers hold four values (De Waele et al., 1993): (a) They have a sense of confidence and faith in life. (b) They believe in their own and others' potential and ability. (c) They are open-minded and curious. (d) They have a sense of autonomy and a desire and ability to express their individuality. Self-managers are people who have the following characteristics (De Waele et al., 1993): They understand their own value system, and as a result, they can develop personal competencies and benefit from self-management opportunities. They are better prepared to manage and direct others. Also, they are sensitive to their own internal conflicts, and are better at understanding and managing competition and conflict with and between others. They are less dependent on their organization and less susceptible to manipulation. That is, they have a sense of their own personal power. They are prepared to contribute to the organization (organizational citizenship), and they contribute to the development of effective group process as they develop themselves.

TABLE 3.1

Self-Management Attitudes and Behaviors

People who are self-managers ...

- Take care of themselves physically.
- Know where and when to set limits to guard their own well-being.
- Are aware of how changes in their lives have an effect on their development.
- Are interested in conscious self-development; set development goals and plans, participates in development activities.
- Believe that their own learning process depends on their own doing; take control over their learning.
- Develop a realistic attitude in coping with life events, especially sudden, possibly stressful changes.
- Know when to say no—for instance, avoid accepting an assignment they feel would be beyond their capabilities; make sure they are prepared for the level of responsibility they take on.
- Know that there are things in their environment that cannot be changed easily or at all—for instance, others' attitudes.
- Accept prior experiences, even if they are painful.
- Prepare for the future through professional training or by learning new skills.
- Balance the energy they expend on different aspects of life (body, emotion, money, love, work).
- Are able to actively cope with disappointments, deceptions, burnout, and depression.
- Are aware that at times their failure to self-manage may affect others negatively (e.g., mismanaging money may have repercussions for others).
- In working with others, particularly direct reports, they are both directive and supportive at the same time, rather than coercive or punitive.
- Encourage others, particularly direct reports, to manage themselves rather than encourage submissiveness.
- Do not wait for the organization to provide opportunities for self-development; take charge of their own self-development.
- In interaction with others, especially supervisors, are responsive to the group and to authority while also expressing their autonomy.
- Set their own standards for success and failure, with knowledge, but not blind acceptance, of others' expectations and standards.
- Stay away from ideologies that do not support development of the person.

Note.   Based on De Waele et al. (1993).

Sensitivity to Social Regulation.   Self-regulation stems from social regulation (i.e., how others influence our lives) and affects how people regulate themselves. People develop different orientations to self-regulation. People who compare their actual self to the way they believe they ought to be (or others want them to be) are oriented to avoid negative outcomes. People who compare their actual self to their ideal are oriented to attain positive outcomes (Higgins, 1998a, 1998b).

Why Self-Regulation Is Important

Self-regulation is important for leaders, managers, and others for several reasons (De Waele et al., 1993): Healthy, adaptive organizations result when managers at each organizational level have personal management abilities, not just when there is exceptional talent at the top of the organization. Recognizing that organizations have limited resources calls attention to the need for people to rely on their internal resources to bring about acceptable conditions. When leaders are not self-managers, negative trends emerge that are the opposite of the positive characteristics of self-managers. That is, leaders who are not self-managers do not take care of themselves; they are not a source of physical, emotional, and spiritual health; and they do not believe that their learning process depends on their own participation.

Self-regulation is also important because leaders become alienated when they are constrained by predetermined strategies or decisions that are not under their control and that they cannot influence (De Waele et al., 1993). In addition the pace of organizational change due to technological, economic, and other factors is often so great that those who are not self-regulators find themselves burned out quickly. Self-management allows channeling personal and interpersonal energies productively, and avoiding wasted time and effort (i.e., people need to manage their time and resources effectively and efficiently).

Barriers to Self-Regulation

Self-regulation is not easy. There are a number of tough barriers to being an effective self-regulator who can translate values into concrete behavior (De Waele et al., 1993). One is the realization of being dependent on other people and organizational resources. Another is the lack of time or opportunity to learn about self-management, perhaps because of the pace of organizational change. Some organizations discourage autonomy, self-direction, and initiative. They may not do so intentionally, but this is the result of rigid adherence to policies and procedures.

A leader's actions can be a barrier to self-regulation. This may happen when leaders stop using their own and the organization's resources, are defensive when interacting with others, ignore or deny realistic feedback about what is actually happening in the environment, and/or are inflexible in the face of change, repeating ineffective behaviors that are anchored in the past rather than the future (De Waele et al., 1993). These barriers can be overcome or avoided when leaders take the initiative to apply their own resources (e.g., knowledge, competence, information, awareness) and the organization's resources to accomplish a particular goal. They can also be overcome when leaders develop meaningful relationships (e.g., with a supervisor), take feedback to heart, make decisions based on a sense of reality, and act with flexibility and a view to change situations and expectations now and in the future. Barriers to self-regulation are dealt with later.

SELF-CONTROL AND SELF-REGULATION

A distinction can be made between the concepts of self-control and self-regulation. Self-control is the process that maintains an active goal, and self-regulation is the process of maintaining one's actions in line with one's self-concept (Kuhl & Fuhrmann, 1988). For instance, the goal to quit smoking may be established because of doctor's orders before the goal has been internalized and self-regulated (i.e., becomes part of the person's sense of self and related needs). Initially, self-control requires a great deal of conscious effort. Slipping up may be punished, for example, by looking bad in front of valued friends or loved ones. The goal becomes self-regulated as the person realizes that it helps achieve other long-term goals (e.g., saving money, not to mention improving health and increasing length of life).

Kuhl and Fuhrmann (1988) outlined dimensions of "volitional competence" (which might otherwise be called willpower), separating them into five domains: self-control (goal pursuit), self-regulation (self-maintenance), self-reflection, inhibition of behavior because of frustration, and inhibition of feelings because of fear of punishment. The component dimensions of each of these are listed in Table 3.2.

Leaders operate in self-control and self-regulatory modes. Those who operate in a self-regulatory mode to pursue a goal are likely to need less time to make decisions related to the goal. They plan and initiate actions at the right times and situations. They are able to control their attention and inhibit troubling impulses to stick with a difficult task.

Self-control based on negative emotions can dominate leaders' behavior and suppress their self-maintenance function. An example would be someone following a goal to please another person, as when a corporate vice president embarks on an action (say negotiating a merger) at the CEO's behest despite having misgivings about the merger. This vice president's self-control is high, but so is her inhibition of other behaviors and personal goals.

Why Self-Regulation Does Not Always Work

There are a number of causes of failure to regulate a leader's behavior. Consider the following (based on Baumeister et al., 1994).

TABLE 3.2

Components of Volitional Competence

(1) Self-control
  • Thinking about your decision (intention control)
  • Thinking out the details (planning)
  • Feeling strong in the face of temptation (impulse control)
  • Learning from mistakes (failure control)

(2) Self-regulation
  • Trying consciously to keep attention stable (conscious attention control)
  • Being absorbed in the matter (unconscious attention control)
  • Considering positive incentives (motivation control)
  • Cheering yourself up (emotion control)
  • Feeling at one with your decisions and choices (self-determination)
  • Having no difficulties with spontaneous decisions (decision control)

(3) Self-reflection
  • Being certain not to become weak (volitional self-confidence)
  • Being optimistic (volitional optimism)

(4) Inhibition of behavior because of frustration
  • Feeling dull (energy deficiency)
  • Suddenly thinking of totally other things (intrusion)
  • Postponing events
  • Feeling obliged to meet others' expectations (alienation)
  • Getting going only if someone threatens to become angry (external control)

(5) Inhibition of feelings because of fear of punishment
  • Constantly asking yourself how you could have done better (ruminative thinking)
  • Maintaining your drive after a failure (emotional perseverance)
  • Finding it possible to abandon an old habit (flexibility)
  • Finding it easy to adjust to a sudden change in rules (cognitive flexibility)
  • Imposing discipline on yourself (pressure/over-control)
  • Imagining how awful another failure will be (negative anticipation)

Note.   Based on Kuhl and Fuhrmann (1988).

Conflicting Standards.   Multiple standards may conflict, so that it is hard to decide which standard to apply. Alternatively, this could be a lack of standards that could provide a basis for self-regulation.

Reduction of Monitoring. Usually, leaders evaluate themselves and their actions against relevant standards. Self-regulation becomes difficult when monitoring breaks down. This may explain, by the way, why attitudes often are unrelated to actual behavior (i.e., people say they believe one thing, but do another). For instance, those who say they believe in helping others do not volunteer when given the chance (cf. Ajzen & Fishbein, 1977).

Inadequate Strength. Self-regulation requires a sort of strength similar to the common notion of willpower. So failure of self-regulation may happen when an individual's strength is weaker than the impulse. It is not that standards disappear or that there is a failure of self-monitoring, but rather the person feels unable to respond in line with the standards. Stopping oneself involves mental and physical exertion. Indeed, suppressing thoughts may lead to an aroused state that was higher than trying to think about a subject. If the physical and mental strength is lacking, then the individual will not be able to overcome the impulse. This has been called "ego control" (the trait of being able to control impulses, desires, and actions; Funder & Block, 1989).

Psychological Inertia. Many actions may be easy to stop early, but may be difficult to stop once they have gained momentum, as if there is an inner force that impels continuing the behavior. Self-regulation requires the least strength when it overrides a response before or soon after it occurs. The longer a bad habit persists, the more difficult it is to stop.

Lapse-Activated Causal Patterns. Breakdowns in self-control have to start with an initial step. Sometimes a person can step over the line and then back off, quickly reasserting self-control. The cause of the initial lapse may be different than the cause of the continued breakdown of self-regulation. For instance, external stress and work overload may cause an initial lapse, giving in to temptation and indulging an impulse. This may result in an unexpected emotional response that results in a snowballing of the behavior. If this response does not occur, then the behavior may stop soon after it starts.

Renegade Attention. Attention management is a good way to nip a bad behavior in the bud. However, losing control of attention may make the behavior much more difficult to stop. The best resistance is to prevent a tempting stimulus. This is the reason why a reformed alcoholic would do well to avoid settings where others are drinking or even talking about it.

Rolling the Snowball. The first lapse may set off reactions that escalate what might otherwise have been a minor lapse. One reason may be a zero-tolerance, all-or-nothing belief. If a lapse occurs, then the cause is lost, thereby making any efforts at further self-control worthless. Another factor contributing to snowballing may be that the initial lapse causes the individual to stop self-monitoring, perhaps in order to prevent feelings of guilt. Another is that the behavior itself (e.g., drinking or the dieter's first bite of deliciously rich food) may lessen the individuals' capacity for self-awareness, so that they cannot reflect on their actions and think through the implications for themselves.

Acquiescence—Letting It Happen.   Human behaviors are rarely the result of inner forces that the individual is totally helpless to stop or control. However, many factors may contribute to the individual's acquiescence. Stress may cause people to want to stop being self-aware for awhile, so they indulge, even in a small way. Unfortunately, other forces may take over, causing snowballing, or, alternatively, the individual may be able to stop.

Misregulation.   People may try to regulate their behavior, but may do so in a nonoptimal or counterproductive way. Therefore, self-regulation may fail, not due to a lack of trying, but because a method was used that produced a different result than was intended. This may occur because of a deficiency in knowledge, particularly knowledge about oneself. The failure may be the result of overgeneralization—the assumption that what worked in one setting will work in another. Alternatively, individuals may believe they can stop when in fact they cannot. People may want to have certain beliefs about themselves, and these may influence their behavior, but they may exaggerate their abilities (particularly their good points). In addition, the culture may support beliefs that may prevent self-regulation. For instance, the belief that persistence leads to success may be culturally accepted and supported, but quitting may be desirable if someone is failing. Students may drink because they believe it makes them more popular, but continuing to drink may block their self-awareness and make them more obnoxious to their peers.

De-individuation.   This is losing self-awareness and feeling apprehensive about being evaluated. This is likely to happen when a person feels submerged in a group of people or when it is unpleasant to think about oneself (as it would be after a failure). People stop monitoring themselves and evaluating their actions in relation to their own personal standards. As a result, they lose their usual restraints and inhibitions, and their behavior may reflect impulses that would normally be held in check.

In summary, this section has reviewed reasons why self-regulation may not emerge. This may happen when leaders face conflicting standards, behave in ways that are inconsistent with their attitudes, weaken their resolve to change their behavior, lapse back to old behavior patterns, make mistakes in self-regulation (e.g., draw wrong conclusions about their behavior), lose self-awareness, or feel apprehensive about being evaluated.

Evaluation Apprehension and Self-Criticism

Low self-awareness and apprehension about being evaluated are causes of deindividuation and loss of self-regulation. Leaders are usually not described as being apprehensive, particularly about being evaluated. However, leaders are often keenly aware of, and hesitant about, how others view them, especially in terms of how they compare to others. Executives are often in a sort of competition, perhaps for a top spot in the organization, or at least for continued bonuses, choice assignments, and job opportunities. They also compete in the marketplace, attempting to bring projects to fruition and contributing to a positive bottom line for the firm and the stockholders. Also, executives are often highly self-critical. Their work demands a lot from them, and they demand a lot from themselves. Although they may not appreciate others' evaluations of them, they are constantly observing their own performance. They may exude self-confidence outwardly, but they may wonder about their ability to meet the ever-changing requirements of their jobs and the uncertain and changing business environment.

Evaluation apprehension and self-criticism may interact to affect leaders' self-regulation. Consider the possible effects of different levels of evaluation apprehension and self-criticism. Note that these are just hypotheses, and research is needed to test them.

High Evaluation Apprehension and High Self-Criticism. These leaders become debilitated. Their performance output is low. They are low in self-efficacy. They have trouble getting things done. They set very high standards and expect too much of themselves. They need coaching and counseling, especially when receiving feedback that is critical.

Low Evaluation Apprehension and High Self-Criticism. These leaders do not care as much about what others think of them, but they are very hard on themselves. They are likely to be outgoing and self-regulated. They emphasize quality and meeting standards, and they seek feedback to see how they are doing. They set goals for themselves, and they do whatever they need to do to overcome barriers to achieving these goals.

High Evaluation Apprehension and Low Self-Criticism. These leaders are outwardly focused. They care more about what others think of them than what they think of themselves. As a result, they do not have much self-insight. Their self-insight is limited to what they think others think of them. They avoid feedback, especially if it might be critical. As a result, they get little feedback. They fear rejection, and so they do not give others a chance to say "no." They plow ahead with their work, worrying more about its quantity (especially if quantity is reported) than its quality. Their prime concern is having others think well of them. When they receive feedback, they need a great deal of encouragement to use it.

Low Evaluation Apprehension and Low Self-Criticism. These leaders are oblivious to others' opinions of them and to their own performance outcomes. They are happy-go-lucky, unstressed by job demands and the press of a high position. They have high self-regard, and they are likely to take more risks than they probably should. However, they have low standards, set low goals, and produce low outcomes.

In short, leaders' evaluation apprehension and self-criticism may combine to affect self-regulation, and with it, attitudes, behaviors, and performance outcomes. Being high in both self-criticism and evaluation apprehension can be particularly damaging personality characteristics. Evaluation apprehension accompanied by low self-criticism may focus the leader's attention more on what others think than what is truly important, and they may avoid feedback that could enhance their self-awareness. Leaders who are highly self-critical, even though they do not care what others think, are likely to be highly self-regulated, although one drawback may be that their standards are so high that they never feel satisfied.

SELF-CONTROL AND IMPULSIVENESS

Logue (1998) distinguished between self-control and impulsiveness. For instance, an insurance company chief executive may spend the firm's money on the latest technology now (impulsiveness) while deferring maintenance on the company's headquarters building (which would have represented self-control). A university department chair may hire an expensive senior faculty member who is no longer productive to boost the department's prestige instantly (impulsiveness) rather than hire an inexpensive junior faculty member with considerable potential.

Self-control is the "choice of a more delayed, but ultimately more valued, outcome over a less delayed, but ultimately less valued, outcome" (Logue, 1998, p. 222). *Impulsiveness* is the opposite—choosing a less delayed, but less valued—outcome. The outcome can be stated negatively or positively. In the decision to purchase technology now while deferring building maintenance, the positive outcome is the increased immediate productivity or perhaps just the status of having the latest equipment (the organizational analogue to "keeping up with the Jones"). The negative outcomes are that the technology may be outdated quickly while the firm's facility will continue to erode, perhaps requiring far greater costs later. In the department chair's decision to hire the senior faculty member, the positive outcome is the instant prestige, whereas the negative outcome is the lack of productivity.

Logue (1998) was quick to point out that the distinction between self-control and impulsiveness does not indicate that one is necessarily better than another. People generally assume that self-control is "good" and impulsiveness is "bad." However, this may not be the case. Delaying gratification may not make sense when a delay may mean never achieving the positive outcome, or when the future is so uncertain that the probability of reaching the delayed goal is very uncertain. Self-control in this sense is not a matter of willpower. Will has less to do about it than understanding the pros and cons of immediate versus delayed action. Logue (1998) pointed to the following factors that predict when a leader will show self-control:

- *Delaying discounting.* This is the degree to which an outcome is valued less because it is delayed. The more events are delayed, the more their distant value approaches zero. Delay discounting causes people to choose outcomes that are less delayed even though they are of less value than the more delayed outcomes.
- *Time horizon.* The longer the time horizon for the delay, the more an outcome is discounted. The more people discount longer time horizons, the more they are likely to act impulsively. Managers on a fast track for advancement do not plan to be in their current jobs for very long. As a result, distant outcomes have less value to them. They want to take actions that will have immediate impact so they can take the credit and move on.
- *Viewing time as passing quickly.* Executives who feel that events are moving quickly and time seems to be passing fast (perhaps because of the challenge of the task or the fun of interacting with valued colleagues) are more likely to wait for delayed outcomes and show self-control.
- *Precommitment.* A strategy to ensure delay is to precommit. The executive can announce that a certain amount of facilities maintenance will occur each year for the next 5 years until the task is complete. That way, several years from now when other investment opportunities arise, the executive will not be tempted to spend the money in other ways. Also, the maintenance will be closer to completion by then, and further expenses from delay will have been avoided.
- *Uncertainty.* The more uncertainty that a delayed outcome will ever be achieved, the less need there is for self-control. Many business leaders operate in an environment of financial uncertainty. This may cause them to maximize control over existing resources instead of trying to obtain long-term goals. Additional information may not be available, or the existing information may be too complex to make a reasonable decision about delay. The best choice may be to go for the short-term benefits.

Sometimes leaders make a short-term decision because they want the immediate value, but they deceive others into thinking they have made the long-term investment. They can do this because others do not have all the information they do. The deception is a way to deflect others' unhappiness with the impulsive decision. The leader may purchase the new technology, but promise to put funds aside for maintenance as soon as the money becomes available (but knowing full well that it will not, or if it does, that other uses will present themselves). Deception may work for the executive in the short run, but in the long run, it will lead to distrust, a marred reputation, and difficulty in working with others.

Logue discussed other situations faced by executives in which the choices are between two negative outcomes. Leaders may show self-control by choosing an immediate but lesser negative outcome, or show impulsiveness by delaying the larger outcome as long as possible. For instance, after investing in a project that seems to be losing money, executives can decide to cut their losses now or wait, hoping for a turnaround, despite the increasingly low probability of success. Waiting will delay the disappointment and anger of those who are still highly committed to working on the project. The executive may hope that investors and financial analysts would see cutting the project now as a positive sign, but still they may take out their immediate frustration by selling their shares and thereby reduce the stock price. Rather than admit they made a mistake and take the consequences early, executives are prone to actually increase the commitment of resources and face the risk of further negative outcomes, essentially throwing good money after bad (a phenomenon in social psychology known as escalating commitment; Staw, 1976). Executives can try to avoid such situations altogether by precommitting to courses of action, for instance, announcing in advance that if the project does not turn a profit in a designated time frame then it will be cut.

Another common business example occurs when executives delay giving a subordinate unfavorable feedback. They may avoid the situation each time some negative behavior occurs, waiting for the opportune moment or for the once-a-year formal performance review and feedback discussion. They may avoid disciplinary action because they do not want to face their subordinate's emotional reactions. The longer they wait, the less likely the problem is to go away on its own and the more unpleasant the task becomes, indeed possibly leading to having to fire the individual. This is why derailed executives are often the last to know that they have a problem. (See chap. 10's, this volume, discussion of how executives overcome such career barriers.) Another example is having to say "no" to employees who want special treatment. Saying "no" is difficult in that no one wants to disappoint someone else. However, saying "yes" may incur other problems, such as having to justify the decision to others or having to treat others in a similar way. Saying "yes" gets rid of the employee for the time being, but reinforces the employees' inappropriate persistence. Avoiding the employee may only increase the intensity of the employee's requests, which is also something the executive wants to avoid.

Another type of impulsiveness occurs when executives lose their temper, perhaps as a result of a subordinate's actions. The subordinate's negative behavior may cease (the subordinate may withdraw or become compliant quickly), but this reinforces the executive's emotional outbursts. However, in the long run, this aggressive management style may very well hurt the executive in a number of ways. The subordinate may not take risks in the future, foregoing opportunities. The subordinate may withhold information. Also, the executive may develop a negative reputation and will have trouble recruiting good people. The bottom line is that leaders need to take into account the long-term consequences of their actions.

Summary

So far, this chapter has examined self-management and the related concepts of self-regulation and self-control (and its opposite, impulsiveness). Leaders need to be good self-managers to use the insights they gain about themselves and their environment, and acquire and use behaviors that keep them on track in terms of their performance, development, and career. Once people assume a leadership role, the assumption is that they have had the experience and gained the savvy to manage most any difficult situation. However, the demands of an executive's position often pose dilemmas that test leaders' ability to maintain self-control. Put simply, self-management is not easy, and many barriers can get in the way, such as the pressure to continually monitor one's own behavior and the uncertainty of situations. The next section considers how leaders' belief in themselves (and their tendency to be self-critical and be apprehensive of evaluation) can support their self-management.

SELF-EFFICACY AND PERFORMANCE
ON TOUGH JOBS

Self-efficacy is a "personal judgment of how well one can execute courses of action required to deal with prospective situations" (Bandura, 1982, p. 122). A leader's expectations of being able to deal with a situation determine how much effort the leader expends on the situation and how long that effort is sustained, especially if there is disconfirming evidence (i.e., the leader does not seem to be succeeding). People who see themselves as efficacious exert sufficient effort to produce successful outcomes, whereas those who do not are likely to stop their efforts prematurely, and as a result, do not do well or fail altogether (Bandura, 1986). In a review of the literature, Stajkovic and Luthans (1998) reported that self-efficacy is related to success in job search, insurance sales, and research productivity of university faculty members. It has also been found to be related to a number of work performance measures, including adjusting to new situations, adapting to advanced technologies, coping with career-related events, generating managerial ideas, and acquiring new skills.

Stajkovic and Luthans (1998) analyzed the existing research to determine the extent to which self-efficacy is related to work outcomes depending on the demands of the situation. Researchers in this field hypothesized that, in general, there should be a positive relation between self-efficacy and work performance. They also hypothesized that the relation between self-efficacy and performance would be strongest when task complexity is low because individuals are able to accurately assess the demands of the task relative to their abilities. However, the relation between self-efficacy and performance should be lower at higher levels of task complexity, especially at the highest level, because individuals have a harder time accurately judging whether their abilities are up to the demands of the task. Complex tasks entail more complex skills for successful performance. For instance, they may require more knowledge, cognitive ability, memory capacity, behavioral facility, information processing, persistence, and physical effort (Bandura, 1986).

Complex tasks may lead to faulty evaluation of both the task requirements and outcomes. In other words, people may not realize how complex the work actually is and that their skills are not up to par. In complex tasks, people may recognize the requirements imposed by certain aspects of the task but not others and, as a result, they ignore or miss certain elements of the task and fail to see that their weaknesses affect their overall performance. In addition, they may not accurately evaluate their actual performance on the task, believing they are actually doing better than they are. Stajkovic and Luthans' (1998) review of the literature supported the hypothesis that whereas self-efficacy is generally related to performance, the relation between self-efficacy and performance tends to be weakest for the higher levels of task complexity.

Group Self-Efficacy

Bandura (2000) noted that groups, like individuals, can develop a sense of self-efficacy. Teams develop a shared impression of the members' collective efficacy. This will affect the goals leaders seek to achieve through collective action. The belief in work group's efficacy will influence how much effort leaders put into the group initiative, their persistence when the group fails to generate a positive outcome quickly or meets opposition, and their resilience in the face of discouragement in tackling the social aspects of a problem. Group self-efficacy is important to leadership and group effectiveness when the task requires interdependent effort, and a weak link can breakdown the entire team's performance (as in a soccer team, as opposed to a team of gymnasts who achieve success independently; Bandura, 2000).

The leader's self-efficacy is tied to the group's self-efficacy. The latter can be viewed from the leader's perspective or the group members' perspectives. It can also be viewed in terms of the each individual in the group or the group as an entity. So, it is possible to measure the leader's perception of each group member's competence, the leader's perception of the ability of the group as a whole, each group member's perception of their own and each other's competence (which can be averaged to derive a measure of group self-efficacy), and each group member's perception of the ability of the group as a whole (which also can be averaged across group measures to derive one index of group self-efficacy).

Leaders who believe in the importance of the collective voice are likely to try to accomplish organizational goals through collective action. They are likely to empower the team to act as a body, valuing both individual contributions and the outcome of the team. Leaders who have little faith in collective action are not likely to delegate tasks to a group. This may hurt organizational functioning, especially if the task demands interdependent effort to be successful.

Summary

Leaders are likely to gain a sense of self-efficacy from the positive experiences that led to their promotion to increasingly responsible positions. To some extent, self-efficacy becomes a self-fulfilling prophesy in bolstering a leader's confidence, persistence, and, ultimately, performance. Nevertheless, self-doubt may emerge, especially as the leader faces novel situations of increasing uncertainty and complexity. The next section addresses missteps that can occur and strategies for handling them.

WHEN SELF-REGULATION GOES AWRY: MISREGULATION AND SELF-HANDICAPPING STRATEGIES

Self-handicapping is a way leaders maintain their self-esteem. It occurs when they deliberately create road blocks to success, increasing their chances of failure. Just as people make excuses for their failures after the fact, wanting to avoid admitting to themselves and others that they were to blame, they set up their own failure as a way of not having to attribute failure to themselves after the event has occurred. As a result, the negative outcome does not threaten their self-esteem. The created handicap confuses the relation between their behavior and the outcome. Their inability did not prevent them from succeeding; rather, it was the environment, others' actions or decisions, or their own laziness (simply not trying). They would rather guarantee their own failure than take the risk of succeeding or having to attribute failure to themselves.

People with a tendency to self-handicap say they are easily distracted, for instance, by noises or their own creative thoughts when trying to read or that they let their emotions get in the way of doing better. They feign illness, procrastinate, or become emotionally upset.

The feelings of doubt and a desire to protect a positive self-image are the motivational basis for self-handicapping. Chronic self-doubt may stem from recurring failures in the past. It may also stem from not being able to determine unequivocally that prior successes were due to one's abilities. Alternatively, self-doubt may be more transitory and may stem merely from lack of experience with the task at hand.

Self-handicapping may be public or private. In public, it is making sure that significant others are aware of the handicap. One will use observable handicaps, such as alcohol consumption, drug use, or lack of effort. In private, the audience is mainly oneself, and it occurs by the explanations one gives oneself (e.g., "I know I didn't try as hard as I could have.").

If success should happen despite the handicap, then the handicap increases the perceived personal responsibility for the positive outcome. The perception is that individuals must be so able that they succeeded despite the difficulty or not really trying. Yet individuals protect themselves in the face of failure. In this sense, leaders cannot lose in guarding their self-image or the image others have of them.

People of low self-esteem are likely to be especially concerned about protecting their public image and self-regard by self-handicapping, whereas those of high self-esteem are motivated to amplify their public and self-image (Arkin & Oleson, 1998; Tice, 1991). Leaders with high self-esteem will seek ways to enhance their likelihood of success and not to protect them against failure, and those with low self-esteem will try to protect themselves against failure at the expense of their own success. Not surprisingly, self-handicappers tend to be underachievers (Arkin & Oleson, 1998).

Self-handicapping is not the only self-protection strategy leaders with self-doubt might use to maintain their self- and public image. For instance, they can withdraw from the situation altogether, get help from others, or delay the task until they have more training and self-confidence. People who have a tendency to attribute outcomes (positive or negative) to causes outside their control are more likely to be self-handicappers. Those who see themselves as in control of outcomes that happen to them are likely not to use self-handicapping as a means of self-protection, because self-handicapping requires making an external attribution for outcomes (Rhodewalt, 1990).

Similarly, leaders who are mastery oriented—that is, interested in increasing their competence, intellectual growth, and learning—are not likely to use self-handicapping. People who have helpless reactions to personal setbacks are likely to pursue performance, rather than learning, goals. They are concerned about demonstrating their ability and receiving positive feedback to affirm their sense of self-competence. As such, they are likely to use self-handicapping as a means of self-protection when outcomes are uncertain.

Although feedback seeking can become a manipulative strategy that feeds into self-handicapping, it is generally a positive way for leaders to regulate their behavior in light of environmental conditions and reactions to their performance. Leaders can use feedback to own up to mistakes, adjust to changing circumstance, shift their course of action, or set new, more achievable, goals.

SEEKING FEEDBACK

People enhance their self-awareness by seeking negative feedback (Ashford & Tsui, 1991). This provides them with an accurate understanding of how others evaluate them. This, in turn, should help them adjust their behavior. Also, people are viewed favorably when they ask for negative feedback. However, they are viewed unfavorably when they ask for positive feedback, which has the appearance of self-aggrandizement (Ashford & Tsui, 1991).

A way to increase managers' accountability to use feedback is to have skilled coaches available to help them review and understand their results. Participation in training—actually taking action to meet development plans—affirms the importance of these plans and the desirability of following through. Linking feedback to a development program that provides training in the areas measured by the feedback survey communicates the importance of feedback. This creates a developmental culture in the organization. Sometimes, leadership development programs start with a feedback process to help the participants target a training path. Evaluating and rewarding leaders for continuous improvement in the areas of the development plan (i.e., not just accomplishing the development goals but applying those goals for performance improvement), and seeing others rewarded for performance improvement, may further increase the importance of development, and feedback helps establish the direction for development. This in turn could increase accountability for using feedback in the future. Overall, these accountability mechanisms establish a climate for development where leaders know they are expected to use feedback for performance improvement (Walker & Smither, 1999).

Feedback is a central theme in this book. It is the foundation for self-insight and development, and, as such, a central aspect of self-regulation. Feedback processes and ways to deliver feedback to leaders are taken up further in chapters 6 and 7, in this volume. To conclude this chapter, consider strategies leaders can adopt to enhance their own and their subordinates' self-management and performance.

WAYS TO INCREASE SELF-MANAGEMENT

The following are practical, relatively inexpensive suggestions to encourage self-management, especially in complex settings (based on Stajkovic and Luthans, 1998):

- *Clarify the task.* Leaders should provide accurate, clear, and concise descriptions of the tasks managers and employees are asked to perform. This will enable them to accurately evaluate the demands of the complex task and accurately regulate their effort and avoid faulty assessment of their perceived efficacy.

- *Provide needed training.* Employees should be trained in the technologies needed to do the job well.
- *Explain how best to do the job.* Employees should be guided in the appropriate means to do the job. Although most tasks can be done in different ways, some methods may be better (more efficient in use of time and energy) than others. Employees may believe they can do the task one way, but if this is not the best way, then they may be spinning their wheels and disappointed in the result.
- *Eliminate or reduce physical distractions.* The work environment should not be cluttered with physical distractions that make doing the job difficult. Physical distractions, such as noise, not only make doing the job difficult (e.g., reading and processing information) but also increase thoughts of failure and stress and reduce coping.
- *Develop and reinforce feelings of self-efficacy.* Employees faced with complex tasks may despair that they do not even know where to begin. So they may be able to benefit from encouragement and demonstrations showing that they already have the needed skills to be successful.
- *Train employees in how to cope with complex tasks.* Employees will not always be able to face a task with self-confidence, at least not at the start. They need to know how to diagnose the needs of the task and recognize that they will learn as they go, acquiring the experience and added skills that help them do better over time. They should realize that ability is not a fixed entity and initial failure is an acceptable way to learn. Also, they need to know how to overcome their initial anxiety stemming from a felt lack of control. They need to be able to live with ambiguity at the start of a task, and give themselves the time to experiment, learn, and adjust to new task requirements.
- *Ensure that training is timely.* Training in new tasks required by a complex job should be provided close to when the employees have to perform the task. Not only is this more efficient from an organizational standpoint in ensuring that employees who need the training most receive it, but it also ensures that the new skills will be applied. If considerable time elapses between training and performance, employees are likely to lose their skills and doubt their ability to do the job when they have to. The same applies to training employees concerning how to cope with change and new task demands. If they do not have a chance to apply the new skills, then the entire efficacy enhancement program will be a waste.
- *Provide clear and objective standards for measuring performance.* Employees should know how they are doing as the task is performed and accomplished. This is especially important if employees are doing part of a complex job. In such a case, not only should they be able to understand the effectiveness of the overall outcome, but they should also be able to judge the effectiveness of their contribution. So measures of performance may be needed to reflect different parts of the overall project. In addition, there should be specific standards for evaluating the quality and quantity of each person's contribution. The stan-

dards provide a way to gauge effectiveness and gear performance to a particular level. If feedback is not available about performance or if the performance measures do not indicate whether they are good or bad, then employees are likely to develop inaccurate estimates of their self-efficacy.

• *Attach personal consequences to employees' performance.* Without personal consequences, employees will have little incentive to appraise their abilities accurately. A major reason that people form self-efficacy beliefs to begin with is because they understand that outcomes they care about depend on how well they perform the job (Bandura, 1997). People take control over their actions because of the benefits they anticipate receiving. So employees must recognize that if they perform well, they will benefit. The nature of the rewards and the outcomes that accrue need to be there, and be clear. Even if rewards are given, if people do not know that after the fact, and expect it before the fact, then they will not exert the initiative to evaluate task requirements, learn needed skills, and exert effort to do the job well.

CONCLUSIONS

Self-regulation flows from self-insight (the topic of the last chapter). Managers and leaders need to regulate their own behavior for maximum effectiveness, and they do so by understanding themselves and those with whom they work. Leaders who are good at self-regulation understand themselves well. They know their strengths and weaknesses, are able to delay gratification, and set achievable goals and reasonable standards for themselves. They are sensitive to their own internal conflicts and have a strong sense of their ability to bring about positive outcomes (self-efficacy). This is important for being able to maintain motivation and adapt to continuously changing role demands and pressures. But it is not easy. Barriers to self-regulation can occur, especially when leaders ignore feedback about critical outcomes.

Self-control refers to maintaining a focus on goal achievement. Self-regulation is acting in a way that is consistent with, and reinforces, one's self-concept. Self-regulation may break down when leaders falter on their standards, become less vigilant in paying attention to the effects of their behavior, or give in to impulses for immediate reinforcement (or procrastinate in facing negative outcomes).

Having a sense of self-efficacy, that is, a belief in being able to tackle difficult situations successfully, is important for a leader's continued self-regulation. People who view themselves as able to bring about positive outcomes are able to sustain their effort and motivation, even when the situation becomes intense and barriers are hard to overcome. Some leaders, who are weak in self-efficacy and find new pressures threatening, may protect their self-image by ignoring feedback and blaming others for failure. Other leaders, who are strong in self-efficacy and welcome new challenges, seek feedback, face problems directly, and make difficult decisions that may mean facing negative outcomes now. There are ways they can avoid unpleasant situations and indeed reduce the risks of failure. These include precommitting to actions that will put a stop to negative outcomes before they get worse and being sure they and the people with whom they work are well-prepared for the complex tasks ahead, thereby giving themselves and others the chance to enhance their belief in their own ability to manage themselves and be successful.

Self-insight and self-regulation are essential ingredients to setting and achieving goals for meaningful career development. This is addressed in the next chapter's examination of the ways leaders form, maintain, and enhance their self-identity.

4

Self-Identity: Personal Directions for Development

Self-identity refers to how individuals view themselves in relation to others—in particular, what individuals do to earn a living (e.g., plumber, teacher, lawyer, physician, researcher, executive), the official roles they take (e.g., leader or elected officer of a corporation, religious institution, or volunteer organization), and what they enjoy and create in their free time (e.g., gardener, photographer, golfer). This chapter addresses a leader's sense of career identity, for instance, as corporate officer, manager, or entrepreneur. Having a strong sense of identity is important because it directs behavior, and viewing oneself as a leader provides a focus for leadership behaviors. The term *career* implies what the person has done, is doing, and plans to do as an occupation. Career is often a dominant part of a leader's life, but not the only part, and a leader's self-identity can have several key components, some of which may have little to do with work. An individual's identity at any given time stems from what has occurred and where one is today (e.g., ones education, job experiences, current responsibilities). It is also prospective in terms of the goals that direct behavior.

The chapter first outlines a theory of career motivation because it highlights the genesis of self-identity. This approach holds that self-identity stems from insight and resilience, building on the first two chapters of this book, which explored self-insight and self-regulation, respectively. The chapter then focuses on how executives develop a sense of leadership identity. Leaders may alter or recreate their identities as they move into different stages of life and confront different life events (e.g., divorce, children leaving home, job change, promotion), and as they change the value they place on different roles and goals. Overall, this chapter is about the meaning of a leader's career identity, its sources, how it relates to other individual characteristics (in particular, resilience in the face of barriers and insight into oneself and the environment), how identity changes over time, and how identity affects leadership behavior.

THE ROLE OF SELF-INSIGHT AND
SELF-REGULATION (RESILIENCE)
IN ESTABLISHING SELF-IDENTITY

One view of the genesis and strength of a leader's career identity is that it requires resilience and insight. This idea stems from *career motivation theory* (London, 1983; London & Noe, 1997). The theory holds that a meaningful identity is one that is an accurate reflection of the individual. Having a meaningful identity is grounded in individuals' sense of insight in understanding their strengths and weaknesses and recognizing the limitations, opportunities, and demands of the environment. Effective, motivated leaders use this insight into themselves and their situation to form a strong sense of identity.

The strength of this self-identity rests, not just in insight, but also in the leader's resilience. This is the leader's ability to overcome career barriers. Leaders who are resilient are self-confident. They are high in self-esteem, and believe in their ability to be effective (self-efficacy, as described in the last chapter). They have a sense of self-control, believing they can make positive things happen for themselves and their companies. They want to achieve, and they respond positively to challenging situations. They are not threatened by negative feedback, but welcome it and use it to identify ways they can adapt. Each of these elements is defined as follows:

- *Career resilience* is the ability to adapt to changing circumstances, even when the circumstances are discouraging or disruptive. It is a disposition consisting of personality variables such as belief in oneself, need for achievement, and a willingness to take risks.
- *Career insight* is the ability to be realistic about oneself and one's career and to put these perceptions to use in establishing goals. It consists of establishing clear career goals and knowing one's strengths and weaknesses.
- *Career identity* is the extent to which one defines oneself by work. It consists of job, organizational, and professional involvement, as well as the needs for advancement, recognition, and being a leader. Viewing oneself as a leader is one form of career identity.

Career identity is the direction of motivation, insight is the energizing or arousal component, and career resilience is the maintenance or persistence component.

Resilience opens the door to insight, which in turn helps to form meaningful identity, and allows individuals to be open to new information—that is, individuals are able and willing to review feedback mindfully rather than categorizing it automatically, ignoring the information, or rationalizing it away.

The survey in Table 4.1 provides a way to assess your own career resilience, insight, and identity.

TABLE 4.1

Assess Your Career Motivation

Answer the following items to evaluate your career motivation:

Indicate the extent to which the following items apply to you. Use a 1 to 5 rating scale where

1 = To a very little extent

2 = somewhat

3 = To a fair extent

4 = Quite a bit

5 = To a very great extent

Resilience

1. ____ I am able to adapt to changing circumstances.

2. ____ I am willing to take risks.

3. ____ I welcome job and organizational changes.

4. ____ I can handle any work problem.

5. ____ I look forward to working with new and different people.

Insight

6. ____ I have clear career goals.

7. ____ I have realistic career goals.

8. ____ I know my strengths (the things I do well).

9. ____ I know my weaknesses (the things I am not good at).

10. ____ I recognize what I can do well and cannot do well.

Identity

11. ____ I define myself by my work.

12. ____ I work as hard as I can, even if it means frequently working long days and weekends.

13. ____ I am involved in my job.

14. ____ I am proud to work for my employer.

15. ____ I believe that my success depends on the success of my employer.

16. ____ I am loyal to my employer.

17. ____ I see myself as a professional and/or technical expert.

To score, average the items within each scale. Some possible patterns of career motivation are:

(A) Average resilience, insight, and identity all high (4 or above): Strong career motivation. Strong foundation for resisting career barriers, maintaining a positive self-image and career direction, and openness to feedback (favorable and unfavorable).

(B) Average resilience and insight high (4 or above), identity low (less than 3): Questioning career direction. Yet strong foundation for re-establishing career identity. Failure is likely to be a learning experience, and the individual is likely to get back on track quickly.

(C) Average resilience weak (less than 3), insight moderate (about 3), and identity strong (4 or above): Strong career identity, but weak foundation. Would have trouble overcoming career barriers. May be open to learning from performance feedback, but may not have the underlying positive self-image to adjust behavior in relation to feedback, re-calibrate one's identity, and formulate potentially successful career goals. This individual may be mired in self-doubt.

Note. These items were adapted from London (1993).

Career identity is a function of retrospective rationality as well as prospective rationality. *Retrospective rationality* occurs when people reflect on their current state, their insight into themselves and the environment, and their ability to overcome career barriers. When they have been successful in overcoming a barrier, when they have been right about their capabilities and demands in the environment, then they come to believe they are resilient and insightful. Also, when they look at where they have been and what they have done in their career, they form a self-identity that matches their experiences.

Prospective rationality is when people look forward to create the type of person they want to be. They decide how they want to change and develop. They do not rationalize current circumstances but generate new conditions, acquire new skills, build their confidence, test their newfound insight, and adjust their identity to allow them to be more successful and/or feel better about themselves and their careers.

Rationalization can be a way for individuals to save face, protect their self-esteem, and turn a career barrier into something positive. Leaders look back on an event and interpret it in a light that fits with their self-image and reputation. For instance, when G. Richard Thoman was suddenly ousted in 2000 as CEO of Xerox (after being hired away from IBM only 13 months earlier), he said in an interview, "The board and I agreed that it made more sense to implement our strategy with an internal team. And I'm a very big shareholder, and a lot of my future net worth is dependent on how well the new management team does" (Deutsch, 2000, p. C1).

Resilience is the bedrock of insight and identity. Resilience gives people strength to accept information about themselves and their environments and to use this information to regulate their behavior. In the process, and as individuals experience successes, learn, and reevaluate their capabilities, they revise their self-perceptions and refine, and sometimes alter, their professional and personal sense of identity. Insight is the spark that allows people to seek new information, motivates them to learn, and provides direction for experimenting with new behaviors. Resilience keeps people going. It allows individuals to maintain this spark as they confront barriers or unexpected conditions that limit their behavior. Together, resilience and insight allow the emergence and refinement of identity.

Sources of Resilience, Insight, and Identity

Resilience is usually well formed by the time people start their careers. They have had plenty of reinforcing experiences as a child and young adult to build their self-esteem (if they are fortunate and able). These experiences give them a sense that they can be effective in bringing about positive outcomes for themselves and generates a sense of wanting to achieve further. As such, resilience is harder to change. It is not immutable, however. Resilience is strengthened as people confirm their abilities throughout adulthood.

Insight and identity are a bit easier to change. They stem largely from information processing. As such, providing people with information about themselves, their environments and opportunities, and their role models and peers will help them calibrate their self-image, formulate goals, and direct their behavior in line with their abilities and interests. When they confront unexpected information, their resilience holds them in good stead as a basis to sustain and reinvigorate their motivation, learn, and continue to refine their insight and identity.

Support for Resilience, Insight, and Identity

This development process suggests ways organizations support people's resilience, insight, and identity. Supervisors provide reinforcement for excellent work, thereby reinforcing the individual's resilience. Supervisors provide unfavorable performance feedback in a constructive way by focusing on behaviors, not attacking the individual's character or abilities. They provide information about the organization (i.e., business goals, job expectations, standards for performance, needed knowledge), especially as changes occur. Career identity is shaped by information about career opportunities (e.g., what it takes to get ahead here and where the job openings will be) and advice about ways to take advantage of them.

Patterns of Resilience, Insight, and Identity

The previous discussion suggests that people who start their careers with reasonably high resilience will be able to use information about themselves and the environment to establish a meaningful, long-lasting career identity. Events do not always go that smoothly. Leaders may redirect their careers because of the barriers they face. They may lose their jobs (and in the process, their principal source of identity). Maybe they made some faulty decisions or decisions that did not work out, not because of poor judgment or lack of foresight, but because of unforeseeable events in the economy or competitive marketplace. They may be able to rise about the failure, attribute it appropriately (perhaps due to a combination of their own actions and uncontrollable events), learn from mistakes that were made (at least not to repeat them in the future), and find another position (perhaps with the help of the outplacement firm hired by the company to help the executive with a job search). The golden parachute may allow displaced executives to maintain a strong financial position and not change their standard of living. These individuals have the resources to overcome their disappointment, bolster their psychological resilience and insight, recover their motivation, and largely maintain their self-respect. Their foundation of resilience and insight serves them well in maintaining or redirecting their career identity. (See the discussion of derailed leaders in chap. 10, this volume.)

Another pattern is leaders who experience failure and question their ability but have the resilience to take appropriate action to restore their belief in themselves. They have a period of self-doubt brought on by the disappointment, and perhaps the surprise, of failure. Often leaders are stunned to lose their jobs. They did not see it coming. Maybe they knew things were not going as well as they would have liked, but they felt their corporate board or other top executives supported them. Losing this support along with their status, the resources they controlled, and the people who followed their direction can be a shattering experience. These individuals take some time to put the events in perspective and regain their drive. They initially question their abilities and judgment, but they eventually realize that they retain the skills, knowledge, and principles that have value. They overcome this temporary self-doubt, perhaps with the help of others (e.g., a supportive spouse, a mentor, a counselor), and seek new experiences. Their underlying resilience is sufficiently strong, and their understanding of their circumstances sufficiently accurate, to rise above their self-doubt. Perhaps they may not truly feel recovered until they find another leadership position. Indeed, they may never forget the loss and self-blame, but they learn from it. (Such frame-breaking experiences are a prime stimulus for learning.) Also, as a result, they feel stronger in their sense of self-worth. Moreover, they may have more empathy for others in similar situations.

Some fallen leaders do not make it back emotionally. They become mired in self-doubt. Eventually, they may achieve small successes and establish new, realistic goals. They may not have ever had a strong foundation of resilience. Their self-esteem and sense of self-efficacy may not have been established in their early lives and careers. They had the intelligence and drive to attain the education and career positions they needed to rise to a leadership role. Perhaps they relied too heavily on one of their strengths, not realizing the need to vary their behavior to suit the situation (e.g., the successful autocratic leader who makes all decisions, even after the firm has grown too large to manage alone). Perhaps they cut some corners in a way that puts them in a precarious position, causing their eventual fall. Maybe they engaged in some unethical or illegal behaviors. Unscrupulous actions may stem from a weak self-image and/or inaccurate insight into themselves and the environment, and the feeling that this is the only way to get ahead (i.e., the ends justify the means). In any case, the result of this pattern may, although not necessarily, be an inability to recover position and sense of identity. (See London & Mone, 1987, for a discussion of these and other patterns of career motivation.)

Summary

Self-identity stems from insight and resilience. Resilience is a result of reinforcement early in life and critical events throughout people's careers that cause them to maintain a positive self-image or doubt themselves. Insight and identity stem from processing information about what's happening in the organization, available opportunities, and performance feedback. The next sections focus more specifically on alternative leadership identities, how they emerge, and how they change over time.

ALTERNATIVE IDENTITIES FOR A LEADER

Leaders are role models, visionaries, and decision-makers. They are responsible for their entire organizations—both for achieving outcomes (i.e., revenue, profit, position in the marketplace) and for how the outcomes are achieved (i.e., safely, legally, ethically, efficiently). They develop organizationwide goals, set direction, assign tasks, and communicate expectations and sometimes methods of operation (e.g., how goals are to be achieved). They monitor others' performance and hold them accountable for achieving their piece of the action. Some leaders behave autocratically, maintaining control and authority. Others involve their staff members in establishing objectives and setting direction. Some focus on operations and others show their consideration and respect for others' expertise, needs, and desires. Some focus on transactions (i.e., setting defined rewards for accomplishing specified goals, perhaps in a certain way) and others focus on transformation (i.e., facilitating others to use their expertise and ingenuity to create a successful enterprise). Some adopt a combination of these styles to fit their own character and the needs of the organization and the people in it. (See the overview of dimensions of leadership behavior in chap.1, this volume.)

The key questions here are whether or not executives view themselves as leaders and, if so, what difference does it make? Is being a leader a central component, or the defining element, of their career identity, and perhaps their overall identity as a person? Does being a leader dominate other aspects of their lives? If so, is this good? Can leaders be effective if they do not see themselves as leaders? Can leaders have balanced lives with other aspects of life having the same importance to them as their role as leader, or does effective leadership require spending most time and energy on being a leader than being anything else? The answers to these questions may vary among executives as they invent themselves as leaders, grow into their leadership role, and establish their own mark on their organizations. However, there may be some immutable standards that define leadership identity.

Contrasting Leadership Styles

As an example of two leadership styles and their connection to self-identity, consider the example of two leaders who recognized that they manage things differently. The presidential campaign between Vice President Al Gore and Governor George W. Bush provided a clear contrast in leadership styles and self-identities. This was reported in a *New York Times* article by Richard Berke (2000) based on in-depth interviews with the candidates and their staffs during the campaign. This is not meant to express a political view but merely to demonstrate different leadership styles. Bush's style was like the corporate executive who sets broad goals, and does not dither with the details, preferring to let his staff come up with ways to implement them. Bush would ask, "Have you told me everything I need to know?" He wasn't above saying that he did not know the answer. When he did not understand, he stopped and asked. When aides talked about the budget, all he wanted to know is, "Are we under or over?" He was removed from the specifics, preferring to rely on people he trusted. Once he believed his aides comprehended his philosophy, he let them develop ideas for him to approve. Explaining his management style, he said, "I don't think anybody knows everything about every subject ... this is a complicated world. The key to the presidency is to set divisions, to lay out the parameters by which decisions will be made and to encourage really good, competent people to serve the country for the right reasons and to build a team" (Berke, 2000, p. A28).

In comparison, Al Gore was more of a micromanager, who was involved in every major move, pronouncement, and decision (Berke, 2000). In contrast to Bush, who was not burdened by needless detail, Gore felt he had an extensive knowledge base (8 years as vice president, 16 years in Congress, as well as a premature attempt to run for the presidency in 1988) that allowed him to be comfortable making well-informed decisions. He immersed himself in policy and logistics. This even went so far as redesigning the logo for his campaign after graphic artists presented him with several alternatives. To Gore, the campaign logo was a hallmark of his campaign and worth his time. This did not occur to Bush. Gore scoured the newspapers several times a day and cut out obscure sections and handed them to staff members with instructions. Bush relied on his wife to sum up news detail, particularly about him. Gore explained his management style in the following way: "I'm not a figurehead here! I've got to know what's going on.... I like the broad brush strokes. But sometimes a significant detail is actually a broad brush stroke in disguise. Sometimes, a significant detail can be a fulcrum around which the rest of the issue turns" (quoted in Berke, 2000, p. A28). Gore's aides felt that he was the driving force behind every major decision, and many small ones. His knowledge and control intimidated aides, particularly those new to his staff who felt that Gore was not interested in their opinions. They had to discern when Gore was open to their ideas. Gore wanted to be briefed, form the opinion, and make the decision. Whereas Bush seemed like the impatient student, Gore seemed like the overbearing teacher (Berke, 2000).

ACQUIRING A LEADERSHIP IDENTITY

Self, or self-identity, refers to all the ways in which a person answers the question, "Who am I?" (Gollwitzer & Kirchhof, 1998). One can answer this in terms of physical attributes, social identities, and relationships (e.g., "I am a student" or "I am the CEO of xyz corporation"). The question can also be answered in terms of self-perceived traits and dispositions (e.g., "I am kind" or "I like sports"). Sometimes identity is a retrospective process. Individuals reflect on what they have done and do as a means of defining themselves. Their identity evolves as they assume different roles. For example, employees may begin to think of themselves as managers when they are appointed to their first supervisory position; executives may begin to think of themselves as leaders when they are appointed to their first general manager position to head a business unit. In part, then, leadership identity is a matter of context and life stage. However, it may also be a conscious choice. For instance, occupational identity is often a conscious choice between available options (e.g., becoming a physician or a chemist; Gollwitzer & Kirchhof, 1998).

Gollwitzer and Kirchhof (1998) reviewed the theoretical processes that have been used to explain the emergence of self-identity. People's need for a self-concept may stem from the fear of death (Greenberg, Pyszczynski, & Solomon, 1986), the fear of social exclusion (Baumeister & Tice, 1990), or a pervasive need to see themself in a positive light (Greenwald, 1980). Self-perceptions may stem from the inferences people make about themselves as they look back at their behavior, feelings, and thoughts (Bem's, 1972, self-perception theory). Alternatively, they observe how others react to them or the roles they play in their lives. Self-verification theory holds that people verify self-related beliefs by selectively interacting with people who support their preferred self-conceptions (i.e., see them in the way they want to be seen; cf. Swann, 1983). Thus, people may actively acquire self-knowledge that supports their implicitly desired view of themselves (e.g., they develop friendships with people who treat them as they want to be treated).

Some elements of self-identity may be stable across situations, whereas other elements may vary depending on what happens or where individuals find themselves (i.e., they are specific to the situation). For instance, people may conceive of themselves as authoritative at home and compliant at work but bright and educated in all contexts. People tend to maintain and enhance their self-evaluation by comparing themselves to others with whom they compare favorably or by associating themselves with others whom they perceive as doing well (basking in others' glory; cf. Tesser, 1988). Some people try to present themselves in a way that puts them in a positive light (Baumeister, 1982). That is, they try to manage the impressions others have of them.

Identity choices, even when they result from careful and possibly difficult deliberations, need to be implemented. Pursuing identity goals is enduring over time. Identity goals are not easily stopped by failure. (Gore's pursuit of the presidency is an example.) Failure experiences may actually enhance pursuing goals associated with the identity. (See chap. 10, this volume, on overcoming career barriers.) An important aspect of identity is the way a person is perceived in the eyes of others. On the one hand, merely thought of by others as having a particular identity affects motivation to pursue the identity. On the other, being recognized in a certain way may hamper goal-directed efforts instead of facilitating them in that there is no need to pursue the identity because the identity has been achieved.

Self-completion theory argues that people set and strive to achieve goals they view as self-defining (Gollwitzer & Wicklund, 1985). Those who fail on a self-defining goal feel more worried, pessimistic, dissatisfied, and blocked than those who fail on the same goal but who do not view the goal as self-defining (Brunstein & Gollwitzer, 1996). For example, two people may want to receive a sizable bonus in compensation at the end of the year. One manager may want to be promoted quickly, and interpret a bonus as recognition of ability and accomplishment and a step toward promotion. The other may need the money to buy a new car. Now assume that both managers receive a much lower amount than they hoped for. The one who wants to advance in the corporation sees the bonus as a self-defining goal. The disappointment may cause the individual to question the goal or to try harder to demonstrate competence and attain outward signs of movement toward the ultimate goal. The manager may even look for a position in another firm where chances for rapid movement upward are higher. In contrast, the other manager may simply turn to alternative ways to make quick money, maybe moonlighting as a consultant for a time. The former manager remains committed to the ideal state and works toward self-completion, and the latter manager does not see the failure in terms of self-identity at all, but rather concentrates on the immediate goal (i.e., earn the extra money).

According to the *theory of self-completion*, when people who are striving for a self-defining goal fail to achieve the goal, come out unfavorably when they compare themselves to others, or receive negative feedback (and thus are denied a relevant symbol of their self-perception), they experience a sense of incompleteness (Gollwitzer & Kirchhof, 1998). They do not accept this passively, but compensate by looking for other ways to achieve their identity goals. This may include presenting themselves to others in the way they want to be perceived. They may do so even if it means ignoring information about what the other individuals expect or want from the relationship. They try to use others as a way to verify their self-identities.

If individuals who have not actually achieved an identity goal receive a sign of goal achievement, even if it is minimal, then they develop a sense of completeness that diminishes their motivation for goal achievement (Brunstein & Gollwitzer, 1996). For instance, when family and friends express pride in their accomplishments (for the aspiring manager, maybe perceiving that the manager has already reached a high status position), the individual's sense of incompletion will diminish, and the individual will not try as hard to achieve the ultimate goal.

Continued pursuit of identity depends on how identity goals are framed in the person's mind. When they are framed as *mastery goals*, motivation to pursue the identity will be less than when they are framed as *learning goals*. Mastery goals have a negative outcome focus (what will happen if you do not achieve the goal?), whereas learning goals have a positive outcome focus (i.e., concentrating on attaining more, as opposed to what has not been attained yet). Some people believe their skills and abilities are fixed. They set performance goals that allow them to determine how capable they are. Others believe that they can grow their skills. They set learning goals to discover their mistakes and how they can improve (Dweck, 1998; Gollwitzer & Kirchhof). For those with performance goals, negative outcomes indicate a lack of ability and lower motivation. For those with learning goals, negative outcomes suggest directions for performance improvement and the need to try new behavioral strategies. Those with performance goals seek signs from past and current goal accomplishment that confirm their identity. Failure suggests to them they lack the skills they need to fulfill their identity. Those with learning goals focus on acquiring new skills in the future. Failure suggests to them that their effort was not good enough, and they need to try harder in the future. So, for example, managers may want to lead a cross-national start-up to be viewed as global executives. This would be a mastery goal. They may try to leverage the experience to gain even higher level positions. Other managers may want a similar experience to enhance their personal growth and capabilities. They may then experiment with their new knowledge in other contexts and continue to enhance their learning. They view themselves as continuous learners, not as masters of a particular role.

As leaders age, they may try to maintain their self-identity by compensating for skill decrements (Gollwitzer & Kirchhof, 1998; Marsiske, Lang, P. B. Baltes, & M. M. Baltes, 1995). They continue self-defining goal pursuits, but in a more limited way. For example, they may narrow their set of goals—essentially, this means trying to do less or do what is in the range of the individual's capabilities. In addition, they may narrow their range of social contacts to a few intimates who treat them in ways that validate their self-identity, rather than having to prove themselves continuously to a wider range of less enduring contacts who would challenge their self-definitional completeness.

Evolving Leadership Roles

As stated earlier, a leader's identity may be a function of contextual changes. Leaders may have to adopt different self-identity's in order to retain their positions. This may happen because of industry or technological changes. Consider the position of chief information officer (CIO). This is changing from a largely technical management job to a position that contributes directly to a firm's business strategy and organization change. CIOs who contribute to their organization's strategy together with other corporate officers need to move away from a detail-oriented mentality to have a larger frame of reference. They need to pay attention to strategic and customer service elements of their jobs as well as the technology. A survey of CIOs found they tend to spend at least half their time outside the information technology division on such initiatives as developing and nurturing new avenues for electronic commerce. As such, the information technology department headed by the CIO is moving from a cost center to a profit center (Siwolop, 2000). Fifteen percent of CIOs now serve on boards of their companies, and 70% are on high-level management teams. Some CIOs have become CEOs. CIOs now develop sales strategies and meet with sales agents, something they would not have done 5 years ago. Cecilia Claudio, CIO at a financial services firm in Los Angeles, said, "People don't look to me as just being a CIO. I'm expected to bring wisdom, to understand all aspects of our business, as well as not work in isolation" (Siwolop, 2000, p. C6). In many companies, technical issues affect every aspect of operations, including product design. This is likely to be a major identity change for some CIOs. Although they may have thought of themselves primarily as chief subject matter experts and supervisors, they are now corporate leaders and strategists.

Summary

A leader's identity is framed by how the role of leadership is viewed by the leader and by others. Leaders who are learning oriented see themselves growing professionally constantly. Setbacks are chances to learn and adapt. Leaders who are performance oriented have a more narrow mind-set. They are outcome focused, and setbacks are reasons for self-doubt. Over time, a leader's identity evolves and is refined, especially as the leader ages in the process and develops a more narrow and perhaps more realistic set of expectations for the present and the future. Leadership identity may also change as the role itself changes, with evolving organizational conditions affecting role expectations. As noted in the last chapter, maintaining leadership identity requires self-regulation, and this is especially challenging in the face of organizational and situational pressures. It also requires individuals to glean information about themselves, others, and the situation to enhance insight. Having a meaningful leadership identity and one that has a basis in reality rests on a foundation of resilience and insight.

PROFESSIONAL IDENTITY
AND ADAPTATION TO NEW ROLES

Ibarra (2000) described the ways in which professionals adapt to new roles by drawing on the repertoire of skills and abilities to try different behavioral styles. They do this through a process of experimentation that has three general stages:

observing role models to determine potential identities, trying alternative "provisional selves," and evaluating these experiments against internal standards and external feedback.

Ibarra drew on Schein's (1978) concept of identity as the foundation for her work. Schein (1978) defined identity as "the relatively stable and enduring constellation of attributes, beliefs, values, motives, and experiences in terms of which people define themselves in a professional role" (Ibarra, 2000, pp. 764–765). Identity is the meaning attached to people by themselves and others. Ibarra argued that professionals adapt to more senior roles by experimenting with new images of themselves as trials for possible, but not yet fully developed, identities. This *anticipatory socialization* is not accomplished in one fell swoop, but is a negotiated adaptation process by which individuals try to improve the match between themselves and their work environment.

Ibarra interviewed 19 management consultants and 15 investment bankers just before they were to make a career transition to a more senior position. The investment bankers were to be evaluated for vice president or director the year following the study, and the consultants had just begun to assume team leader and client manager roles. Ibarra organized the interview responses into the three components of her model of the adaptation process: observing role models, experimenting with provisional selves, and evaluation. Each is described here:

1. People observe role models through two processes:
    (a) *role prototyping*—discerning what constitutes a credible role perfomance; for example, asking themselves, "What do people in this position do to project an effective image?"
    (b) *identity matching*—the process of comparing and contrasting role models with themselves as a way to explore images of how they might fit in their new role. For instance, they might determine, "Yes, I see. I can do that" or "That's just not me."

2. Experimenting with provisional selves involves two types of imitation strategies and true-to-self strategies:
    (a) *wholesale imitations*—the professional mimics the role model in dress, mannerisms, style of writing, time spent at different tasks, etc., adopting the role model's personal without much adaptation
    (b) *selective imitation*—adapting different elements of several role models' personas to create a new persona
    (c) *true-to-self strategies*—the professional's dominant concern is authenticity, that is, they want people to see them as they see themselves. They disdain "faking it" and refuse to imitate others to improve their effectiveness. Instead, they work hard so that others, especially their clients, see the value of what they can contribute

3. Evaluation occurs in two ways, which may be combined:
  (a) *internal evaluations*—professionals evaluate themselves on the degree of congruence between their provisional styles of behavior and their conception of the demands of the role. Styles that they feel good about are maintained and internalized in changes in self-concept. Styles that do not seem to work are revised or discarded and new behaviors tried.
  (b) *external evaluations*—professionals observe, and ask for, others' reactions to their performance. For instance, after a meeting, they might ask colleagues, "How do you think that went? What do you think the clients thought about my presentation?" Positive feedback gradually reinforces the changed behavior and a new self-identity begins to emerge. This is an iterative process, and the new self-concept develops over time.

This adaptation process has several outcomes: It affects the speed of adaptation. Behaviors that receive positive feedback and that feel right and match the individual's true self are likely to be retained and enhanced quickly. Behaviors that receive negative feedback and/or do not feel right require the individual to go back to the drawing board to try new approaches. Another outcome is the degree of change in self-identity. Some people may realize they can be effective just the way they are. Others may try new ways of behaving and realize they have talents never realized before. They essentially grow into the senior position. This is indeed likely as they move from mostly technical support positions to responsibilities that rely greatly on interpersonal relationships. Sometimes people form new, relatively unique approaches to the role, developing innovative styles that stand out and add tremendous value to client interactions. Eventually, the effectiveness of the new role becomes apparent, and the role and the reputation of the professional solidify in the professional's mind and the perceptions of colleagues in the company and clients.

Versatility

Kaiser and Kaplan (2000) developed the concept of versatility in being able to adjust to new situations. Their formulation is based on the concepts of forceful and enabling leadership styles. These styles were described in the first chapter. Here, they suggested a way to capture the likelihood that leaders will change aspects of their identity because of changing conditions. Table 4.2 provides a simple measure of each style and a way to calculate versatility. Versatile leaders can be forceful and enabling when necessary. This affects both their behavior toward others and the way they see themselves. The next section extends this idea of self-perception and versatility to understanding the way leaders try to manage how others see them.

TABLE 4.2
Evaluate Your Leadership Versatility

Use the following items to evaluate your leadership versatility: Use the following 3-point scale:
1 = too little, 2 = the right amount, 3 = too much

Forceful Leadership Style

_____ Forceful

_____ Aggressive

_____ Competitive

_____ Critical

_____ Dominant

_____ Intense

_____ Outspoken

_____ Self-assertive

_____ Tough

_____ TOTAL Forceful Score

Enabling Leadership Style

_____ Enabling

_____ Appreciative

_____ Cautious

_____ Caring

_____ Compassionate

_____ Gentle

_____ Mild Responsive to others

_____ Understanding

_____ Considerate

_____ TOTAL Enabling Score

A total score of 18 on each scale would be optimal in that it would indicate versatility in being able to be forceful or enabling when necessary.

Now, calculate your versatility based on the *Polarity Index* = Absolute Value of (Total Forceful Score–Total Enabling Score)

Versatility: The closer the forceful minus enabling score is to zero, the more versatile you are.

Too forceful: Someone who is too forceful would have a forceful score greater than 18 and an enabling score less than 18. (Forceful minus Enabling would be greater than 0. The higher the score, the more forceful the individual.)

Too enabling: Conversely, someone who is too enabling would have an enabling score greater than 18 and a forceful score less than 18. (Forceful minus enabling would be less than 0. The lower this score, the more enabling the individual.)

Note. This scale was adapted for this book based on the work of Kaiser and Kaplan (2000). For the actual items and the scoring method used in their research, contact Rob Kaiser, Kaplan DeVries Inc., 1903 G. Ashwood Ct., Greensboro, NC 27455. E-mail: rkaiser@kaplandevries.com.

SELF-PRESENTATION AND THE
COMPLEXITY OF SELF-VIEWS

Identity translates to the way people present themselves to others. Identity is a "highly complex, integrated mental representation of who one is that is stable and consistent across time" (Rhodewalt, 1998, p. 375). People filter information to maintain their self-views. Also, they are driven to maintain positive self-views (self-enhancement theory; cf. Jussim, Yen, & Aiello, 1995). People engineer their "social realities" to maintain and verify their beliefs about themselves (Swann, 1983). However, self-perceptions can fluctuate to some degree depending on recent events (e.g., feedback) and behaviors (e.g., behaving in a way that tries to convey a particular impression to others, which, as a by-product, affects an individual's own self-view). This is a self-reinforcing process in that people are attending to behaviors that are congruent with self-knowledge.

As leaders try to convey an impression that is contrary to, or at least different from, their self-view, they may actually change their self-conception, at least a bit, to be more consistent with the impression they are trying to convey. To put it another way, they fool themselves, even if they are not convincing others. In this way, the self can become a network of concepts, some of which may actually be contradictory at times. When contradictory self-views occur, people may need to resolve the dissonance, perhaps by denying to themselves the way they really are or, eventually, recognizing that one view is indeed false and they should stop kidding themselves. The inconsistent information is only temporary. Nevertheless, while it lasts, it may carryover into other feelings, behaviors, or actions (Rhodewalt, 1998). For instance, when leaders act in a self-deprecating manner at work that is inconsistent with their usual positive self-image, they may do so for a time at home as well. However, this may not last long. This carryover affect has been found in actors who take on the personality profiles of the characters they portray as they develop the character during rehearsals and performances. This has been found to have an effect even 1 month after the play's closing (Rhodewalt, 1998). This carryover is unlikely to happen if the assumed characteristics are too far afield of the individual's true self, however.

Individuals present themselves to others in a certain way, calling to mind behaviors and characteristics in their past that are consistent with the presentation. This biased filtering of self-knowledge then carries over to other situations. This lasts only as long as the self-presentation remains relevant. If individuals are forced to think about counterexamples (i.e., ways in which their own behavior has conflicted with the self-presentation), then they are likely to give up the self-presentation. However, if they believe they will have to continue the self-presentation (i.e., in future performances of a play or, to use a work situation, in subsequent job interviews), then they will maintain the self-view and seek consistent information to lend some credence to it in their own minds. Essentially, they are bound to this self-view as a public identity, and this is important for maintaining the carryover effect (Rhodewalt, 1998).

The leaders most likely to display this self-presentation carryover effect are those who are high in social identity. These are individuals whose self-identity is rooted in social experiences, roles, and relationships (Rhodewalt, 1998). Others whose self-concepts are inclined to be influenced by how they present themselves to others are those who have a broad range of behaviors and attributes they can accept about themselves. These individuals are more accepting of inconsistent information about themselves. They do not see themselves as the same in all situations. People who have a stronger tendency to maintain self-consistency and have a narrow range of behaviors and attributes they accept about themselves are likely to feel less responsible when they are asked to behave in a discrepant manner. However, this does not mean they will feel good about it. They will feel the same, if not more, discomfort as those who change the direction of the discrepant behavior to resolve the feelings of dissonance (Schlenker & Trudeau, 1990, described in Rhodewalt, 1998).

Leaders who have a highly complex view of themselves (i.e., who have well-articulated, finely differentiated, multifaceted self-concepts) are likely to have a harder time incorporating a new and inconsistent self-presentation into their identities. This is compared to those whose self-concepts are low in complexity in that they think of themselves in simple, undifferentiated ways. If these individuals try to present themselves differently, they think of themselves as a different person more easily than those who have a more precise, and finely differentiated self-view (Rhodewalt, 1998).

This might be called the "Homer Simpson" effect, after the crude, simple-minded, and sometimes immoral patriarch of the cartoon Simpson family. Homer occasionally takes on contrary personae, for instance, the hero, the entrepreneur, or role model. These personae never last, but while they do, Homer views himself in a new light and behaves accordingly. The new self-image and self-presentation last as long as the outcomes are positive. In Homer's case, his incompetencies invariably catch up to him and failure ensues, just as any person's true characteristics eventually emerge. Homer easily reverts to his true self with only a whimper of disappointment. Others who are more complex and invested in self-enhancement might have a harder time adjusting to their true selves, although they might have been less affected by the false persona in the first place.

CONCLUSIONS

This chapter showed how leaders develop a sense of self-identity that is tied to their leadership role. This identity may be simple or complex, with multiple components and different styles and demeanors depending on the situation. It may be associated with their power base, their role, their expertise, the resources they command, or the respect others have for them. One element of constancy may be the adherence to a set of ethical values that guide their behavior.

In general, people try to achieve goals that are self-defining. Career identity is the direction that leaders set for themselves. It rests on a foundation of resilience (which includes the idea of self-efficacy) and insight into one's strengths and weaknesses, others' expectations, and available opportunities. Leaders' patterns of resilience, insight, and identity may vary as new feedback and other sorts of information arise and as circumstances change. Failures may alter a leaders' sense of identity. However, those with strong resilience and insight are likely to change the situation or change their identity to match the new conditions and challenges.

Leaders adapt to new roles by drawing on their repertoire of skills and abilities. They observe others, try alternatives modes of operating, and evaluate the outcomes. Versatile leaders are able to vary their style (i.e., enabling or forceful) depending on the conditions. This versatility may be a part of their identity. That is, they do not think of themselves in just one way or the other. Those who are not so versatile, however, may develop an identity based on a dominant consistent style.

Leaders act in a way that conveys their identity to others. More than likely, they want people to have a consistently positive view of them. Their self-image and the way they present themselves may not be how others actually see them. Leaders who have complex, differentiated views of themselves may have a harder time making a substantive change in their identity, as compared to those who have a fairly simple (some might say, shallow) self-image that is likely to change as behaviors change.

This chapter concludes the first section of the book. Chapters 2 through 4 examined psychological processes that are the underpinnings of leadership behavior and motivation: self-insight, self-regulation, and self-identity. The next section covers organizational support mechanisms for enhancing these processes and establishing leadership that meets organizational needs. This discussion begins in chapter 5, this volume, with the examination of the leadership development process and how organizations establish a comprehensive system for leadership development. Subsequent chapters discuss feedback processes and methods (e.g., 360-degree feedback), executive coaching, and alternative leadership development methods.

II

Support for Leadership Development

5

The Leadership
Development Process

The second section of this book considers organizational programs and methods that support leaders' self-insight, self-regulation, and self-identity. This chapter outlines the components of leadership development as a systematic process contributing to continuous growth. It is systematic in that multiple components work together over time to foster individual learning, performance, and career advancement, as well as organization development for continued financial success. This chapter outlines the components of a leadership development system from both the individual and organizational perspectives. Case examples show how several large firms approach leadership development in terms of assessing skill gaps, effecting immediate needs for organizational change, and preparing for the future. Individual development is recognized to be a key part of organizational performance, and an organization's performance management systems need to drive individual development as well as financial success and customer satisfaction.

LEADERSHIP DEVELOPMENT AS A SYSTEM

These days, organizations realize that their ability to be competitive requires attracting, retaining, and developing top leadership talent. Development is important because effective leaders want continued learning opportunities. Development is also critical for a business to stay ahead of the competition. In addition, the nature of leadership in today's complex, continuously changing organizations poses new challenges. Executives manage work teams, often across geographic and cultural boundaries. A conference on leadership development sponsored by the Conference Board and the Center for Creative Leadership cited revitalizing leadership in an established high growth organization and leadership issues during mergers and acquisitions as key challenges ("Leadership Development: Present Challenges/Future Opportunities," 2000). Another leadership challenge is managing collective work (McCauley, 2000a). This requires leading departments and people who are working in coordination across functions to accomplish goals, as compared to individuals or departments working independently on their specific functions. Collective work requires setting direction, creating alignment, facing adaptive challenges to unexpected situations, and maintaining employees' commitment and energy.

Cynthia McCauley, Vice President for New Initiatives at the Center for Creative Leadership headquartered in Greensboro, North Carolina, argued that leadership development requires a systemic lens to understand leadership requirements and merge together elements of learning about the system (McCauley, 2000a; also see McCauley, Van Velsor, & Moxley, 1998). This is the approach taken by the Center's leadership development programs to help managers and executives develop sustainable leadership capacities—those that will serve them well as business needs change. The Center defines leadership development as enhancing the organization's capacity to carry out tasks in increasingly complex situations. To do this, the leader needs interpersonal and cognitive competencies to manage people and their relationships, and the organization's implicit, if not explicit, principles of how leadership should get done (e.g., whether it is expected that leaders will set direction by fiat, mutual influence, or finding a common ground among diverse views). Leadership education and training need to be implemented in relation to other systemic factors in the organization, including rewards, performance feedback and reviews, and production systems. Also, this needs to recognize the specific needs of the situation, such as the degree of interdependence among individuals and work groups.

Components of a Leadership Development System

A leadership development system may be thought of from two perspectives: the organizational and the individual. From an organizational perspective, leadership development begins by assessing skills in the organization and comparing them to skill needs anticipated in the future. From an individual perspective, leadership development begins by assessing a current or prospective leader's talent and determining areas for development. The organization then provides the resources to enable individual development. So, leadership development can be viewed from these different perspectives, but the system is one and the same. Overall, the goal is to instill in the organization and its people a developmental mind-set. That is, leadership development, and indeed the development of all employees, is an important performance strategy for future success.

Consider the following components of an integrated leadership development program aimed at meeting individual and organizational needs across levels of the organization and over time:

- *Corporate needs analysis*: This entails considering leadership position requirements for today and the future given anticipated industry trends and business strategies. Organizations estimate the number and types of leaders likely to be needed at different levels of the organization and in different business units, say 5 to 10 years from now. This has implications for the numbers and types of talented managers to recruit now and the sort of development they require to be ready for the future.
- *Overall assessment of talent at different organizational levels*: Information may be available from assessment centers, performance appraisals, and employee attitude surveys (e.g., 360-degree feedback, upward feedback, or customer surveys). The data can be averaged across employees as an indicator of organizational needs. Also, the data serve as input for assessing each manager's individual development needs.
- *Skill gap analysis*: Skill needs are analyzed at the organizational level (e.g., "We need more leaders with global experience to be general managers in our increasingly international businesses. This is particularly a problem because so many global companies lack this talent.") and at the individual level (e.g., "I need more business experience abroad if I am going to move up in this company, given that we are expanding through a variety of international joint ventures.").
- *Early identification of talent*: Companies use aggressive recruitment strategies, nomination from supervisors, and performance appraisal and assessment center data to identify young managers who have the potential to be developed as leaders of the business for the future.
- *Development planning*: Individuals determine the skills they wish to strengthen and the weaknesses they need to overcome based on data about their capabilities and performance and on information about organizational opportunities. This has implications for the goals they establish for learning and development (e.g., the kinds of job experiences and training they want).
- *Support for development*: Individuals are responsible for their own development. Organizations are responsible for providing the enabling resources and ensuring that sufficient leaders are taking advantage of developmental opportunities. Development planning is increasingly a part of the organization's formal performance management programs. When managers at all organizational levels assess their subordinates' performance, they also assess their developmental needs. This becomes part of performance review discussions between managers and their subordinates. As such, development becomes a business goal for the individual and the organization. Companies usually offer a host of development programs, including executive coaches, training classes, workshops focusing on actual business problems, challenging developmental projects, and job rotations.

• *Ongoing assessment and development*: Organizations repeat the aforementioned processes, conducting corporatewide leadership job analyses and skills assessments, at least once every 3 to 5 years. Individuals repeat this process at least annually, constantly calibrating their skills and career goals in relation to opportunities within (and often outside) the organization. Feedback allows them to determine whether or not changes in their behavior are producing the performance outcomes and skill acquisition they desire. Organizations eventually establish a development-oriented corporate culture to support the value of learning and encourage individuals' sense that they can alter their behavior and learn new skills to meet changing business conditions and strategies. Individuals eventually acquire a learning mind-set. They track what is learned as well as the positive career outcomes that learning produces.

McCall (2000) summarized the important ingredients for leadership development programs: He stated that systematic programs should have a conceptual foundation (e.g., Microsoft's focus on adaptive challenges and convictions and connections) and should use measurements to be sure that the organization's goals for development are being accomplished. They should use experience as a teacher by focusing on learning that comes from real initiatives, such as job assignments. Also, leaders should be held accountable for their role in development as teachers and coaches. In general, top executives should never be satisfied with the status quo in terms of leadership skills and the leadership pool of talent. The organizations should continuously calibrate, revise, and refine the skills and training needed to ensure a competent pool of leaders for today and the future. The notion of leadership is changing in the high-tech world (McCall, 2000). Today's heroes of business are not leaders, but young entrepreneurs who got rich quickly without building lasting organizations. These firms get into trouble when they grow and recognize they do not have a bank of junior managers who are ready to assume leadership roles in setting a vision and managing people to accomplish it.

SOME CASE EXAMPLES

The following cases show how organizations have recognized the importance of leadership development to their continued success. These organizations have designed programs to assess their current leadership capabilities and close the gap between the leadership skills available now and the anticipated need for different leadership skills to meet business goals. The cases show that leadership development should fit the organization's specific objectives, business environment, and the ways it does business. They also show how to apply the key ingredients of leadership development already reviewed.

Bristol-Myers-Squibb

Bristol-Myers-Squibb is a global health products and services company with 53,000 employees and 40% of sales outside the United States (Dowell, 2000). In 1994, its new CEO saw flat earning projections and increased competitive challenges. His goal was to double sales and earnings and move the firm from a value company to a growth company. To do this, the firm wanted to change the role of manager from judge to coach. A four-pronged leadership development approach was established to support this strategy: Leaders should envision, engage, enable, and evaluate. A new, ratingless performance management system was developed, called the Performance Partnership Model. Ratingless means that instead of using numbers to categorize each employee on a set of performance dimensions, supervisors write narrative reports that describe the employee's strengths and areas for improvement. The model expects managers to engage in a continuous cycle of coaching employees on behaviors they could change ("actionable coaching"), setting expectations, observing behavior, and providing feedback.

To implement this new process, the company's top executives worked with the human resources department to conduct a leadership development planning review. They found that only 27% of the company's midlevel managers were promotable now, and they wondered how they could create a growth company with such a limited talent pool. They created a Position Profile for each job. This included competency requirements (what the person does), leadership behaviors (how the person will do the job), the experiences necessary, the knowledge desired (which may be obtained by formal education or experience), and the learning value of the position (opportunities and challenges presented by the job). Managers and executives could review 1,200 position profiles on the internet, see the opportunities and organizational needs, and understand what it will take to get ahead in the new business environment.

By 1998, the number one growth priority for the firm was to develop the depth, breadth, and diversity of talent at every level of the organization. To help achieve this, the company established a career development Web site that provided information about job opportunities, skills needs, and online learning. Senior leaders are expected to pay attention to leadership development as part of their responsibilities. They act as role models for development, engaging in career planning and continuous learning for themselves, and supporting the development of those who work for them. Also, they can find out whether or not directions for their own and others' development are aligned with corporate goals and business direction.

Johnson & Johnson

Johnson & Johnson's (J&J) goal for leadership development is to identify talented young managers who can move upward in a global, decentralized organization. J&J has 90,000 employees in 190 different operating companies. Its goal is to grow from a $20 billion business to a $50 billion business. The organizational culture has been changing within J&J, shifting from a culture in which each unit is operating as an island unto itself to promoting opportunities for cross-unit integration and alignment of systems. The company is less hierarchical. It is faced with a fast-paced, competitive environment with increased focus on costs and the need for continuous innovation and teamwork. The company runs an executive conference annually for its top 1,000 leaders across the business. This keeps executives apprised of developments throughout the business. It also emphasizes that J&J is still one firm with a solid foundation of values. Indeed, development is embedded within the firm's written credo:

> We are responsible to our employees, the men and women who work with us throughout the world. Everyone must be considered as an individual. We must respect their dignity and recognize their merit. They must have a sense of security in their jobs. Compensation must be fair and adequate, and working conditions clean, orderly and safe. We must be mindful of ways to help our employees fulfill their family responsibilities. Employees must feel free to make suggestions and complaints. There must be equal opportunity for employment, development and advancement for those qualified. We must provide competent management, and their actions must be just and ethical ("Johnson & Johnson Credo," 2000).

J&J's Talent Scope project was to build a pool of up-and-coming leaders who represent and enact the company's values in a global environment and who are able to adapt to situational changes. The process creates a dialog between supervisors and subordinates about career development. They consider positions and developmental experiences across business units and functions.

Microsoft

At Microsoft, talented college graduates were hired and promoted rapidly in an environment where the demand for leaders exceeded the supply (McHenry, 2000). Microsoft, similar to other vastly successful high-tech firms, is largely a volunteer organization when it comes to the ranks of top executives. That is, many are so wealthy that they can forego working if the spirit moves them. As a result, implementing standards and responsibilities is difficult. Expanding their role in leadership development is a way for them to ensure the ongoing viability of their investment. The employee attitude survey asks employees to evaluate their managers on their support for career development (e.g., "My manager cares about my career."). This shows that the company cares that managers take their responsibility for subordinate career development seriously. A key dimension of effective leadership in Microsoft is adapting to change and challenges. The leader's role is to galvanize energy to solve problems. Their model is based on a formula.

Adaptive change is a function of dissatisfaction with the status quo, vision, and momentous first steps that overcome resistance to change. Effective leaders in Microsoft need to have strong, clear convictions and calm, open connections to people (the C^2 model). This simple model resonates with executives and gives them a common framework for discussion.

About 70% of leadership development in Microsoft is on-the-job training. Another 10% takes place in courses and self-study. The remaining 20% happens through feedback and coaching. Development events sponsored by the training department go beyond lectures to getting participants involved in solving real business problems. For instance, the leading change course asks participants to redesign a unit, review the plan with executives and organization development experts, and implement the change. The Learning from Others course uses 360- degree feedback surveys, assessment results, and executive coaching.

Shell Oil

As a vast company, with $25 billion in revenue and 16,000 company-owned service stations in the United States alone, Shell Oil Corporation operates throughout the globe. It maintains a "grow your own" philosophy when it comes to filling management positions (Hofmeister, 2000). The company requires managers to have strong technical knowledge and understanding of marketing, because both are key aspects of their business. Six thousand managers live outside their home country on international assignment.

Shell has an extensive assessment process for high potential managers who tend to be in their early to mid-forties in age. It takes place over the course of 6 months, and includes a structured interview with a team of executives, a business management simulation, role plays (including a task force role-playing exercise simulating interaction with, and contribution to, a group effort), and cognitive testing. It measures such skills as championing a customer focus, building a shared vision, demonstrating personal and professional mastery, maximizing business opportunities, delivering results, motivating (coaching and developing), and valuing diversity. Each participant is rated "green" (excellent), "yellow" (some strengthening needed"), or "red" (substantial development needed) on each of these skills. The results are presented in an assessment report that is used to establish a development plan. Each participant in the leadership development program is assigned a mentor, however, the participants themselves are held accountable for their own development.

Cisco Systems

When John Chambers was named CEO of Cisco Systems, the computer networking equipment manufacturer, in January 1995, the firm employed 3,000 people and had approximately $2 billion in annual revenue. In 2000, the number of employees had increased to 30,000, and revenues had increased to almost $20 billion annually. Competition and technological change forced the company to move faster all the time. In order to respond and keep his company first in the marketplace, Chambers set out three prime responsibilities for himself: (a) Set the strategy. (b) Recruit, develop, and retain the leadership team to implement the strategy. (c) Develop a company culture that is focused on enhancing customer success ("Cisco—From 3,000 employees to 30,000 employees in 5 years," 2000). One way Cisco does this is to link manager's pay to customer satisfaction. It also views its leaders and managers as a team, not as individuals who operate in isolation and then coordinate activities and outputs. Chambers' view of leadership development is integrally tied to this corporate philosophy of customer satisfaction and teamwork. He articulated 9 managerial tasks and characteristics that are the basis for the company's selection and development process. Leaders need to be able to do the following:

1. Attract, retain, and develop new employees at the speed the company is growing.
2. Model and instill trust and integrity.
3. Maintain industry knowledge.
4. Build teamwork.
5. Explain to team members what is expected of them.
6. Listen and communicate and listen some more (which is hard to do in such a fast growing company).
7. Maintain customer focus.
8. Enhance people skills.
9. Consciously build a corporate a culture that fosters customer satisfaction and teamwork.

Using Assessments of Leadership Talent to Effect a Corporate Turnaround

Heine (2000) described an example of a huge merger that doubled the size of an unnamed company. The merger presented a tremendous integration issue of how to bring the two firms together. The merger raised such basic questions as, "Does the new, combined firm have the talent it needs to achieve its goals and be competitive?", "What kind of talents are needed?", "Does the new firm have enough talent now?", "Can it develop the talent it needs from the ranks of current managers?" These were especially cogent questions because half of the 23 senior executives would be ready to retire in from 3 to 5 years. They were also cogent because senior management's job complexity had increased considerably after the merger. This posed the need to identify executives for the future who could turn around the business as the competitive environment changed.

The company had used an executive assessment center to evaluate its top executives. The two-day center, which used management simulations to assess participants' abilities, was combined with results from a 360-degree feedback survey and coaching for development planning, behavior change, and performance tracking. Although the assessment center data were collected mainly as feedback for development, participants recognized that the company could use the information at any time to make decisions about them.

The merger entailed a stronger firm taking over a weak firm. The new CEO and VPs wanted to understand the talent resident in the new organization, so they turned to the human resources department to provide data on the top executives from the assessment center process. Whereas the data were originally derived for purely developmental purposes, the CEO and VPs examined the data to see where executives fell on key dimensions of performance. The results showed which people needed the most development, and the areas that they needed to develop. The results also showed that people were ready to assume more responsibility. As a result, the data could be used to make new assignments, pulling weak people from the top of the weak segment of the business and reassigning strong people to fill these positions. These changes were the start of an overall business turnaround that reduced employees by 27%, and dramatically increased sales and on time delivery.

Hillenbrand Industries

Steven McMillen, director of Executive Development and Performance Improvement at Hillenbrand Industries, initiated leadership development by establishing a leadership competency model that outlined key competencies needed by the corporation. After assessing leaders and managers current skills, McMillen concluded that the company needed to accelerate the development of executives who could be designated as "ready now" to meet the firm's aggressive growth goals. He and his staff, working with a consulting firm, created a web technology-driven learning management system. The system provides leaders with tools such as 360-degree feedback, coaching, and distance/online learning. It also provides a way for the firm to track and analyze the effectiveness of leadership development in terms of how many people were participating and at what levels (McMillen, 2000).

Summary

These cases demonstrate the key ingredients for an effective leadership development program. Each case applies a number of these components. Most corporate programs began because top executives perceived a weakness in the current organization that could be corrected by a change in management talent. For instance, consider Bristol-Myers-Squibb's desire to enhance earnings by encouraging managers to view leadership development as a managerial responsibility. The value of a conceptual base for leadership development was evident in Johnson & Johnson's credo and Microsoft's focus on adaptation to change. Shell Oil demonstrated the value of early identification of managerial talent. Cisco Systems showed how to translate such a broad goal for improvement into specific leadership dimensions for development. Several of the firms used web technology to provide managers with ongoing information about career and learning opportunities as well as actual training. Hillenbrand Industries used 360-degree feedback survey results as one method to track the effectiveness of an accelerated development program. Given the general business objectives that led to the program, the companies usually turned to financial measures of improvement, such as sales data and customer satisfaction, to assess their program's bottom-line, long-term success.

DEVELOPMENT AS A DIMENSION OF INDIVIDUAL AND ORGANIZATIONAL PERFORMANCE

Development is part of most organizations' performance management system. That is, development is recognized as integral to effective individual job performance and overall organizational performance. Essentially, development becomes a goal itself—one that, of course, is aimed at producing higher levels of effectiveness and, from the individual's point of view, improved career opportunities. Directions for development stem from the organization's business objectives, which include goals for revenue, profit, customer satisfaction, and business process efficiency. Development refers to the leader's own development and the leader's role in developing subordinates.

Multiple Indicators of Performance

As introduced in the first chapter, Kaplan and Norton (1996) formulated the concept of the balanced scorecard (BSC) for managing individual and organizational levels. The balanced scorecard (BSC) translates a company's vision and strategy into a coherent set of performance measures that starts with business units, which are then applied to each executive on down throughout the organization. The process begins with top executives establishing corporate strategy along a set of mutually supportive components usually organized into five areas: Finance, Customers, Internal Business Processes, Personnel, Systems, and Organizational Development, and Personal Leadership Development. Each element may have a number of indicators for tracking performance. For instance, financial objectives may be measured by a variety of indexes reflecting revenue and expenses. Customer goals may deal with market share, loyalty, and satisfaction with product and service. Business process objectives may refer to indicators of efficiency and effectiveness, such as just-in-time delivery, product quality, and output per employee. Employee development objectives may deal with personnel and organizational development. Measures of employee education, skills, participation in training and development, satisfaction, and teamwork may be indicators of employee development. These all may be important to the organization's continued viability. Indeed, they may all contribute to the first three performance domains (business process, customer, and finance).

A company's balanced scorecard defines each of these elements, establishes tracking measures, sets ambitious yet realistic objectives on each measure, and tracks performance over time. The measures and goals for each performance area are designed to fit the organization. The process of establishing these benchmarks starts at the top and works down as each business unit, department within the business unit, and area within the department, outlines its respective performance indicators and goals. Ultimately, each manager has a unique set of performance objectives that covers the five areas and contributes to the department, business unit, and overall organizational objectives. These individual objectives and measures serve as a basis for regular performance evaluation and feedback.

This focus on multiple, strategic categories helps leaders in the following ways:

- translates a generic vision into a strategy that is understood and can be communicated
- creates a management system for the long run concentrating on strategic objectives, not operational tasks
- identifies strategic initiatives that close performance gaps
- starts top down: uses the corporate BSC as a template for business unit and communicates strategy throughout the organization; clarifies and gains consensus about strategy
- aligns departmental and individual goals to the strategy; drives down to individual performance scorecards
- promotes cross-functional efforts directed toward accomplishing corporate strategy
- links strategic objectives to long-term targets and annual budgets
- uses multiple strategies and measures to drive toward unity of purposes
- communicates and informs, does not control
- identifies the customer and market segments in which the unit will compete and the measures of the unit's performance in these targeted segments
- applies strategic values and strategic objectives that are specific, measurable, achievable, relevant, and time-bound
- ensures that plans and actions are strategically linked to corporatewide objectives
- recognizes that organizational and individual performance is multidimensional
- focuses on multiple strategic categories (finance, customer, internal business process, people and organization development, personal development, action learning, technology)

Employee, Systems, and Organizational Development Objectives

One goal in the balanced performance scorecard deals with resource development. This includes the development of people, systems, and the organization itself. The goal of resource development is to ensure that the human, technological, and structural resources of the corporation contribute to internal business processes that drive positive customer and financial outcomes. Analyses of these areas may show substantial gaps between current abilities and requirements to meet goals for business success in the future. Closing these gaps requires investing in employee training, implementing new technological systems (including advanced information technology), and ensuring that the systems and procedures of interdependent departments fit together (Kaplan & Norton, 1996). Possible measures of employee capabilities, motivation, involvement are listed in Table 5.1.

An Example of a Performance Management Program

Table 5.2 presents an excerpt from a performance management program developed for a major corporation. The entire program would outline the major strategies of the organization and the key performance objectives related to each strategy. Under development, the document would explain to managers and executives that development is a key part of their role in the business and that it will be measured as part of the performance management process. The section in Table 5.2 focuses on giving and receiving feedback and coaching as important performance elements. The guideline outlines the purpose for this element of the program, outcomes, steps, and possible activities, including encouraging subordinates' development. As such, it is an excellent prelude to the discussion in the forthcoming chapters on feedback methods and coaching.

Personal Leadership Development

Another performance category in the balanced scorecard focuses on leaders setting strategic objectives for their personal development that will contribute to the attainment of financial, customer, business process, and people and organizational development objectives. In doing so, they need to understand the company's leadership requirements for today and the future, assess their personal strengths and weaknesses, and establish a personal development plan to build strengths and, where possible, overcome weaknesses.

For instance, a leader's *strategic objective* for personal development may be to:

TABLE 5.1
Possible Measures of Employee Capabilities, Motivation, and Involvement

* employee satisfaction
* involvement with decisions
* recognition for doing a good job
* access to sufficient information to do the job well
* active encouragement to be creative and use initiative
* support level from staff functions
* overall satisfaction with the company
* employee retention
* unwanted departures (loss of intellectual capital, percentage of key staff turnover)
* employee productivity
* revenue per employee (may lead to too much pressure to achieve an ambitious target)
* motivation, empowerment, and alignment
* measures of suggestions made and implemented
* measure length of time for process performance to improve by 50%
* measures of employee confidence in top management
* managers exposed to the balanced scorecard (BSC) concept, % of staff exposed to BSC, % of top managers with personal goals aligned to BSC, % of staff with personal goals aligned to BSC and % of employees who achieved personal goals
* information systems capability measures: real-time availability of accurate, critical customer and internal process information to employees on the front lines of decision making and actions
* organizational procedures showing alignment of employee incentives with overall organizational factors, and measured rates of improvement in critical customer-based and internal processes

* Enhance your leadership competencies—establish your leadership development plan to respond to competency gaps evident from data, for instance, from the company's 360- degree feedback survey for managers.
* Enhance your business and technical competencies—establish your business and technical competency development plan based on gaps evident from discussions with your direct reports, peers, and your manager and from the 360-degree feedback survey.

Measures of success on this performance dimension may be evaluations from others (e.g., from the 360-degree feedback survey, and/or supervisor observation and ratings). Outcomes from development planning could include participating in planned training, survey ratings showing improvement in desired areas, and supervisor recognition.

TABLE 5.2

Excerpt from a Corporate Performance Management Program

A company's performance management program outlines the steps managers are expected to follow in setting strategic objectives, giving and receiving feedback and coaching, evaluating performance, and awarding performance-based compensation. The following excerpt from a company's performance management program describes the processes of giving and receiving feedback and coaching. As such, the program lets managers know what the company expects them to do to support their subordinates' development and enhance their performance. Also, the program provides ideas and recommendations for carrying out this step of the performance management process.

Giving and Receiving Feedback and Coaching

The purpose of this phase of the company's performance management process is to:

- Be sure you know how well you are doing in accomplishing your strategic objectives.
  - Feedback provides you with information about how close you are to your targets. This allows you to make changes so you can accomplish your targets by the end of the performance year.
- Use feedback effectively.
  - Coaching doesn't evaluate you or your performance (saying you or your performance are good or bad), but rather provides advice, ideas, or encouragement to help you accomplish your targets and achieve your strategic objectives.

The focus of feedback and coaching may be on any one or more of the following topics:

- business goals for this year
- immediate problems on the job
- performance improvement
- skills needing development
- problem performers in the work group
- ways to enhance teamwork among subordinates and/or peers
- planning for next career move
- planning for long-term career/life goals

Outcomes of Feedback and Coaching

As a result of this phase of the performance management process:

- Your direct reports will feel that ...
  - they can discuss performance issues openly.
  - they can be honest with you about their feelings.
  - you don't judge them.
  - at performance appraisal time, you evaluate their performance fairly.
  - you are a valued resource.
  - your door is always open to their ideas and problems.

112

- You will feel the same way because you have received feedback and coaching from your manager and peers.
- Performance will become an acceptable and frequent topic of conversation.

In starting this phase of the performance management process, remember that feedback is information on how close you are to your targets. Coaching doesn't evaluate you or your performance as good or bad. Rather, coaching provides advice, ideas, and encouragement about how you can achieve your targets. You participate in feedback and coaching throughout the year.

As an executive, you receive feedback and coaching from others, especially your manager. Feedback is also likely to be available from your coworkers, customers, and an external coach.

You are also expected to provide feedback and coaching to your direct reports. This is part of every manager's job.

Feedback and coaching occur when they are needed, not just at designated time periods. However, there should be informal performance discussions at the end of the first and third quarters, and formal performance reviews at midyear and at the end of the year.

Steps for Giving and Receiving Feedback and Coaching:

- Collect information from a variety of sources (this may be objective data about performance outcomes, such as cash flow, or subjective data, such as customer and/or employee satisfaction).
- Hold an informal performance discussion at the end of the first and third quarters. The purpose is not to evaluate performance but to provide feedback and coaching. (Formal performance evaluations occur at midyear and at the end of the year. These also provide feedback and may include coaching for performance improvement.)
- When an event occurs, provide your feedback as soon as possible. Also, set times aside to discuss performance. Don't wait for the formal, once-a-year appraisal discussion.
- Provide feedback and coaching to your direct reports and peers; expect feedback and coaching from your manager and peers.

Recommendations:

- Recognize the difference between coaching and evaluating. Coach is providing advice and guidance, not making a value judgment about whether one's performance was good or bad.
- Start a discussion by asking for a self-assessment (e.g., "How do you think that went?", "What could you have done differently?").
- Be open to new ideas.

Possible Activities for Employee Development

Your goal may be to enhance your or your direct reports' leadership competencies, such as the ability to set and communicate strategy, convey enthusiasm for business objectives, demonstrate support for employees' development, providing employees with on-going feedback and coaching, measuring performance and establishing performance-based compensation.

Begin by reviewing data, such as 360-degree survey feedback results, to determine skill gaps. Identify weaknesses you want to improve and/or skills you want to enhance. Formulate a development plan for improvement on these skills. Specify learning or training experiences.

Another goal may be to engage in a continuous learning process to enhance personal contributions. You will need to acquire needed business knowledge and technical skills in order to keep up with changing demands of the business and technological advancements.

113

Activities for employee development include training courses, seminars, and computer-based programs that may be instructor led or self-paced. Self-development activities may include reading a book related to a needed skill, finding a mentor or role model, or watching a skill building videotape.

Learning takes place on the job as well as in the classroom, and vehicles for training include information communication, access to information databases and related resources, and a host of increasingly sophisticated and less costly technologies, such as the computer, CD-ROMs, and videos.

Self-Assessments

Self-appraisals should be incorporated into the performance appraisal discussion. Start the discussion by asking for your direct report's view of his or her own performance. Your role as a supervisor, then, is to provide praise when it is deserved, clarify your expectations if need be, and suggest changes in behavior or activities to meet strategic goals.

Asking for, and discussing, self-assessments in the appraisal process help to:

- increase the direct report's dignity and self-respect.
- place the manager in the role of counselor or coach, not judge.
- encourage the direct report's commitment to goals and development plans that emerge from the discussion.
- avoid the subordinate's defensiveness.

Note. This is based on an actual program developed for a major corporation by Edward Mone and Manuel London.

Conclusions

This chapter examined how organizations formulate leadership development strategies to fit current and emerging business needs. It showed that organizations establish performance management programs that incorporate leadership development—both self-development and the development of employees in a leader's charge—as part of a multidimensional approach to performance. An example offered performance management strategies that enhance employees' skills and abilities along with technological and organizational systems. Another example focused on leaders' roles in developing themselves and those who work for them.

Each performance element needs to be measured to track success, and examples of performance indicators were given. These measures are fed back to leaders and managers to make changes in their own behavior and the systems for which they are responsible. As such, feedback is an important part of leadership development. This was evident in the earlier chapters on self-insight, self-regulation, and self-identity. The next chapter addresses the critical role of feedback. This prepares the groundwork for the subsequent chapters on 360-degree feedback and coaching.

6

Feedback Processes

Feedback is central to leadership development. It is the key to leaders' self-insight. Without feedback, leaders would be in the dark about the effects of their decisions and actions on their organizations and their relationships. Feedback stems from a number of sources. Some feedback comes from objective data: information about finances (reports of expenses and revenues), human resources (data on employee turnover, numbers attending various training courses, salary surveys in the labor market outside the firm), and business processes (error rates, projects completed on time, inventory). Other feedback comes from subjective data: comments or ratings from one's supervisor, subordinates, peers, customers, and/or suppliers.

Leaders are sensitive to performance feedback because of its tie, and potential threat, to their self-identity. Chapter 2, this volume, reviewed insight formation processes, and suggested that leaders, especially those with positive self-images, are likely to discount negative information. On the one hand, some negative information should indeed be ignored or attributed to external factors. On the other hand, to ignore or discount unfavorable feedback may miss the opportunity for change that could have positive benefits for the leader and the organization.

This chapter covers the basic elements of feedback processes that apply to most everyone, including leaders. These elements need to be taken into account in developing support mechanisms for leadership development. This foundation is necessary to fully understand the leadership development support mechanisms, in particular, feedback surveys and coaching, described in the next two chapters. This chapter begins with a primer on the value of feedback, explaining why it works and what can be done to maximize its benefit. The way people respond to feedback, particularly in relation to its sign (positive or negative) is tied to self-regulation processes. Methods are discussed for making feedback constructive, rather than destructive. Self-assessment questions are offered to help leaders understand their reactions to feedback and how they use the feedback to enhance their insight and identity. The chapter then examines how to create an organizational culture that supports feedback, where feedback is expected, welcomed, and integrated in the way leaders do business.

ENHANCING THE VALUE OF FEEDBACK

Job Feedback (London, 1997a) covered the elements of feedback in detail, including sources and characteristics of feedback, methods for giving feedback, and encouraging the effective use of feedback. Here some of the major concepts are outlined as background to understanding the role of feedback in leadership development, in particular, the benefits of feedback, findings from research about the effects of feedback, and conditions for effective feedback.

Benefits of Feedback

Feedback is valuable for many reasons. It directs, motivates, and rewards behavior. It is the basis for development and career planning, and it contributes to building effective interpersonal relationships. It is an important element in learning. We know that people learn by modeling others, trying new behavior, and receiving feedback on how well they are doing.

Feedback conveys information about behaviors, and it conveys an evaluation of those behaviors (whether they were good or bad, right or wrong). Knowing whether you succeeded or failed is not enough. Feedback must provide accurate, timely, and specific information about how the leader's behavior led to performance improvement. Feedback provides insight about individuals and about the way the environment affects the stability and direction of their career behavior. It allows individuals to avoid the use of inappropriate performance strategies in the future that could occur if feedback is inaccurate or delayed.

Feedback has reward value in and of itself, not just because of the financial or other concrete rewards tied to positive performance. That is, people feel good knowing they did well. It contributes to increased self-awareness and willingness to engage in self-assessment. Also, it improves the organization's service quality and customer responsiveness.

Effects of Feedback

A review of the literature resulted in the following conclusions about feedback. (This section is adapted from London, 1997a, pp. 14–15, based on literature reviews by Ilgen, Fisher, & Taylor, 1979; Larson, 1984; London, 1988; and Nadler, 1979.)

Feedback directs behavior; that is, it keeps goal-directed behavior on course. It influences future performance goals, essentially creating objectives for achieving higher levels of performance in the future. Actually, positive feedback is reinforcing in and of itself.

Feedback enhances learning. It increases employees' abilities to detect errors on their own. It helps employees realize what they need to know and what they need to do to improve. Feedback increases motivation by demonstrating what behaviors contribute to successful performance. It helps people clarify their beliefs about the effects of their behavior. Feedback increases the salience of the information and the importance of the feedback process.

Feedback increases in the amount of power and control employees feel. This applies to both the source of feedback and the recipient. Feedback increases employees' feeling of involvement in the task. Feedback about individual performance coupled with information about environmental conditions and opportunities helps employees form a career identity that is challenging and potentially rewarding.

In negotiations, feedback is a mechanism for evaluating offers. In decision making, feedback about the results of the decision helps groups and individuals recognize cognitive biases (e.g., the tendency to overly weight information that is worded negatively) and to avoid these biases in the future.

Conditions for Effective Feedback

For feedback to have a positive effect, it should be clear, specific, and easily understood. The source and recipient need to interpret it in the same way.

Feedback should be given frequently. Moreover, it should refer to elements of performance that contribute to task success and that are under the recipient's control. It should be from a credible source and be accompanied by explanation and used so the recipient understands the source of the feedback and how it can be applied to improve task performance.

Also, feedback should take into account the recipient's ability to comprehend the feedback. For instance, the provider of feedback should consider the extent to which the feedback conforms to the recipients' cognitive ability to process the information. In other words, the feedback should not be too detailed. The provider should also consider whether the feedback will encourage the recipient to think about the task from others' perspectives. Moreover, the feedback should prompt the recipient to think about ways the feedback can be applied to improve job performance.

Another consideration in giving feedback is the recipient's sensitivity to feedback, or the extent to which the recipient wants to learn and is able and motivated to process information from different sources. Recipients who are not motivated to use the feedback are unlikely to benefit from it. This motivation may be influenced by the context, that is, what is happening in the organization and the demands and stressors experienced by those who give and receive feedback. For instance, employees who initially felt threatened by feedback may welcome it when suddenly under increased pressure to complete an ambitious project. In addition, accountability mechanisms are likely to affect the perceived usefulness of feedback. Employees will give feedback more attention if they are held responsible for giving and using it.

THE ROLE OF FEEDBACK
IN CHANGING SELF-INSIGHT

DeNisi and Kluger (2000) outlined five basic assumptions of how feedback operates: (a) People regulate their behavior by comparing feedback they receive with a goal or standard of performance. (b) Goals and standards are arranged in a hierarchical order. (c) People are limited in their ability to process information, so only gaps between feedback and standards or goals that receive attention will regulate behavior. (d) People attend to feedback that focuses goals or standards in the middle of the hierarchy (those that are not the most long term and important, on the one hand, and those that are not the most immediate or trivial, on the other). People tend to avoid feedback that threatens their self-concept, especially feedback that addresses personal characteristics as opposed to specific task behaviors that they can change. (e) Feedback interventions alter the locus of attention by focusing on goals and standards in the middle of the hierarchy that specify behaviors as opposed to personal characteristics. Feedback that focuses on the latter is likely to have a negative effect (especially if it is unfavorable and does not confirm the individual's positive sense of self-efficacy), whereas feedback that focuses on the former is likely to have a positive effect (especially if it suggests specific directions for behavior change).

Higgins Self-Regulatory Model.   People focus their attention on their "ideal self" (what they aspire to be as they work on tasks they want to work on) or their "ought self" (what others expect them to be as they work on tasks they are supposed to work at or are forced to work at) (Higgins, 1987). When focusing on the ideal self, people have a *promotion* or learning focus. That is, they concentrate on trying to achieve goals that they set for themselves. When focusing on the ought self, people have a *prevention* focus. That is, they concentrate on trying to avoid failure and punishment. Negative feedback under a prevention focus causes people to work harder to avoid punishment, such as disappointing spouses or parents. Positive feedback under a prevention focus tends to cause people to maintain effort but not work harder to improve, because there is no incentive to do better. Positive feedback under a promotion focus spurs people to greater effort, whereas negative feedback under a promotion focus tends to be disheartening, making the gap between the desired self and actual self too great to overcome.

Effects of Sign of Feedback

A question that arises in the feedback literature is whether receiving positive feedback is more or less motivating than receiving negative feedback. It could be that receiving positive feedback spurs people on to greater heights or, alternatively, causes them to rest on their laurels and do nothing extra. It could also be that receiving negative feedback discourages people from working harder or, alternatively, causes them to work harder to overcome the performance gap and show others that they can do better.

Prevention and Promotion Mind-sets. Van-Dijk and Kluger (2000) argued that the effects of the sign of feedback depend on the individual's focus on preventing failure or promoting success. Drawing on Higgins (1998a, 1998b) theory of self-regulation, a prevention focus can be activated by security needs, strong obligations, or framing a situation in terms of loss or non-loss. A promotion focus can be activated by nurturance needs, strong ideals, or framing a situation in terms of gain or non-gain. Individuals who have a prevention focus are sensitive to the presence or absence of punishment. They avoid potentially punishing situations and try not to do things that could engender punishment. Those who have a promotion focus are sensitive to the presence or absence of rewards. Rather than avoiding actions or behaviors that have possible negative outcomes, they actively engage in behaviors they think will have positive outcomes.

To summarize Van-Dijk and Kluger's (2000) thesis, if the task is something individuals want to do and they want to succeed (they have a promotion focus), then doing well motivates them to work even higher, but failing causes them to do little more. If the task is something individuals have to do and they better not fail (they have a prevention focus), then failing causes them to try harder, but succeeding causes them to do little more. In other words, positive feedback is consistent with a promotion focus, and negative feedback is consistent with a prevention focus. So, if people receive positive feedback under a promotion focus or negative feedback under a prevention focus, then they will have higher motivation than people who received feedback that is inconsistent with their regulation focus. This is because feedback that is consistent with their self-regulation focus causes higher arousal emotions. For example, failure under a prevention focus causes anxiety, whereas success under a promotion focus causes elation. Feedback that is inconsistent with self-regulation focus causes low arousal emotions. For example, failure under a promotion focus causes dejection, whereas success under a prevention focus causes quiescence (Van-Dijk & Kluger, 2000).

Assessing the Joint Effects of Promotion Versus Prevention Focus. To understand prevention and promotion focus, think about the scenario Van-Dijk and Kluger (2000) used to test their theory. They asked students, police officers, and military personnel to answer the following: Think about how you would feel in each case: elated, anxious, dejected, or calm? Consider the four scenarios:

Scenario A (prevention focus, negative feedback): Imagine you are working on a job that you have to keep because you are afraid of being left without income. Now, suppose your boss tells you that you have been doing poorly during the first 6 months.

Scenario B (prevention focus, positive feedback): Now, imagine again you are working on a job that you have to keep because you are afraid of being left without income. Suppose your boss tells you that you have excelled during the first 6 months.

Scenario C (promotion focus, positive feedback): Next, imagine you are working on a job that you always wanted to have and that you want to develop and advance in the job. Suppose your boss tells you that you have excelled during the first 6 months.

Scenario D (promotion focus, negative feedback): Finally, imagine again you are working on a job that you always wanted to have and you want to develop and advance in the job. Suppose this time your boss reveals that you have done poorly during the first 6 months.

According to Van-Dijk and Kluger (2000), you would feel anxious in Scenario A, calm or quiescent in Scenario B, elated in Scenario C, and dejected in Scenario D.

How the Favorability of Feedback Affects Reactions to It.   It might be expected that negative feedback will motivate managers to engage in development activities. However, the actual effect may be to demotivate (or demoralize) managers or cause them to ignore or deny the results. People think that positive ratings are more accurate than negative ratings (D. Stone & E. Stone, 1985). People are more satisfied with positive ratings than negative ratings (not surprisingly; cf. Podsakof & Farh, 1989). This is consistent with self-enhancement theory, which holds that people respond more positively to information that is consistent with a positive self-image (Schrauger, 1975). Feedback that is inconsistent with the way individuals view themselves was received as less information and resulted in less development than feedback that was self-confirming (Pearce & Porter, 1986). Comparative information (self–other feedback) focuses attention away from the actual behaviors and task and toward the individual, thereby threatening the individual's self-image (DiNisi & Kluger, 2000). So, for instance, a feedback report that provides information about others to allow self–other comparisons may set up a situation that is evaluative oriented, even if the data are meant solely for development.

In addition, Ferstl (2000) examined the effects of feedback sign and regulatory focus on intentions to exert more effort. Specifically, students in an introductory psychology class who stated they enrolled to fulfill ideals (promotion focus) versus obligations (prevention) were asked to imagine receiving negative, neutral, or positive feedback about their course performance. They then indicated their effort intentions. The results were partially consistent with Higgins' (1998a, 1998b) self-regulation theory. After receiving positive feedback, those under the promotion focus indicated higher intentions of effort and stated this was because they enjoyed learning about the subject matter compared to those under the prevention focus. However, following negative feedback, those under the prevention focus did not indicate higher effort intentions than those under the promotion focus. However, they tended to be more likely to indicate they preferred to devote time to other classes or pursuits (a sour grape response tantamount to the negative information, essentially saying, "I didn't want to take this course anyway").

GIVING FEEDBACK

A key element of whether or not feedback is valuable depends not just on the content of the feedback, but on the way it is given (see Table 6.1). This depends on the relationship between the leader and the source of the feedback, who is likely to be the leader's manager.

DiNisi and Kluger (2000) recommended a number of ways to improve the effectiveness of feedback (p. 134). They suggested focusing on the task and task performance only, not on the person or any part of the person's self-concept. Feedback should be presented in ways that do not threaten the ego of the recipient. It should include information about how to improve performance. Also, it should include a formal goal-setting plan along with the feedback. In general, the feedback should concentrate on information relating to performance improvement and avoid information concerning the performance of others.

Causes of Inaccurate Feedback

Several factors may cause inaccurate feedback or make it less effective. For example, whereas people often use unfavorable adjectives to describe others, while they use favorable adjectives to describe themselves (Langer, 1992). Managers generally view discussing feedback as unpleasant and so they avoid or postpone the discussion or rush through it (Meyer, 1991)). Supervisors do not like to give unfavorable feedback to subordinates they like.

Poor performing subordinates receive less feedback than high performing subordinates (Larson, 1986). However, when managers do give negative performance feedback, they tend to be more specific than when they give positive performance feedback in order to be as helpful as possible to the poor performer (Larson, 1988). Unfortunately, managers delay evaluating and giving feedback to

TABLE 6.1
Guidelines for Giving Feedback

Feedback should . . .

- Be given as soon as possible following the behavior.
- Allow ample time for discussion.
- Be conducted in a private setting.
- Not be given when the supervisor or subordinate are frustrated, angry, or tired.
- Encourage self-evaluation by the subordinate.
- Use factual information.
- Initially be descriptive rather than evaluative.
- Be specific.
- Focus on behaviors, not personality.
- Be related to an expected task.
- Demonstrate interest in, and concern for, the subordinate.
- Respect the subordinate's dignity and opinions.
- Exhibit a trusting climate.
- Demonstrate that the supervisor is prepared for the review.
- Reflect adequate collection of information.
- Ensure that the supervisor and subordinate understand what has been discussed.
- Encourage input from the subordinate.
- Address both effective performance and areas needing improvement.
- Review the consequences of not effectively addressing a performance problem.
- Use effective verbal and nonverbal communication skills.

Note.   Adapted by London (1997a, p. 90), based on Hillman, Schwandt, and Bartz (1990).

moderately low performers, and they evaluate them with more positive distortion than they evaluate moderately high performers (Benedict & Levine, 1988).

Other reasons for poor feedback stem from poor ratings. Here are some of the errors people make in evaluating others' performance:

- Leniency—the tendency to be too favorable.
- Severity—the tendency to be too unfavorable.
- Halo—the tendency to allow perceptions of one performance dimension to influence perceptions of other, unrelated performance dimensions.
- Similarity—the tendency to give overly favorable ratings to ratees who are similar to the rater on characteristics that are unrelated to performance (e.g., age, race, or gender).

- Central tendency—the tendency to evaluate everyone as middle of the road on all aspects of performance.
- First impression—the tendency to allow one's first impression of the ratee to influence ratings.
- Recency effect—the tendency to allow a recent incident to influence judgments of performance dimensions for the entire performance period.

Constructive and Destructive Feedback

Some people feel there is no such thing as constructive feedback. They believe all individuals are so averse to feedback that they view any critical information as potentially damaging. This chapter has suggested ways that supervisors can provide feedback to limit, if not eliminate, the negative sting.

Consider the distinction between constructive and destructive feedback (Baron, 1988, cited in London, 1997a, pp. 17–18). Feedback is *constructive* when it is specific and considerate and when it attributes good performance to internal causes, such as the individual's effort and ability. Also, it is constructive when it attributes poor performance to external causes, such as situational factors beyond the subordinate's control. This assumes that the external attribution is justified. That is, it does not blame people for negative outcomes that are not their fault. Feedback is constructive when it empowers the recipient and concentrates on ways the recipient and source can both win. It is constructive when it increases the recipient's sense of independence and self-control. That is, it encourages and reinforces a can-do attitude, while it increases goal clarity and challenges the recipients to do better or overcome disabilities or barriers on their own. Constructive feedback allows a controlled expression of feelings. It leads to increased mutual trust and confidence.

Feedback is *destructive* when it focuses on general comments about performance, uses an inconsiderate tone, or attributes poor performance to the individual's characteristics. Destructive feedback uses threats (i.e., "Here's what will happen if your performance doesn't improve ..."). It generates feelings of low self-efficacy (i.e., a "can't do" rather than "can do" attitude).

In general, supervisors are more willing to give feedback when their subordinates can control the results, the results are positive, and they get along well with the subordinates (from London, 1997a, p. 17). Also, supervisors are more willing to give feedback when they believe their subordinates will agree with them and perceive that the information is important. Supervisors are more likely to give feedback when they depend on the subordinates for getting the job done (which is likely to be the case) and when they feel a responsibility to provide the feedback (they recognize that giving feedback is part of the supervisory role). Supervisors are more likely to give feedback when performance results are tied to organizational rewards and when there are positive norms in the organization for giving feedback (e.g., it is an expected and usual process throughout the business unit).

Steps for Conducting a Performance Review

Now, here is a 12-step structure to follow when conducting a performance review (from Silverman, 1991, pp. 142–143; also in Fletcher, 1986, pp. 5–6, and London, 1997a, p. 102):

1. Explain the purpose of the review meeting.
2. Ask the employee to summarize accomplishments and developmental needs related to the most important responsibility.
3. Summarize accomplishments and development needs from the supervisor's perspective.
4. Reach agreement on what developmental steps should be taken.
5. If there is a gap between current and expected performance on the most important responsibility, then diagnose the causes of the discrepancy (whether the outside environment, the organization, the manager, and/or the employee).
6. Develop action plans to improve performance on the major responsibility.
7. Do the same for remaining major responsibilities.
8. Summarize overall performance in relation to each major responsibility and review action plans.
9. Compliment the employee on accomplishments.
10. Set a time and date to discuss any needed changes in responsibilities and performance standards for the next performance review period.
11. Have other sources of feedback available (e.g., from peer ratings or customers). This reduces defensiveness and should mean less need for feedback per se and more willingness to discuss the results.
12. Practice frequent communication about performance feedback. Managers who have the most frequent communication with their subordinates the rest of the year have the most productive appraisal interviews.

Goal Setting Principles

Goal setting is integral to the feedback process. Feedback works best when goals are set in advance. The goals provide a benchmark or standard of comparison for evaluating the meaning of the feedback. Also, goals should be set or revised in response to feedback. Consider some generally accepted principles for goal setting (based on Latham and Wexley, 1981, p. 126; in London, 1997a, p. 105): Outlining specific goals leads employees to higher performance than telling them to do their best. When employees participate in goal setting, they tend to set higher goals than when the supervisor assigns them without the employee's input. As long as employees perceive a goal as reasonable and achievable (e.g., they have control over the factors essential to attaining the goal), then the higher the goal, the better they perform. Also, employees must receive ongoing feedback on how they are doing in reaching their goals.

FEEDBACK ORIENTATION

Although some people are averse to feedback, others welcome it. London and Smither (in press) called this attitude "feedback orientation." People who are high in feedback orientation are generally those who like feedback (i.e., have an overall positive affect toward feedback and an absence, or a low level, of evaluation apprehension), seek feedback, and process feedback mindfully and deeply. Also, they are sensitive to how others see them. Moreover, they believe in the value of feedback: It offers insights that may help the recipient become more effective and take actions in response to feedback that enhance their effectiveness. In addition, they feel responsible for doing something about the feedback. As discussed earlier, these are all important aspects for feedback to have an impact on developmental behavior.

Table 6.2 provides some items that have been used to assess *feelings* about feedback in general. Table 6.3 presents items, developed by London and Smither (1997), to assess a leader's *reactions* to feedback. These items can also be used to examine followers' reactions to the leader's change in behavior as a result of the feedback.

Support for Feedback Seeking

Seeking feedback can be risky business because it affects self-image. Lack of source support and negative peer reactions add to the psychological cost of seeking feedback. Asking for feedback under these conditions lowers the value of the likely feedback and risks that others, including the source, will think less of the employee for asking. In such a case, the desire for performance feedback competes with the desire to maintain a positive image. In research testing this, Williams, Miller, Steelman, and Levy (1999) found that the supportiveness of the feedback source and reactions of peers to feedback affect the extent to which employees seek feedback in front of others. In particular, people will be more likely to seek feedback if the supportiveness of the source and peer reactions are positive.

In this research, college students participated in a computer simulation involving a time management task that required them to allocate a week's worth of hours to a variety of student-related activities. For each of four trials, they could bypass feedback or raise their hand to receive feedback. In one study, the experimenter (the source of the feedback) voiced support prior to the task by saying, for instance, "I would be happy to give you feedback.... This task is new to you all, so the feedback just lets you know you are on the right track." In the

TABLE 6.2
Measures of Feedback Orientation

Consider how you would respond to the following items measuring feelings about feedback and willingness to request feedback.a (Note: These could be rated on a scale from 1 = low to 5 = high.)

- I like being told how well I am doing on a project.

- Even though I may think I have done a good job, I feel a lot more confident of it after someone else tells me so.

- Even when I think I could have done something better, I feel good when other people think well of what I have done.

- It is very important for me to know what people think of my work.

Now, consider your propensity to ask for feedback. Would you agree with the following?b

- I think my boss would think worse of me if I asked him or her for feedback.

- I would be nervous about asking my boss how he or she evaluates my behavior.

- It is not a good idea to ask my coworkers for feedback; they might think I am incompetent.

- It is embarrassing to ask my coworkers for their impression of how I am doing at work.

- It would bother me to ask my boss for feedback.

- It is not a good idea to ask my boss for feedback he or she might think I am incompetent.

- It is embarrassing to ask my boss for feedback.

- I think my coworkers would think worse of me if I asked them for feedback.

- I would be nervous about asking my coworkers how they evaluate my behaviors.

- It is better to try and figure out how I am doing on my own rather than ask my coworkers for feedback.

---

aFrom Fedor, Rensvold, and Adams (1992; reprinted in London, 1997a, pp. 11–12).
bFrom Ashford (1986; reprinted in London, 1997a, p. 12).

unsupportive condition, the experimenter told participants, "I will give you feedback if you request it, but I may not be able to get it to all of you right away; there are several of you in the room and only one of me." Also, a confederate would always be the first person to request feedback in each of the groups of participants, and this would be a demonstration of either supportive and enthusiastic feedback or quick and abrupt feedback. The results showed that participants requested feedback significantly more often in the supportive condition.

In a second study, Williams et al.(1999) included the same supportiveness manipulation and added a peer reaction manipulation to assess the effects of peers' expressed value and usefulness of the feedback would be in influencing others' feedback seeking. In the positive peer reaction case, the confederate who received the initial feedback repeated the feedback given, and indicated the feedback helped. For instance, the confederate said, "Oh, so I need to be

TABLE 6.3
Items Measuring Perceptions of Feedback Results

In general, what were your reactions to the feedback?

- The feedback results were easy to understand.
- The feedback results didn't have much value to me.
- I learned a lot about myself from the feedback results.
- The feedback results said more about the people who rated me than they did about me.
- The feedback results showed that the raters had an ax to grind.
- I agreed with the feedback results.

To what extent did the leader ...

- Disagree with the results.
- Try to rationalize or explain away negative feedback.
- Explain why he underrated himself.
- Attribute the results to factors beyond his control.

What actions were taken?

- I shared my feedback or written developmental plan with my superior.
- After receiving my 360-degree feedback, I had a constructive discussion about my performance with my superior.
- I shared my feedback or written developmental plan with my peers.
- I shared my feedback or written developmental plan with my subordinates.
- As a result of the feedback, I promised myself that I would try to improve.
- I changed my behavior as a result of the feedback.
- I improved my performance as a result of the feedback.

Since receiving your feedback, has the leader ...

- Learned new leadership skills.
- Set goals for performance improvement.
- Volunteered to attend leadership training.
- Discussed my results with others.
- Asked others for additional feedback.
- Asked others for explanation or more precise information about your performance.
- Asked others how you're doing on the job.
- Asked others how you can do better on the job.
- Initiated a discussion with your superior about your development needs and plans.
- Initiated a discussion with your peers, subordinates, or friends about your development needs and plans.

Table 6.3 continues

Table 6.3 continued

- Initiated a career planning discussion with your superior.
- Read a book or magazine article about a leadership skill you want to develop.
- Prepared a written plan concerning your developmental goals and activities.
- Asked your superior for assignments that will help you improve leadership skills.
- Made a verbal commitment to your superior to make improvements in your skills or performance.
- Made a verbal commitment to your peers, subordinates, or friends to make improvements in your skills or performance.
- Set specific goals for personal development.
- Targeted a specific skill for improvement.
- Requested coaching from your superior.
- Requested coaching from a peer or subordinate.

giving more time to volunteer activities, but I'm doing fine on studying." Then the confederate would say, "that helps" in a positive way. In the negative peer reaction case, the confederate responded to the feedback by asking about an activity that was not mentioned and stated, "that doesn't help much." The results showed that positive source supportiveness and peer reactions increased feedback seeking.

These findings indicate that supervisors can reduce the psychological costs of feedback by stating their willingness to provide feedback. Similarly, the costs of feedback are lower if fellow workers are willing to ask for feedback and have a positive experience.

Responding to Failure

In the course of learning a new job or task, people are likely to experience failure. People usually react to negative feedback by decreasing their goals, discounting, or rejecting the feedback. These are self-protection mechanisms. Others are listed in Table 6.4. Of course, another reaction to negative feedback is to try harder. People usually respond to positive feedback by exerting less effort or increasing their future goals (cf. Bandura & Jourden, 1991; Locke and Latham, 1990; Nease, Mudgett, & Quinones, 1999). However, these reactions may depend on whether this is initial feedback or repeated feedback. Also, people may vary in their reactions to feedback depending on their sense of self-efficacy, or the extent to which they generally see themselves as able to use their capabilities to be successful on the job. Those with high self-efficacy are likely to increase their effort in response to initially negative feedback as com-

TABLE 6.4
Self-Protection Mechanisms

Self-protection mechanisms are ways people affirm their self-image, especially in response to failure. Examples include:

Denial

- Reacts negatively to feedback
- Blames others for failure
- Never admits mistakes
- Inhibits other's performance
- Accurately perceives one's own performance [Inverse]
- Frequently asks for feedback [Inverse]
- Gives credit where it is due [Inverse]
- Accurately perceives other's performance [Inverse]
- Accurately describes events [Inverse]

Giving up

- Abandons difficult tasks
- Avoids being compared with better performers
- Tunes out others who perform better
- Would leave a job because co-workers perform better
- Negative feedback lowers performance
- Dislikes better performers
- Tries hard on difficult tasks [Inverse]
- Sticks to tasks until succeeds [Inverse]

Self-promotion

- Makes sure others know about successes
- Asks for praise
- Concerned about status symbols
- Talks about own good performance
- Makes others feel compelled to say good things about his/her performance
- Does not admit one's own contribution to a group's success [Inverse]

Fear of failure

- Points out own strengths when criticized
- Afraid of failure
- Gets upset by own poor performance

Table 6.4 continues

Table 6.4 continued

- Tries to prevent others from doing well
- Tries to convince others they are wrong
- Tries to raise others' opinions of self
- Downplays own weaknesses
- Concerned about making the "right" career moves

Note. From Wohlers and London (1989; in London, 1997a, p. 124).

pared to those with low self-efficacy (Bandura, 1986). However, if the negative feedback continues, individuals with high self-efficacy are likely to be less accepting of the feedback. Also, over time, for individuals who maintain their acceptance of the feedback, an individual's sense of self-efficacy is likely to decline with repeated negative feedback.

Nease et al. (1999) found this in a laboratory study of 80 undergraduate students participating in a computer naval air defense simulation. When feedback was negative over the course of three trials, students with initially high self-efficacy decreased their acceptance of the feedback. People in such a situation are likely to become increasingly frustrated with the idea that their efforts are unsuccessful, and they begin to doubt the accuracy of the feedback. Those with low self-efficacy who received negative feedback probably expected and, therefore, accepted the negative results. Those with higher acceptance of negative feedback tended to decrease their self-efficacy for this task by the third trial.

Individuals with initially low self-efficacy tended to reject repeatedly negative feedback, presumably because the feedback did not fit their self-concept for this task. High self-efficacy individuals did not change their acceptance of positive feedback when it occurred over time, presumably because this is just what they expected.

These results indicate that people tend to protect their initial self-concepts at the start of the task. Consistent with self-verification theory, they reject information that does not fit their self-perceptions. Even those with initially low self-efficacy tended to deny positive feedback rather than increase their sense of self-efficacy. Those who did maintain a level of acceptance of negative feedback, however, tended to decrease their self-efficacy, but this occurred only after repeated (three) trials of the task.

Self-verification theory holds that people believe that information supporting their self-concept is more diagnostic than information undermining (fails to support) their self-concept (Jussim, Yen, & Aiello, 1995; Nease et al., 1999; Swann, 1987). People believe feedback is valid when it matches the way they already view themselves. When feedback confirms their self-expectations, people attribute the feedback to their personal characteristics. However, when feedback contradicts their self-expectations, they attribute the feedback to the source (e.g., "The rater doesn't know me well enough," or "The rater doesn't like me."). People with low self-efficacy are more willing to accept negative feedback, admit it is accurate, and take responsibility for it.

Responses to failure are discussed further in chapter 10. Failure, or at least setbacks, can be learning experiences. People who welcome feedback are likely to be continuous learners. They are always looking for ways to benefit from their experiences. Chapter 11 examines continuous learning. The next section considers how feedback fosters continuous learning.

Fostering Continuous Learning

Continuous learning is the process by which individuals acquire knowledge, skills, and abilities throughout their career in reaction to, and anticipation of, changing performance requirements (London & Mone, 1999). Becoming a continuous learner requires having a strong and ongoing awareness of the need for, and value of, learning. Continuous learners anticipate learning requirements and identify areas for future job requirements and implications for needed skill updates. They set development goals related to these job requirements. As they participate in learning activities, they request feedback to test the relevance of their goals and track their progress in achieving them. London and Smither (1997) predicted that leaders would react positively to feedback and incorporate periodic feedback into a process of continuous learning when they are high in resilience, self-efficacy, self-attribution (attributing the feedback to their own behavior rather than factors beyond their control), and accountability.

They also suggested organizational interventions to create a feedback culture (London & Smither, in press). These are ways to enhance the quality of the feedback, emphasize the importance of feedback in the organization, and provide support for using feedback. These are listed in Table 6.5.

The Performance Management Process

Positive reactions to feedback occur slowly over time as the leader becomes used to receiving feedback, the feedback focuses on behaviors, and the feedback leads to improvements in behavior or performance. This encourages continuous learning unless there are countervailing forces, such as disconfirming or contradictory feedback. As was suggested in chapters 2 and 4 in this volume, self-insight and self-identity change as the leader gains self-confidence with improving feedback.

TABLE 6.5

Ways to Create a Feedback-Oriented Organizational Culture

1. Enhance the quality of feedback.

- Train for supervisors and others about how to provide useful feedback.
- Create clear standards concerning valued behaviors that are relevant to organizational goals.
- Provide clear performance measurements.
- Provide reports tying individual performance to bottom-line departmental or organizational (e.g., financial or operational) indexes.
- Provide time to review and clarify feedback results with others, such as one's supervisor.

2. Emphasize the importance of feedback in the organization.

- Expect top-level managers to serve as role models about how to seek, receive, and use feedback.
- Ensure that everyone receives feedback (i.e., it's not voluntary) and uses feedback to guide development.
- Encourage the importance of informal (or "in the moment") feedback.
- Involve employees in developing behavior/performance standards.
- Ensure that performance improvements following feedback are recognized and rewarded.

3. Provide support for using feedback.

- Provide skilled facilitators to help recipients interpret formal (e.g., multisource) feedback, set goals, and track progress.
- Train and reward supervisors for coaching.
- Encourage feedback recipients to discuss their feedback with raters and other colleagues to help clarify the feedback and reach a shared agreement concerning behavior expectations and changes.
- Provide feedback recipients with freedom to act on the feedback (giving them a sense of self-control).
- Provide opportunities to learn.

Note.   Based on London and Smither (in press).

Smither and London (in press) predicted that, over time, positive reactions and emotions following feedback lead to a sense of optimism and a will to do better, and negative reactions and emotions lead to a sense of failure and frustration. Positive feedback orientation helps the individual control and channel emotional reactions from feedback to focus on its behavioral implications. Coaching and other forms of support help individuals deal with their emotional responses to feedback, allowing them to concentrate on its behavioral implications. Moreover, leaders process feedback more deeply, find more personal meaning in the feedback, and make internal attributions that lead to goal setting when they are high in feedback orientation and the organization has a strong feedback culture.

CONCLUSIONS

This chapter began with an outline of the benefits of feedback, the effects of feedback, and conditions for effective feedback. It examined the ways feedback can change self-insight. Leaders compare their feedback to goals and standards they set for themselves (e.g., their ideal self) or that others set for them. The effects of the sign of feedback (positive or negative) depend on the individual's focus on preventing failure or promoting success. Positive feedback is motivating for people who have a promotion focus (meaning they want to succeed) but results in no extra effort for people who have a prevention focus (meaning they want to avoid failure). Conversely, negative feedback causes harder effort for people who have a prevention focus, but results in no extra effort for people who have a promotion focus.

The chapter then turned to guidelines for giving feedback in a constructive way. It concluded that feedback should not focus on an individual's characteristics because this concentrates attention on the self rather than the task. Instead, feedback should focus on behaviors. There are a number of reasons why feedback may be inaccurate, including common rating errors, such as leniency. Feedback is most effective when goals have been set and when goals are set as a result of the feedback. People are likely to become more comfortable with giving and receiving feedback over time. This was referred to as "feedback orientation." Steps were offered to make a performance review discussion more productive. In general, feedback is part of a performance management process that supports continuous learning.

The next chapter describes 360-degree feedback surveys as a vehicle for providing performance feedback. Then, in chapter 8, the discussion turns to how executive coaching supports the use of feedback for self-insight and identity.

7

360-Degree Feedback

360-degree feedback (also called multicource feedback) collects ratings from subordinates, peers, supervisors, internal customers, or some combination. In some organizations, just upward (subordinate) ratings are gathered. The ratings may be collected by paper-and-pencil questionnaire, computer, or telephone system. The survey may be administered annually, semi-annually, or quarterly. The results may be fed back to the managers in a variety of ways: in a written (computerized) report sent to the manager, during a workshop that explains how to use the report, or in a one-to-one session with an external coach.

The benefits of 360-degree feedback are that it contributes to individual development by providing information on worthwhile directions for learning and growth while it promotes organizational development by specifying dimensions of leadership behavior that are important in the organization. Also, it clarifies management's performance expectations recognizing the complexity of managerial performance—that leaders and managers need input from these different sources for a comprehensive view of their performance.

Sometimes the feedback is used solely for the development of the manager, and the results are not provided to the supervisor or others in the organization. That is, the intention is for managers to use the results to understand themselves better and consider areas for development and performance improvement. Other times, the results are used both for development and administration—that is, in addition to encouraging managers to consider the implications of the results for their development, their supervisors are given the results to help make decisions about the managers (e.g., whether a manager is ready for promotion or a pay raise). This is more threatening, of course. Also, when raters know the information may be used to make decisions about the manager they are rating, they may be more lenient (London, Wohlers, & Gallagher, 1990).

This chapter examines the content of 360 and upward feedback surveys, reviews the literature on their use, with particular attention to whether or not raters agree with each other and the effects of the feedback on a leader's development and change in performance. It then offers some recommendations for increasing the value of multisource feedback.

SURVEY METHODS

By way of example, Table 7.1 presents an upward feedback survey, sample report, and outline of a set of guidelines to help leaders and managers use the results. The items might be developed by the human resources department and/or a consulting firm working with the department staff. The goal in writing items is to ensure they make sense to the respondents, adequately reflect important aspects of performance, and ask for information that the raters have had a chance to observe directly. In a multisource survey, peers may be asked different items than subordinates, for instance, because they have a different perspective on the leader. Peers may not know about the extent to which the leader supports subordinates' career development. Subordinates may not know the extent to which the leader cooperates on interdepartmental team efforts. However, there would be a set of core items to which all raters respond as a way of comparing ratings from different rater groups.

Online Surveys

In order to make the assessment process easy and fast, 360-degree feedback surveys can be offered online. Survey consulting firms offer a variety of online instruments for self-assessment and to collect ratings from others, such as supervisors, subordinates, peers, and customers. Topics range from management and supervisory development to professional and functional expertise. Responses are confidential. The method has instant turnaround, because the results are computer scored and provided to each leader and summarized across leaders. Respondents receive questionnaires via e-mail, and return their questionnaires in the same way, thereby enhancing the response rate. The result is better quality data and better participation. These surveys can be developed just in time in that leaders can decide when they want survey feedback results (e.g., they are having some problems in getting team members to work together, and they wonder how they can manage differently to improve the group's interaction and progress). Then they use internet technology to construct their own surveys, determine who should receive them by e-mail, deliver the survey, calculate the results, and present them with a report.

TABLE 7.1
Sample Upward Feedback Survey

Instructions: An important aspect of leadership is the management of people. This survey focuses on your satisfaction with the relationship you have with your supervisor. Use the numeric scale below to rate your supervisor. Indicate the number that best describes your rating. Use "N" to indicate you have had insufficient opportunity to accurately gauge your degree of satisfaction. Your responses will be averaged with those from other subordinates who also report to your supervisor.

Scale:

1 = Very dissatisfied

2 = Dissatisfied

3 = Somewhat dissatisfied

4 = Somewhat satisfied

5 = Satisfied

6 = Very Satisfied

N = No opportunity to observe

_____ 1. Jointly sets performance objectives with you.

_____ 2. Supports you in developing your career plans.

_____ 3. Motivates you to do a good job.

_____ 4. Gives you authority to do your job.

_____ 5. Provides the support necessary to help you do your job (e.g., advice, resources, or information).

_____ 6. Understands the work to be done within your work group.

_____ 7. Is available to you when needed.

_____ 8. Encourages innovation and creativity.

_____ 8. Encourages innovation and creativity.

_____ 9. Holds employees accountable for meeting performance objectives.

_____ 10. Keeps commitments.

_____ 11. Allows adequate training time for you.

_____ 12. Provides ongoing performance feedback.

_____ 13. Provided a useful performance appraisal within the past year.

_____ 14. Conducts productive staff meetings.

_____ 15. Demonstrates trust and confidence in you.

_____ 16. Treats you with dignity and respect.

_____ 17. Informs you about issues affecting you.

_____ 18. Balances the work load fairly.

Table 7.1 continues

Table 7.1 continued

_____ 19. Communicates the reasons for his/her actions.

_____ 20. Supports and backs you up.

_____ 21. Has the subject matter knowledge to do the job.

_____ 22. Fairly evaluates your job performance.

_____ 23. Represents the group effectively to others (e.g., to clients, to management, or at meetings).

_____ 24. Insures that you get credit/recognition for your work.

_____ 25. Encourages open, two-way communication.

_____ 26. Modifies his/her position based on feedback from you (e.g., ideas, plans, or solutions).

_____ 27. Provides opportunities for you to develop new skills.

_____ 28. Strives for quality in spite of time pressure.

Sample Feedback Report

	Self-Rating	Subordinate Rating	Mean Range Low	Mean Range High	Number Responding to Item	"Norm"[1]
1. Jointly sets performance objectives with you.	5	3	1	4	7	3
2. Supports you in developing your career plans.	4	4	2	4	8	4
3. Motivates you to do a good job.	6	5	3	6	8	4
4. Gives you authority to do your job.	5	4	3	5	8	3
5. Provides the support necessary to help you do your job (e.g., advice, resources, or information).	6	4	2	5	7	4

[1]Norm is the average of subordinate ratings for the item across all managers in the unit.

Outline of a Guide for Interpreting Results

An interpretation guide would ask the manager receiving the report to compare his or her self-ratings to the average subordinate ratings.

The number of responding subordinates is an indication of the degree to which the results represent the work group. Data would not be presented if four or less subordinates responded to an item.

The "norm" provides a comparison to how managers overall were perceived by their subordinates.

The guide would include information about training and developmental experiences available that would be useful for each category of items.

_____

Note. Adapted from Wohlers and London (1989, in London, 1997a, pp. 48–49).

TYPICAL REACTIONS TO SURVEY FEEDBACK

The following are typical reactions to multirater survey reports. They demonstrate that the reactions are not necessarily all positive:

> "I never look at the numbers. All I care about is the write-in responses. They really tell me something. But most of my people don't write anything."

> "The first time I got my feedback report I kept it in my desk drawer for three months before tossing it. I just couldn't bring myself to open it up. Some of my friends told me how much they studied their results, so the second year we did this, I forced myself to look at the report. There were a few problems I needed to fix, but I was pleased to see some really positive results."

> "I hate this. It's not a subordinate's place to rate me. Subordinates' opinions are tied to what they think I think of them. Either they want to brown nose me with positive ratings, or they want to punish me for rating them down."

> "I loved the feedback. It gave me a chance to concentrate areas I need to improve. I learned a lot about myself that I really hadn't thought about before."

> "The feedback report was very useful. I showed it to my boss, and we had a great discussion about what the results meant for me. My boss helped me put together a training plan to improve my performance."

> "The results were confusing. There was a lot of disagreement among the people who rated me."

> "I distributed my results at a staff meeting, and I had an honest discussion with my staff about what they mean and where I need to improve. Some of them were embarrassed at first. They were reluctant to talk, I think, because they thought I would know who provided what ratings if they spoke up. After awhile though, they could see I really wanted to understand. They talked about what the raters "might" have meant, not that they agreed necessarily. They gave me a number of examples, saying "Remember when this and that happened. Here's what you did.... This is the kind of thing the raters might have meant.""

These comments demonstrate that feedback in general, and multisource feedback in particular, is not always warmly welcomed. It can be a threatening experience, especially for people who are not inclined to seek feedback. Also, the feedback report is not a stand-alone event. As discussed later in the section on understanding how feedback affects performance over time, the report is one part of a developmental, performance improvement process that includes other factors, such as sources of feedback, support from one's boss and work group, planning for development, and organizational support for implementing these plans (e.g., the opportunity for developmental job experiences and training workshops).

PARADOXES OF USING 360-DEGREE FEEDBACK

Ghorpade (2000) noted that whereas 360-degree feedback provides useful performance information, the method has major problems relating to privacy, validity, and effectiveness. Part of the difficulty arises because there is no consistent method of design and delivery of 360-degree feedback. There are many forms of 360-degree feedback programs, ranging from traditional vertical ratings of performance appraisal to sophisticated systems that gather, analyze, and disseminate behavioral data for individuals and teams at all organizational levels. Many 360 programs lack strategic context, and do not focus on how the process can provide a competitive advantage. He outlined the following five paradoxes of 360-degree survey feedback programs and suggestions for managing them:

1. The use of 360-degree feedback for development gets tangled with the appraisal process, creating the potential for confusion and erosion of its utility as a method for development. This may be overcome in one of two ways: Keep the program solely as a development tool, and establish clear rules for information sharing so that recipients and raters know who has access to the information and how the information will be used. Alternatively, if 360-degree feedback is to be combined with performance appraisal, then do so gradually as part of a comprehensive performance management program. Raters and ratees will become used to participating in the process, will understand its value, and will be less likely to sabotage the process or limit the usefulness of their ratings (e.g., make all lenient judgments) if they think the information is to be used primarily for promotion or pay decisions.

2. The use of multiple raters from different constituencies broadens the scope of feedback data and is touted as one, if not the, major advantage of 360-degree feedback. However, more information does not necessarily mean better feedback. Possible solutions to this paradox are coupled with the next paradox dealing with anonymous ratings.

3. Also, anonymous ratings are more honest than signed ratings, but may not necessarily be more valid in capturing meaningful performance information. Ghorpade (2000) recommended not worrying as much about increasing the number of rater groups providing ratings but rather focus on the value of the feedback for development. So, for instance, peers may not be the best group to provide feedback about a leader's supervisory behavior. Instead, ask rater groups for information concerning behaviors about which they know. Also, Ghorpade recommended providing raters with guidance and training, including descriptions of the major competencies they are rating so they have a common understanding of the performance dimensions. Another recommendation is to provide raters with the chance to detect their own rating biases before they actually rate anyone. Data from prior surveys, or a test survey, can be presented to raters in a training session so that they see and understand possible rating errors.

4. Structured, quantitative, and generic feedback is easy to collect, but may have limited value, and may be misleading. The generic questions may be too general to provide really useful information. Also, workplaces may not be

comparable, so comparing mean results between departments within the organization, or between organizations, may be misleading. Ghorpade (2000) suggested collecting both qualitative information (written responses) and quantitative ratings. Also, context-specific performance dimensions that relate to the strategy and specific demands of the department and organization should be included along with generic performance dimensions that apply in most situations.

5. Involving management in the process of gathering and processing the data is legitimate and inevitable, but may reduce the data's credibility by causing fear or mistrust about how the information will be used. Ghorpade (2000) recommended assigning administrative tasks to one designated manager, preferably someone in the human resources department or to someone whose involvement will enhance trust, such as the corporation's ombudsperson or organization development specialist. In one organization, the principal coordinator was a long-term executive who was responsible for organization development. He was well-known and respected throughout the organization as a person who did what was right, not what was best for him.

EFFECTS OF FEEDBACK ON DEVELOPMENT AND PERFORMANCE

Several previous studies found that upward feedback improves ratings. These were reviewed by Walker and Smither (1999) and are summarized here:

- Subordinates perceived performance improvement among supervisors who received upward feedback (Hegarty, 1974).
- Skill increases and increased self–coworker agreeement in performance ratings occurred 2 years after receiving multisource feeback (Hazucha, Hezlett, & Schneider, 1993).
- Subordinate ratings improved over time in a study of 48 store managers in a retail clothing chain (Bernardin, Hagan, Ross, & Kane, 1995).
- In a sample of 238 managers of a large organization receiving upward feedback 2 months apart, managers whose initial feedback ratings were low or moderate improved (Smither et al.,1995). The managers whose first feedback ratings were low maintained their performance improvement for a third and fourth administration as long as 2½ years after the first (Reilly, Smither, & Vasilopoulos, 1996).
- Follower ratings of student leaders at the U.S. Naval Academy improved after upward feedback was given to the leaders, and those receiving the lowest performance ratings initially improved the most (L.E. Atwater, Roush, P., & Fischthal, A., 1995).
- Upward feedback ratings were collected at two points in time separated by 10 months for two randomly selected groups of supervisors from a state

police agency. One group received feedback after the first administration, and the other did not. The group receiving feedback improved significantly, but the other group showed no significant improvement (L. E. Atwater, Waldman, D. Atwater, & Cartier, 1998). In the feedback group, those who were most accepting of the feedback improved the most, and those who were cynical improved less.

- Walker and Smither (1999) studied 252 managers over five annual administrations of an upward feedback program (ratings from subordinates). They found that managers who initially were rated as poor or moderate in performance by their subordinates showed significant improvements in performance over the 5-year period. The managers who improved the most were those who met with their subordinates to discuss their results. Also, the same managers improved more in those years when they met with their subordinates to discuss the prior year's results than when they did not. This showed that what managers do with the upward feedback affects its benefits. Walker and Smither reasoned that the value in meeting with subordinates stemmed from further understanding of the results and increased feelings of accountability for doing something with the feedback.

Accountability

Increasing attention is being given to the accountability of ratees to use the feedback to guide performance improvement. Often, a confidential feedback report is given to the ratee for developmental purposes only. It is not shared with the supervisor, and the ratee is not required to discuss or share the results with others. One way to enhance the ratee's accountability to use the results is to require that the ratee use the report to construct a development plan and share the plan with the supervisor (Dalessio, 1998). Later, the supervisor can evaluate the extent to which the developmental goals were achieved.

An additional approach is to encourage ratees to discuss their feedback results with the raters (e.g., a group of subordinates) (London, Smither, & Adsit, 1997). This is similar to the traditional performance feedback discussion that supervisors hold with the subordinates they rate except that here, the recipient of the ratings initiates the conversation with the raters. Also, of course, different rater groups are involved. The discussion can center on clarifying the feedback results and having ratees commit themselves to changing their behavior. The discussion may increase the time and effort the ratee spends thinking about and absorbing the feedback results. Raters have the chance to clarify the feedback results and give ratees some ideas for improvement. Setting goals for improvement and publicly committing to performance improvement also increases the likelihood that the ratee will work toward accomplishing those goals (Walker & Smither, 1999). In addition, because direct reports and the supervisor are aware of the goals, they can help the ratee work toward improvement.

London et al.(1997) argued that multisource feedback will not be effective if ratees are not accountable for using the feedback for performance improvement, raters are not accountable for the accuracy of their ratings, and management does not provide resources to support behavior change. They suggested that accountability is the Achilles Heal of 360-degree feedback in that survey procedures do little to hold raters accountable for the accuracy of the information they provide or hold ratees accountable for using the feedback. A dilemma is that raters prefer anonymous ratings (low accountability), whereas target managers (ratees) prefer confidential feedback (low accountability) and prefer that the multisource feedback not be used for formal appraisal. Also, corporations do not always provide the resources needed to help managers develop. If a change is made to hold raters and ratees accountable, then other problems may emerge. For instance, ratings may be more lenient than if they were anonymous, and raters may use their ratings to affect how the recipient of the feedback will view them (i.e., use it for impression management purposes). However, if raters and ratees are not accountable, then will they take the process seriously?

London et al. (1997) suggested that different approaches to multisource feedback offer different levels of accountability. In particular:

1. *Traditional survey feedback.* This is an organization-wide employee opinion or attitude survey. Employees complete the forms anonymously. The items ask about a wide variety of issues (e.g., benefits, working condition) as well as a section on supervision. The results are aggregated across all employees in the organization, with separate results reported for each department. The results are used by top management to track employee attitudes. Leaders can request results from their own units. When they do so, they have no obligation to use the information. In this case, there is low rater, ratee, and organization accountability.

2. *360-degree survey feedback as a resource for each leader.* Leaders receive confidential multisource feedback. Ratings are made specifically about the individual leader. The leaders are encouraged, but are not required, to share the feedback with their work team and hold discussions with the team to gain clarity about the meaning of the results. The leaders use the feedback to set development goals for themselves. Raters are anonymous. Management provides no support or resources for interpreting the results or creating development plans. Here again, rater, ratee, and organizational accountability are low.

3. *Survey results presented with guidelines for use of the feedback.* Leaders receive confidential multisource feedback. They are encouraged, but not required, to share the feedback with their team and use it for development. Raters are anonymous. All of this is similar to the last situation. However, now the organization provides some written guidelines or resources related to the dimensions being rated (e.g., books, training programs, or tips on how to improve specific skills). Accountability of raters and ratees is low here too. However, organizational accountability is a bit higher.

4. *Survey feedback incorporated into formal appraisal.* Leaders receive multisource feedback. Raters are anonymous. The results are not confidential, but instead are given to the leaders who incorporate the feedback into their formal performance appraisal where it may affect compensation, promotion, job assignments, or other decisions about the leader. The organization may or may not provide resources to support personal development. Here, only the leader's accountability to use the information is high. Rater and organizational accountability are low.

5. *Survey feedback linked to training.* Raters provide anonymous feedback. Leaders receive confidential feedback during an off-site leadership training program that focuses on the skills being rated. The leaders are encouraged to share their development plan with their boss. In this case, rater accountability is low, manager accountability to use the information is moderate, and organizational accountability to provide resources for development is high (if only because the feedback is built into the design of a leadership development program).

6. *Facilitator-guided use of feedback.* Raters provide anonymous feedback. The leader's feedback report is sent to a coach who reviews the feedback and presents it to the leader. Together, they formulate some reactions and development plans. They may arrange a meeting for the leaders and their work group. The leaders share initial reactions and plans with the group. Raters offer additional guidance and specific, constructive suggestions. The leaders prepare a development plan and share the plan (but not the feedback on which it is based) with the boss. The coach meets with the leaders 1 month, 3 months, 6 months, and 9 months after the leaders receive initial feedback (to help formulate goals and action plans, share approaches others are using, direct the leader to appropriate resources, and monitor progress). Here, rater accountability is moderate, the leader's accountability is high, and the organization's accountability is also high, by virtue of providing a coach to at least encourage development planning.

7. *Survey feedback linked to assessment center.* Raters provide anonymous feedback. Leaders receive feedback during participation in an assessment center that measures and provides feedback on the same dimensions rated by coworkers. Leaders prepare a development plan and are encouraged to share it with their boss. Management provides some written guidelines or resources related to the dimensions being rated. Rater accountability is low, whereas leader accountability and organizational accountability are both moderate in this case.

London et al. (1997) also suggested interventions to facilitate accountability. These are listed in Table 7.2. They suggested that the organization can establish an environment that highlights and promotes the use of survey feedback results.

TABLE 7.2

Interventions to Encourage Ratees' Accountability to Use Feedback

- Requiring that recipients explain feedback results to their boss and make commitments for improvement
- Repeating surveys over time (i.e., not just doing a survey once and expecting it to change behavior)
- Discussing feedback results with others (supervisor, peers, subordinates) in a constructive, nonthreatening way.
- Providing normative ratings to encourage ratees to think about how their results compare to others
- Rewarding supervisors for supporting subordinate development
- Involving subordinates in writing survey items that define the boss–subordinate relationship
- Involving customers in writing survey items
- Ensuring that items reflect behaviors that are desired by the organization and so convey the organization's expectations for effective managerial behavior
- Engaging in team building activities that foster mutual support
- Linking feedback to training programs and development opportunities (i.e., ensuring the feedback recipients have a chance to participate in development activities that are aimed at enhancing their strengths and reversing their weaknesses, as reflected in the feedback)
- Using facilitators or coaches to guide the use of feedback

Note. Based on London, Smither, and Adsit (1997).

Accountability and Self-Ratings. Evaluations of self and others may depend on how people communicate. People's positive bias in evaluating themselves is likely to be lower when they are evaluating their contribution to a group that meets face-to-face than when evaluating their contribution to a group meeting electronically. Weisband, S. and Atwater, L. E. (1999) discovered this in a study of 105 business students participating in a group discussion. Assigned to 3-person groups, they used electronic media to communicate or meet face-to face. This finding may occur because in electronic communication, people focus more on the effort they exerted. Others' effort is less visible. Another explanation is that people feel less accountable for their self-evaluations. They worry less about being able to justify their contributions to others in the electronic group than in the face-to-face group. However, in evaluating others, they tend to be more accurate about others' contributions in the electronic situation than face-to-face. In face-to-face interaction, they are influenced by how much they like the people they are rating. They tend to rate the people they like more highly than those they do not like. However, in electronic communication, actual contributions (e.g., the number of task relevant remarks) are more highly related to evaluations than in face-to-face communication. People seem to be able to focus more clearly on actual contributions made by others in electronic media, however, they seem to be more biased in their self-evaluations in electronic media.

Perceptions of Fairness

The manner in which employees react to feedback affects the extent to which they process the information mindfully to enhance their self-insight, adjust their self-concept, and change their performance (as discussed in chap. 2, this volume). In particular, Flint (1999) suggested that managers' reactions to feedback depend on their perception of the outcomes (distributive justice) and the fairness of the appraisal process (procedural justice). Research has shown that when distributive justice is low (i.e., ratings are less than the ratees felt they deserved), the perceptions of the fairness of the rating process influence whether the results are used to improve performance in the future (Brockner & Wiesenfeld, 1996).

Drawing on a resource-based model of procedural justice of Thibaut and Walker (1975), Flint (1999) suggested that people perceive that procedures are the fairest when the participants have control over the process. They may have control over the decisions or outcomes, or they may have influence (voice) over the process (process-control). That is, they have a chance to present their point of view, if not actually make the decision. In multisource performance appraisal, this would mean that leaders who are rated have some say in the process used to arrive at the ratings (e.g., suggesting items on which they will be rated or nominating the raters). In addition, they may have a chance to provide self-ratings. Self-ratings tend to lack reliability (i.e., they tend to be unrelated to supervisor and peer ratings, whereas peer and supervisor ratings tend to be highly correlated; cf. Folger & Cropanzano, 1998, p. 126). Nevertheless, self-ratings are a way for leaders to express their viewpoint on their own performance. Flint argued that including self-ratings can lead to better employee attitudes about the appraisal results from others, more tolerance of managerial criticism, and high work performance (as found by Bassett & Meyer, 1968). Because having the chance to express disagreement with the ratings is important for acceptance of the results, supervisors should be trained in how to handle challenges to their own ratings and those provided by other sources (Flint, 1999).

Leaders prefer to receive feedback from identifiable individuals, but raters, not surprisingly, prefer to be anonymous (Antonioni, 1994). Flint's (1999) solution was to overcome difficulties associated with anonymous feedback by giving leaders the chance to express their concerns with the appraisals at the time of feedback.

Flint (1999) also suggested that the group values model (Lind & Tyler, 1988) affects reactions to feedback. This model holds that long-term relationships involving groups are more important than control. According to this model, leaders will react more favorably to the ratings they receive if the raters are perceived as neutral (making ratings based on facts, not opinions), trustworthy (they will rate in a fair and reasonable way), and have standing (are recognized by the leaders as familiar with their work).

Rater Agreement

Another study of changes in performance following feedback was conducted by J. W. Johnson and Ferstl (1999), who collected data from 1,903 managers in an accounting firm. The managers received subordinate ratings at two points in time separated by from 12 to 18 months. Those who were initially overraters (i.e., they rated themselves more favorably than they were rated by subordinates) had lower self-ratings and higher subordinate ratings at the second time. This is the group that would have the most difficulty accepting feedback that is incongruent with their self-image, as per chapter 2's (this volume) discussion of self. However, this study found that overraters tended to improve their performance regardless of their initial performance level—that is, whether they were fairly high already and just rated themselves higher than their subordinates saw them or whether their self-ratings were generally low and their subordinates saw them as even lower. In general, receiving lower ratings from subordinates compared to self-ratings provides direction for performance improvement and impetus to be more stringent in rating oneself the next time (J. W. Johnson, Olson, & Courtney, 1996). The feedback provides people with the information about what behaviors are expected and valued by the organization, the particular elements of performance they need to improve, and ways they can improve their performance, such as training courses or job assignments. Assuming the people who are rated poorly want to improve, they will be motivated to use the feedback to enhance their performance before the next ratings are collected.

The J. W. Johnson and Ferstl (1999) study found that upward feedback does not have positive effects for all performers. Those who were initially underraters (they rated themselves less favorably than they were rated by subordinates) had higher self-ratings and lower subordinate ratings at the second time. Receiving higher ratings from subordinates compared to self-ratings suggests that all is well and there is no need to adjust behavior and there may even be room to slack off. Underraters simply have less motivation to change their behavior.

If J. W. Johnson and Ferstl (1999) had not examined differences between over-and underraters, then upward feedback would have appeared to have very little or no effect on performance change. The effects of overraters simply canceled out the effects of underraters, and those whose self-ratings initially agreed with subordinate ratings did not change their performance. Self-ratings usually are higher than ratings made by others (cf. Smither et al., 1995), and so receiving lower subordinate ratings is more likely than receiving higher subordinate ratings, and performance tends to improve for overraters. In the J. W. Johnson and Ferstl (1999) sample, overraters were a lower proportion of the overall sample than might be found in other studies.

Information about self–other discrepancies would not be likely to change performance for underraters, so J. W. Johnson and Ferstl (1999) suggested that feedback reports should be adjusted for this group and for those who are in agreement. For these groups, they suggested that the self–other discrepancy not be highlighted. Rather, emphasis should be placed on the absolute level of the ratings or a comparison to the norm group. The report should provide information about how the ratees are doing relative to optimal performance or in comparison to other managers in the organization. This may help motivate them to enhance their performance and provide information about how to do it—that is, which performance dimensions to concentrate on and ways to do it.

Effects of Monitoring the Environment for Performance Feedback on Self-Supervisor Agreement. Williams and M. A. Johnson (2000) found that employees' self-assessments are more likely to agree with their supervisors' ratings of performance when the employees seek feedback through monitoring. *Monitoring* is attending to, and taking in, information from the environment (Ashford & Cummings, 1983). These are covert seeking behaviors that require seekers to interpret cues in the environment. Although this may not result in accurate or complete feedback, it may be sufficient to provide valuable information about performance. Another way to acquire feedback is through direct inquiry. This may result in less ambiguous, more accurate, and more timely information. However, individuals may be hesitant to ask for feedback because they are concerned about what others will think of them for asking. They do not want to call attention to negative aspects of their performance and they do not want others to feel they do not have a handle on their own performance outcomes or they are not confident in their own abilities. Williams and M. A. Johnson (2000) asked college students working on campus to complete a survey that asked about the frequency of their feedback seeking and the extent to which they monitor their environment for feedback (e.g., "How often do you compare your coworkers' performance to your own?" and "How often do you pay attention to casual remarks made by others regarding your performance?"). Respondents were more likely to indicate they obtain feedback by monitoring their environment than asking for feedback directly. Also, agreement between self and supervisor ratings was higher for individuals who reported higher frequency of monitoring. Moreover, individuals who reported low frequency of monitoring and who were rated highly by their supervisor rated themselves much lower than their supervisors. This indicates that those who do not monitor may not have an accurate view of how highly their supervisors view their performance.

Intentions to Use the Feedback for Development

Maurer and Palmer (1999) addressed the general question: What do ratees do when they initially receive developmental feedback? Do they dismiss the ratings and not intend to do anything, or do they respond with intentions to improve on the rated skills that indicate improvement is needed? Their theory of planned behavior argues that intentions to engage in improvement are a function of three variables: the belief that improvement will yield favorable outcomes, others' expectations for improvement, and belief that improvement is possible. The resulting intentions are theoretically related to actual improvement. Also, intentions and perceived beliefs about capability (i.e., control over one's behaviors) interact such that improvement is higher when both intentions and perceived behavioral control are high. Another variable that should be associated with intention to improve is perceived accuracy of the ratings. Leaders are more likely to respond to feedback if they believe the feedback is accurate.

Studying 127 telecommunications company managers who had just received performance feedback reports based on anonymous peer and subordinate ratings of four behavioral dimensions of performance (leadership skills, coaching skills, facilitating subordinates' work, and team-building skills), Maurer and Palmer (1999) found that intention to engage in voluntary development activities following feedback was related to three variables: (a) perceived outcomes or benefits of improvement, which were highly related to spending time on off-the-job development, such as participation in courses, as opposed to on-the-job development, such as meetings with subordinates and peers and seeking coaching; (b) perceived social pressures of improvement, showing that "voluntary" development behavior can be related to both perceived rewards (a pull) and social pressures (a push); and (c) perceived control over improvement.

Perceived control interacted with intentions to produce behavior change. That is, the more the managers believed they could improve, the more they intended to react to the feedback by trying to develop their skills. This suggests that it is important for managers to realize they are able to control their behavior and indeed they can use performance feedback to guide their development and successfully improve their performance. Interventions to help managers understand they are capable of improving may help make the feedback more useful. Bandura's (1982) self-efficacy theory suggests that people can increase their self-confidence for a behavior by engaging in activities that result in success. The experiences of success persuade individuals that they are able to perform the behavior. Another way to increase self-confidence and the sense of self-control is to show individuals role models who are similar to them and who have been able to engage in the behavior and improve their performance. Support and encouragement for improvement in an environment where others are improving and being more successful as a result can increase others' self-confidence such that they too can improve.

Maurer and Palmer's (1999) study also showed that peer performance ratings repeated 9 months after the initial feedback showed positive performance change for those managers who had indicated they would engage in voluntary development activities off-the-job if they believed they had high control over their future performance. Their performance was significantly lower if they said they would try to improve but they believed they had little control over the outcomes. Also interesting was the finding that perceived social pressures were related to intentions to improve by engaging in on-the-job activities. In addition, different social and intrinsic outcomes differentially predicted intention to participate in development. Intrinsic outcomes, such as personal satisfaction and having more interesting work, were associated with participating in off-the-job development activities. Peer outcomes, such as more positive interpersonal relations, were associated with intention to participate in on-the-job activities. Perceived accuracy of the ratings was not significantly related to intentions.

Managers Give Importance to Subordinate Ratings

In a sample of 2,163 managers who participated in a week-long leadership development program that began by reviewing their 360 feedback results, subordinate ratings were more highly related to developmental goals set at the end of the development program than were supervisory ratings (Brutus, London, & Martineau, 1999). The managers may realize that their effectiveness depends on their ability to work through others, particularly subordinates. The managers may be accustomed to using indirect feedback cues from subordinates because they rarely get direct feedback from them. Also, subordinate ratings were the average of ratings from different subordinates. These averaged results may represent a more uniform and stronger message (assuming a reasonable level of interrater agreement), and a message that is directly related to the purpose of the leadership development program. Moreover, subordinates know the most about managers' leadership behavior, and so their ratings are likely to carry more weight than supervisor ratings when setting leadership development goals.

Demonstrating managers' sensitivity to subordinate ratings, L. E. Atwater, Waldman, D. Atwater, and Cartier (2000) conducted a field experiment of an upward feedback program in a policing agency. In this study, 110 supervisors were randomly assigned to one of two conditions: a survey-only group in which supervisors and subordinates completed surveys of leadership behavior at two times separated by approximately 10 months, and the supervisors received feedback only at Time 2; and a feedback group in which supervisors and subordinates completed surveys at both points in time, and the supervisors received feedback after each survey. The results showed no significant improvement in subordinate ratings for the feedback or survey-only group. Self-ratings decreased from Time 1 to Time 2 for the feedback group but not for the survey-only group. This suggested that increased self-awareness or a desire to have self-ratings be more consistent with subordinate ratings. Future research needs to investigate whether more accurate self-ratings could prompt leaders to develop areas of weakness.

The study measured supervisors' feeling of organizational cynicism with a scale that included items such as, "It is hard to be hopeful about the future because people at (agency X) have such bad attitudes," and "People at (agency X) get credit they don't deserve for work they don't do" (L. E. Atwater et al., 2000, p. 296). Supervisors who were more cynical about organizational changes, as measured by a cynicism scale at Time 1, were less likely to be rated highly by subordinates at Time 2. This suggested that the more cynical supervisors were less motivated to change their behavior, or, more generally, were less interested in exerting energy to improve the overall organization.

Another result correlated the cynicism measured at Time 1 with an index of commitment to subordinates measured at both points in time. Commitment was measured by items such as, "I am willing to put in a great deal of effort beyond that normally expected in order to help my subordinates by successful," and "I feel a sense of loyalty to my subordinates" (L. E. Atwater et al., 2000, p. 296). Cynicism at Time 1 was negatively related to commitment to subordinates at Time 2 for supervisors in the feedback group but not for supervisors in the survey-only group. This indicates that more cynical supervisors are less committed to their subordinates once they have received feedback and know what their subordinates think of them. This reinforces the idea that cynicism reduces the motivation to change, particularly after feedback. In general, commitment to subordinates is a meaningful outcome in and of itself, in addition to performance improvement. Higher ratings from subordinates resulted in higher commitment to subordinates, whereas lower ratings from subordinates resulted in lower commitment. This indicated that negative feedback had a negative effect on subsequent attitudes.

At Time 2, supervisors who had received feedback at Time 1 were asked about their reactions to the feedback and their attempts to change. Supervisors who found feedback to be more valuable and had set improvement goals had higher Time 2 ratings from subordinates. This is consistent with Walker and Smither (1999) and Brutus, London, and Martineau (1999), who indicated that subordinate ratings that are well-received and prompt a leader to set development goals are likely to result in changed behavior.

The Importance of Psychological Safety for Effective Learning

As suggested at the outset of this chapter, feedback is potentially threatening, especially feedback with implications for important work and life outcomes.

Using 360-degree feedback for development alone promotes psychological safety. This is key to positive learning outcomes.

In designing a model of team psychological safety and learning behavior, Edmondson (1999) showed how organizational structures (support and coaching from the leader) and feelings of psychological safety and efficacy affect learning behavior (seeking feedback and reviewing errors). Her ideas apply to individual as well as group learning. She cited Dewey's (1922) classic definition of learning as "an iterative process of designing, carrying out, reflecting upon, and modifying actions" (Edmondson, 1999, p. 353). Extending this concept, she noted that learning is "an ongoing process of reflection and action, characterized by asking questions, seeking feedback, experimenting, reflecting on results, and discussing errors or unexpected outcomes of action" (Edmondson, 1999, p. 353). The learning process unfolds as gaps in plans are discovered, changes are made accordingly, assumptions are tested, and different ideas and courses of action are openly discussed. These ideas build on conceptualizations of learning as dependent on attention to feedback, experimentation, and recognition and processing of failure (e.g., Schön, 1983). Errors are a valuable source of information in showing that something did not work as planned. Learning behavior is time consuming, and as such, risky. This is especially the case for people engaged in highly routine repetitive tasks with little need for improvement. This is less so for people facing change or uncertainty, for whom the risk of wasting time would be small in relation to the possible gain. Even for people engaged in routine tasks, Edmondson noted that learning behavior may be effective for intermittent process improvement.

Edmondson's (1999) model emphasized that learning requires psychological safety. This is essentially a tacit belief (unspoken, taken-for-granted, and not directly attended to) that people can be trusted. Psychological safety is necessary for people to feel secure and capable of change.

Intention to Use Feedback

Williams and Lueke (1999) developed a comprehensive model to understand the long-term effects of 360-degree feedback on developmental behavior (intentions to participate in development and actually choosing a coach). Their model proposed that three factors influence intentions to use the feedback: self-efficacy (feeling good about one's ability to use the feedback effectively), perceived constraints (the resources or lack thereof that allow using the feedback to improve performance, i.e., the availability of training or the time to practice and improve), and feelings about the system (e.g., its fairness and accuracy). These three factors will be more positive when the raters agree with one another in providing a consistent picture of performance. Furthermore, consistency of feedback is likely to have a more positive effect on self-efficacy, perceived constraints, and system reactions when the following conditions are present: social support for using the feedback, prior positive experience with the feedback process, and (c) perceived knowledge of how the performance appraisal system works in the organization.

Williams and Lueke (1999) studied 63 managers in a financial institution. The 360-degree feedback process had been in place for 3 years prior to the study. On the average, the managers were 41 years old, had been with the institution for almost 10 years, and had participated in the 360-degree feedback twice before. Forty three percent of the managers were women. They completed a survey 2 to 3 months after receiving their most recent feedback. The survey measured the variables in the model, for instance, perceived system support, feelings about the system, intentions to improve, and whether they had obtained a coach. They were also asked to evaluate the value of the different sources of feedback. The result showed that the managers valued subordinate feedback, as opposed to peer and supervisor feedback, as the most relevant and appropriate source. Managers who received highly inconsistent ratings were most likely to perceive situational constraints, especially when they did not understand how the appraisal system worked. Reporting constraints after having received inconsistent feedback may be a form of self-protection or rationalization, as if to say, "There's nothing I can do about this," or self-handicapping in not knowing how to use the inconsistent information. The study also showed that managers who received highly consistent ratings and perceived high support reported the lowest level of constraints.

The study also showed that managers whose self-ratings were consistent with their subordinate ratings had higher self-efficacy judgments. Interestingly, however, if the self and subordinate ratings were consistent and they had more experience with the system, then they reported lower self-efficacy judgments than if they had inconsistent ratings and lower experience. Williams and Lueke interpreted this to mean that as managers gain experience with the feedback system, and if ratings are inconsistent, then their self-efficacy for improvement decreases. Their motivation probably decreases because they are not sure they can make changes in their performance to generate more consistent ratings. Those with less experience have not had a chance to see this. Managers who had more consistent ratings with subordinates and more experience with the system had the most positive reactions to the feedback.

These results showed the importance of consistency in ratings on desire to use feedback for development. They also showed the importance of experience and knowledge about the system on how the feedback affects reactions. Managers who received consistent ratings (ratings that disagree with their own), and who have more experience with the system, were likely to have more positive reactions to 360-degree feedback. The consistency in the ratings may reflect their efforts to improve over time. Those who had experience receiving inconsistent ratings were likely to be frustrated by the process, develop feelings that their efforts to improve failed, and be less satisfied with the whole process. Reactions to the system were lower for those with low experience and consistent ratings, perhaps because they have not had the time to fully understand or appreciate what the consistency means. Future research is needed to test Williams and Lueke's model more completely, in particular, to investigate how the components in the model affect actual participation in development over time and future performance and consistency of ratings.

RECOMMENDATIONS FOR 360-DEGREE FEEDBACK

DeNisi and Kluger (2000) emphasized that feedback interventions are more likely to be effective if they keep the employee's attention focused on task goals, and are least likely to be effective if they shift focus to the self. "Unfortunately, several aspects of 360-degree appraisals often increase the likelihood that focus will move towards the self, while other aspects of typical 360-degree systems decrease the likelihood that any feedback will be effective for other reasons" (p. 135). Their recommendations for increasing the beneficial impact of 360-degree feedback are summarized in Table 7.3.

THE $64,000 QUESTION:
SHOULD FEEDBACK RESULTS BE USED
FOR ADMINISTRATION OR ONLY DEVELOPMENT?

Some companies use 360-degree feedback exclusively for managers' development. Others use the information to make decisions about managers. Table 7.4 summarizes pros and cons for using 360-feedback for administration (based on London, 2001). Basically, the fear is that 360-degree feedback will be more threatening and less accurate if it is used for decision making. Yet, many corporate executives want to act on the information if it is available. Fortunately, there are some ways to have the best of both worlds. One possibility is to introduce 360 as a developmental tool, and then, after several administrations, provide it as input to supervisors for performance evaluations. This may occur over a period of years, especially if the survey is administered only once a year. Be sure that managers know that this is what is planned from the start. This will help managers get comfortable with the process over time, and recognize its value. They can be encouraged to share their early results with their supervisor. They will see how they use the results in understanding the performance of the managers who report to them, and as a consequence, will appreciate how their own supervisor may use similar data about them. Another way to ease into using the survey results for administration is to provide the data to executive coaches who help managers understand their initial results. Alternatively, deliver the results during a training workshop so that managers can learn how to use the feedback report. As new managers are hired, the first several administrations of feedback

TABLE 7.3

Ways to Enhance the Effectiveness of 360-Degree Feedback

General Recommendations

- Avoid using 360-degree appraisals for decision making, at least when it is first introduced in the organization.
- Tell employees if ratings are being used for decision making.
- Help employees interpret and react to the ratings.
- Minimize the amount of data presented to employees.
- Do not have all raters evaluate employees in all areas.
- Include a formal goal-setting component in the system.
- Implement a 360-degree system regularly.
- Evaluate the effectiveness of 360-degree appraisal systems.

Recommendations for Different Components of 360-Degree Feedback Systems

- Use comparative or normative data to focus attention on self (runs the risk of decreasing performance).
- Include a goal setting program because goal setting increases the effectiveness of feedback.
- Repeat feedback with information about improvement because frequent feedback with messages about the degree of improvement increases feedback effectiveness.
- Recognize that feedback on complex tasks may interfere with performance.
- Provide information about correct solutions, but avoid the impression that fixed solutions work in any situation.
- Recognize that multiple sources of feedback (the essence of 360-degree feedback) may be inconsistent and confusing, and allow recipients to focus on the most favorable information.
- Offer coaching to help employees deal effectively with feedback, particularly if their coach encourages them to formulate accurate hypotheses about how to improve performance.
- When starting a multisource feedback process, use the information just for developmental purposes. Use of feedback for administrative purposes rather than just for development increases anxiety, which is likely to result in performance decline. It may take two or three time periods for raters and managers to become comfortable with the process.

Note. Adapted from DeNisi & Kluger (2000, pp. 136–137).

can be used solely for development to give them a chance to feel comfortable with the organization's performance management process.

With this compromise in mind, consider the following guidelines for implementing 360-degree feedback:

- *Clarify purpose and build trust.* Leaders should be clear about the way the survey results will be used. There should be no surprises. For instance, suddenly announcing that the results will be used to make decisions when leaders

TABLE 7.4
**Pros and Cons for Using 360-Degree Feedback
for Making Administrative Decisions**

Pros for Use for Administration

- The information from different sources can be valuable input for making decisions about people.
- Performance judgments from many raters are better than those from any one rater.
- Feedback surveys quantify judgments about important aspects of performance.
- The company paid for the survey and should get as much benefit as possible from it.
- Raters may respect the survey process more, and pay more attention to providing accurate ratings, if they know the information will be used to make decisions about leaders who are rated.
- Using the data to make decisions increases the attention that leaders pay to their feedback results.
- The survey results supplement other sources of performance information.
- The survey is especially useful for evaluating leaders who are not monitored closely and who work with diverse organizations.

Cons Against Use for Administration

- Supervisors will feel they have less discretion in evaluating a subordinate manager's performance if they have to use the 360 survey results.
- Using 360 to evaluate leaders, as opposed to giving them advice, engenders defensiveness and rationalization, which detracts from focusing on developmental needs.
- Managers are wary of feedback from subordinates and peers. Managers are not open to negative feedback to begin with, and they don't want to hear negative comments from people who work for them.
- Knowing that your supervisor has the results can be stressful and threatening.
- Managers will question the raters' motives (e.g., "They don't like me anyway," or "They just want to get on my good side.").
- If managers nominate their own raters, they don't necessary choose impartial people.
- Managers believe that raters may sabotage the ratings because they are anonymous.
- Raters don't have to justify their ratings, and so ratees may not have much confidence in their accuracy.
- Receiving feedback is stressful, especially if it is inconsistent with one's expectations or self-image.
- Supervisors may not have the skill or motivation to help their subordinate managers deal with the feedback results.

Note. Based on London (2001).

thought the results would be used only for development would undermine leaders' trust in the process in addition to their trust in the organization.

• *Separate development from administration, even if the same information is used for both purposes.* That is, be sure the discussions about administrative decisions are separated from using the feedback results to establish development goals. This will limit defensiveness and help focus the discussion on career development objectives and skill and knowledge areas for development.

• *Consider customized, on-demand surveys for intermediate use* (may be delivered via the internet). Leaders can get accustomed to using these informal surveys for their own use when they need them, and as a result, make seeking feedback and using ratings a routine part of the managerial role.

• *Incorporate into a balanced set of performance measures.* The rating results then become one source of data among multiple performance indicators.

• *Introduce new managers to the process slowly.* Recognize that other managers acclimate to the process over time, and newcomers need the same consideration and time to adjust.

CONCLUSIONS

Multisource feedback is an area that is rich in theory, research, and practice. The field is moving beyond its original focus on whether self-ratings agree with ratings from others to whether feedback recipients use the information to improve their performance and development. Although self–other agreement may be important and interesting from the standpoint of self-insight, and perhaps this is the heart of 360 feedback in terms of its effects on motivating people to change behavior, there is a new focus on the context in which 360 is used. Tornow and London (1998) emphasized that 360 should be viewed as part of a long-term performance leadership *process* that is embedded in an organization context. London and Smither (2001) distinguished between individual and organizational feedback orientation as factors that affect readiness to accept, and support for, feedback. DeNisi and Kluger (2000) indicated that feedback concentrating on behavior relevant to the task is more productive than feedback threatening to the individual as a person.

The following are 10 ideas that emerge from the current state of multisource feedback:

1. Off-the-shelf, vanilla-flavored 360 that does not reflect the specific needs or characteristics of the organization is not likely to produce behavior change or performance improvement.
2. Organizational policies, culture, and performance systems are likely to influence the effectiveness of a feedback process.

3. The feedback report should not be a desk-drop. Support for feedback is important. Individuals certainly know this already but do not always act on it in building 360 programs.
4. Individual feedback may be counterproductive in team settings. Consideration must be given to different foci for feedback, including both process and outcome information and focusing on behavior of the overall team.
5. There is a difference between process and outcome feedback. Both may be necessary. Process feedback pinpoints factors that produce outcomes and specifies behaviors that need to be changed to enhance outcomes. Process feedback over time indicates the extent to which behaviors have changed. Outcome feedback over time indicates the extent to which the behaviors have had the desired effect. If outcomes do not improve, then the wrong process information may have been provided.
6. Tasks vary in the need for different types of feedback. In teams, some tasks require more adaptation and more coordination than others, and the content and direction of the feedback should reflect this need.
7. Individual differences may affect readiness to accept and use feedback. These include cognitive ability as well as attitudes, expectations, and motivation to learn.
8. Ratings may reflect the situation and the raters in addition to, or even instead of, the performance of the ratee. Feedback processes may be more successful if they allow for a dynamic interaction between rater and ratee.
9. Higher ratings may not be desirable, and a low gap between self and other ratings may not show real self-understanding. Self-understanding requires more depth than can be provided from 360 feedback alone. However, 360 can be a valuable adjunct when combined with other information to produce self-insight, self-objectivity, and social sensitivity.
10. Support factors, such as coaching, vary in their effectiveness. More information is needed about how they work and what can be done to increase their value. This is especially true of coaching, which is highly popular and for which there is little empirical literature.

Now, consider some overall questions that need to be answered by future research on multisource feedback:

1. What are the specific elements of 360 that make it work better than other forms of feedback? This is still a basic question that needs answering.
2. How does 360 feedback work within the context of team performance. Are team processes and team characteristics just the sum of individual member behavior and characteristics, or are there qualitatively different constructs that distinguish the team as an entity and its individual members?

3. How can feedback be calibrated over time to ensure the best mix of process and outcome and team and individual feedback; and how should this mix change as the learning experiences and capabilities change and shared behavioral expectations and behavioral schemata evolve?

4. How do individual differences, organizational roles, task requirements, organizational culture, and environmental support work together to affect feedback over time?

5. What interventions can promote the benefits of the dynamic interaction between raters and ratees over time (i.e., how can the double-feedback looped process be enhanced)?

6. What are different ways to allow the receiver of feedback to calibrate its meaning and context? Do norms help? How is it possible to account for role, level, task, and culture differences within an organization?

7. What are the challenges in designing a context-specific feedback process in terms of having bases for comparisons, such as norms and standards? How is it possible to account for changes in job requirements over time? Maybe standardization should not be a concern. What is needed is a customized approach that will be of most value when used in conjunction with other support mechanisms. As such, just-in-time, customized feedback collected, analyzed, and delivered by the internet and used in conjunction with coaching may be best for development. More standardized methods can be used for administrative approaches.

The next chapter examines coaching, another increasingly popular support mechanism for leadership development.

8

Coaching Processes

This chapter investigates the role of the coach in supporting leaders' career development and performance improvement. As noted in the last chapter, many organizations hire external coaches to help top leaders process their 360-degree feedback. Coaching has really blossomed as a central force in leadership development. There is much less research on the topic than there are "how to" books and materials. Nevertheless, the existing literature outlines many worthwhile ways to approach coaching and enhance its value. This chapter reviews the literature on coaching. It describes the purpose and process of coaching and ways to make coaching more effective. Although the prime focus is external coaches who are hired on a consulting basis to work with top executives, the chapter also discusses how managers at all organizational levels can become effective coaches to their subordinates and peers.

BACKGROUND

The coaching profession has grown dramatically during the last few years. Tyler (2000) reported the following: Membership in the International Coach Federation, headquartered in Washington, DC, was 2,300 and growing at a rate of 100 members per month. There may be as many as 10,000 professional coaches worldwide. One consulting firm estimated that 59% of organizations now offer coaching or developmental counseling to their managers and executives. Coaches meet with their clients two to four times per month for from 30 to 60 minutes. Coaches use a combination of methods. Ninety-four percent of coaching is conducted by telephone, 45% by e-mail, and 35% in person. From 55% to 70% of clients report the following benefits: enhanced self-awareness, setting better goals, a more balanced life, and lower stress.

This section considers why coaching is so popular, the background needed to be an external coach, the cost of coaching, and how coaching is part of the supervisory role.

The Value of Coaching

Coaching is especially helpful in today's business environment. Kilburg (2000) argued that traditional leadership styles stem from a hierarchical, industrial view of organizations during the last two centuries. Planning, organizing, and controlling, however, do not work as well in motivating and empowering a workforce to deal with unpredictable, often chaotic business environments across the globe. Executive coaching is valuable in this environment in helping leaders understand themselves and their environments, including others' and their own emotions, thoughts, and defenses as well as interpersonal relationships and conflicts. As an example, CSX Transportation in Jacksonville, Florida, uses coaches for high potential employees and executives to help them see the company as a whole and recognize the ways their actions affect others (Tyler, 2000). CSX believes that coaching helps executives keep pace with the need for constant development. Coaching keeps managers interested and motivated. Coaches work one on one with individual executives, focusing on exactly what they need when they need it. Unlike training, coaching is tailored to each individual. It is always on target, as long as the coach is doing a proper job.

Coaching has gained popularity because coaches provide a safe way for leaders to discuss their business problems and interpersonal issues that may be quite sensitive. As external experts whose sole role is to help the executives they are hired to support, coaches can be honest, help the executives own up to problems that may arise from their behavior, and suggest ways the executives can change their behavior. Also, coaches can be sounding boards, listening and providing their opinion as executives discuss new ideas without risk of what others in the organization might think.

Coaching works well when participants are highly motivated to learn, that is, when they want to enhance their self-insight and apply feedback to improve their work relationships. The coaching process facilitates the use of feedback for a number of reasons (Harris, 1999). The coach is able to develop a close, personal relationship with the executive. Coaching sessions provide opportunity to work through problems and issues that arise over the course of the coaching process. Coaching provides ongoing support and reinforcement, which is often not present in a standard, one-shot training program. The coaching process is designed to fit the specific needs of the executive, rather than being a predesigned training program targeted to the typical employee. Coaching provides an objective, honest atmosphere for high-level executives to discuss their concerns, weaknesses, and other issues.

Coaching does not work when the executive being coached is not motivated and/or the coach is inexperienced or incompetent (Harris, 1999). Also, some competencies can only change so much, and some are not easily developed. For instance, communication skills can be defined behaviorally, learned, practiced, and improved, as long as the executive is motivated to improve and devotes energy and time to improving. Being outgoing and personable may be harder to learn if it does not come naturally, although even the shyest executive can learn to be more forthcoming in interpersonal relationships.

Coaches' Credentials

Coaches usually bring a wide range of experiences to the role, often having been executives themselves. Some coaches are psychologists by training. Others are experts in management and leadership development. Many have their own favorite assessment tools and techniques to evaluate the executive's leadership style, although they will also follow processes developed by the executive's company and work with data about the executive collected by the company. Coaches may be independent consultants whose business comes from word or mouth, or they may be partners or employees of management consulting firms. Executives may seek a coach on their own, but usually, if they are part of a large company, the human resources department may arrange for a cohort of external coaches on whom executives can draw. The human resources department explores the coaches' credentials before placing them on a recommended list or assigning them to leaders.

The Cost of Coaching

Coaching can be costly (say, $3,000–$12,000 per executive for several coaching sessions and follow-up telephone calls—enough time to help the executive process feedback and formulate a development plan—and far more if the coaching continues; Harris, 1999). However, this cost needs to be weighed against the cost of other developmental experiences, say a weeklong off-site workshop sponsored by a training company or a university with a high tuition (perhaps $4,000 or more for the week, not including travel and living expenses). Coaching is very focused and direct and does not require leaving the office, although it helps to have a quiet, uninterrupted place for meetings.

Leaders as Coaches

Thoughts of coaching usually bring to mind external executive coaches. However, leaders and managers can be coaches to the people who report to them. They can also be mentors to others in the organization. Coaching is part of the role of supervisor and mentor. Although internal coaches have limitations, and supervisors, especially, are neither impartial sounding boards nor management development experts, they should be expected to help their subordinate formulate ways to develop and improve their job performance, and as such, contribute to a development-oriented organizational culture. This is discussed further later in the chapter.

JUST WHAT IS COACHING?

Harris (1999) interviewed five executive coaches to gather their understanding of the definition of executive coaching, why it works, its limitations, and the future of the process. Integrating the respondents' ideas, Harris arrived at the following definition: Executive coaching is "an on-going, one-on-one learning process enabling people to enhance their job performance" (p. 38). Ongoing means that it will last several months to a year. Moreover, it entails a close relationship between the executive and the coach. Coaching is less teaching and more helping the executive "learn how to learn."

Kilburg (1996) defined executive coaching as:

a helping relationship formed between a client who has managerial authority and responsibility in an organization and a consultant who uses a wide variety of behavioral techniques and methods to help the client achieve a mutually identified set of goals to improve his or her professional performance and personal satisfaction and, consequently, to improve the effectiveness of the client's organization within a formally defined coaching agreement. (p. 142)

Executive coaching is practical, goal-focused one-to-one learning. Coaches provide executives with important feedback that they would normally never get about personal, performance, career, and organizational issues. Coaching allows executives to address the kinds of issues that often go unattended in the rush of everyday business life. In a coaching relationship, these issues take center stage (Hall, Otazo, & Hollenbeck, 1999).

The goal of coaching is to move valued executives from where they are to where they want to be in terms of the performance of their work groups as well as their personal effectiveness and career success (Evered & Selman, 1989, cited in Witherspoon & White, 1997). Coaching helps executives learn, grow, and change.

Kinlaw (1996) defined superior coaching as "a disciplined conversation, using concrete performance information, between a leader and an individual or a team that results in the continuous improvement of performance" (p. 21). According to Kinlaw (1996), coaching is results oriented (leads to performance improvement); involves a disciplined interaction to create essential characteristics, develop critical skills, and use a core coaching conversation; requires a trained coach; and begins with values such as the belief that people want to be competent and (given the necessary help) want to be more competent, the belief that people should be given the chance to demonstrate their competencies on a continual basis, and the recognition that superior performance does not stem from control but rather engendering employees' commitment to perform at the best of their ability.

This links back to earlier discussions of self-insight, self-efficacy, learning, and accountability in chapters 2 and 7 of this volume. Coaching is especially useful for people who are open to information about themselves, who want to increase their effectiveness, who seek feedback, and who are serious about using feedback, and indeed, feel they are accountable for using feedback and establishing and implementing a development program for themselves. Coaching will not be useful for those who are resistant to feedback, who do not have the self-confidence to deal with information that is inconsistent with their self-image, and who do not feel any responsibility for seeking and using feedback.

These values emerge when employees understand what they are doing and why it is important, have the competencies to perform the jobs that are expected of them, feel appreciated, feel challenged, and have the chance to improve when they make mistakes.

Foster and Seeker (1997) viewed coaching as part of a performance management cycle that drives continuous learning. Performance measurement is the heart of the cycle ("If you can't measure it, you can't manage it," p. 16). The cycle revolves around planning, coaching, and evaluating for performance enhancement. According to Foster and Seeker (1997), "Coaches are motivators of people and teams. They inspire others to work hard and continually improve. They are the consummate observer and subject-matter expert. They may not be able to play at the same level as their star players, but that's okay. They don't have to. The task of a coach is to help others perform better" (p. 9). Coaching consists of helping to monitor performance, diagnosing performance problems and deficiencies, determining directions for performance improvement, sharing constructive feedback, and creating a supportive environment.

Waldroop and Butler (1996) characterized coaching in the following way: "Coaching requires understanding someone's problem behavior in context, deciding whether the problem can be remedied, and encouraging the person to adapt" (p. 111). They described coaching as just plain good management, requiring such generic management skills as keen powers of observation, sensible judgment, and an ability to take appropriate action. The goal of coaching is the same as the goal of good management: Do the most with available organizational resources.

Senior leaders increasingly think of coaching as an important part of their role (Kilburg, 1996; Tichy & Charan, 1995). The higher executives are in the organizational hierarchy, the less feedback they are likely to receive (Saporito, 1996). Performance reviews (and presumably other forms of feedback) at senior levels are less frequent, systematic, informative, and useful (Graddick & Lane, 1998). They also noted that executives may need performance reviews and feedback more than any other group in the organization due to several factors:

the sophisticated and more ambiguous nature of their jobs, the fact that their responsibilities and priorities tend to change often, the serious organizational consequences of ineffective performance at that level, and their typically high need for achievement, recognition, and career progress.

Coaching Goals

Coaching has several goals: behavior changes needed for performance improvement, handling business problems (could be problem performers, problem people outside the department, tough business objectives, etc.), career development (e.g., next jobs, preparing for changes in the business), and continuous learning. The coach and executive determine the direction of the coaching relationship together as they move along. This may take several sessions to develop, or it may be evident from the start.

Witherspoon and White (1997) conceptualized four potential coaching goals: coaching for skills performance, development, and/or coaching for the executive's agenda—that is, the specific problems and issues perceived by the executive. Each varies on the dimensions of clarity, consensus (i.e., the extent to which people tend to agree about the end for coaching and be strongly committed), and control (i.e., people believe they have a good chance of achieving their learning goals). Consider each of these possible goals and their implications for a successful coaching process. Coaching for skills is generally high in clarity, consensus, and control. Coaching for performance improvement is likely initially to have fuzzy goals, with more time required to reach clarity, consensus, and control. Coaching for performance may be critical for the executive's long-term viability and career success, even though it may appear to be less urgently needed than coaching for skill development. Also, coaching for performance improvement may be more threatening than coaching for skills. In coaching for performance, the coach may need to confront the executive's ineffective attitudes, low confidence and commitment, and blind spots about weaknesses. Coaching for performance helps executives assess their performance and obtain feedback on their strengths and weaknesses. Goals in coaching for career development may be unclear or lacking altogether. Learning is focused on a future job, which may not even exist now. This type of coaching can be intense and analytical, and may represent more threat to some learners. It has a deeper focus on personal growth than coaching for skills or performance. Coaching sessions focus on development for a future job by helping executives discover strengths and weaknesses, determine where growth is needed, and consider how to fill the gaps. In addition, coaching for the executive's agenda may or may not have clear goals. Indeed, the goal may be broad or open-ended. Coaching may be tied to an organization's priorities, for instance, to help implement specific change.

Possible Outcomes

What do executives and their companies hope to gain from coaching? The following are some possible outcomes: increased self-awareness, behavior change, performance improvement, relationship improvements, persistence, flexibility, tolerance, and emotional control (Witherspoon & White, 1997).

Graddick and Lane (1998) found two major reasons why executive coaches are hired: first, to help talented executives who are "in trouble" because of behavioral or style deficiencies and, second, to help executives through critical transitions such as having to lead a major change effort.

Mone (1988) emphasized that coaching should not be limited to dealing only with poor performers. Instead, it should be focused on growth, rather than performance deficiencies. Also, it should not be focused solely on preparing people for promotion, but instead should include a broader focus on gaining more responsibility and autonomy in the current job and enhancing technical and managerial skills. Coaching is also an ongoing process rather than a once-a-year planning activity.

Internal Versus External Coaches

There is a difference between the immediate supervisor as coach and an external, professional consultant/coach. An external coach is not necessarily as adept, skilled, or experienced as the executive. The external coach may become familiar with the executive's company over time, but will probably never have the familiarity with the company's culture and people enjoyed by internal coaches. However, this may not be necessary to be an effective coach. The external coach brings broad experience, an open and objective frame of mind without being evaluative or judgmental, and fresh ideas and different perspectives.

Witherspoon and White (1997) described the value of an external coach. The external coach is an objective outsider, free to question and engage the executive on major issues, which is harder for insiders to do. The external coach poses little threat and can be very effective when the executive wants more insight to support a decision, more options and creative suggestions for actions, support for change management, and a guide through unknown or unexplored areas. The external coach acts as a sounding board by offering feedback and suggestions to support or supplement the executive's ideas. The external coach should work with the firm's human resources department to help the executive assess the situation in a systematic way. For instance, the coach may use attitude survey results, derived from the company's employee survey, to diagnose key issues and set an agenda for change.

Hall et al. (1999) argued that external coaches are preferable when extreme confidentiality and anonymity are required, where a coach with experience in a wide range of businesses is needed, or when someone is needed to "speak the unspeakable." Internal coaches are preferred when knowing the company culture and politics is critical, when easy availability is desired, and when personal trust and comfort are at a premium.

A supervisor as coach explicitly states when coaching is happening, tries to be an objective sounding board, and makes suggestions, rather than giving instructions or directives. The supervisor can initiate formal coaching conversations and/or have a series of short sessions, really using even chance meetings as opportunities to give nonevaluative observations and specific, behaviorally oriented advice.

An external consultant may not know the executive or organization at first and interprets feedback solely from instruments. Internal consultants know the organization and its people. Feedback may be augmented from other sources (Wilkes, Nellen, & DelCarmen, 2000). Harris (1999) reasoned that internal coaches have the chance to build long-term, informal relationships with executives and managers. External consultants might be able to develop a greater sense of trust on the part of the executive and have more freedom to use assessment tools, such as personality inventories. Harris conjectured that individual differences between coaches may account for more variance in trust than whether the coach is internal or external. Overall, both external coaches and supervisors as coaches reinforce positive change, do not punish failure but rather focus on learning, and provide constructive feedback.

THE COACHING PROCESS

Information is the heart of coaching. At the outset, information is needed to diagnose the situation. As things move forward, information is needed to track behavioral change and assess the effects of this change on key outcomes. This requires determining relevant performance measurements and observations, collecting the data, gathering other information, and processing the results.

Coaching should take into account extra-work issues (e.g., politics, interpersonal relationships) and non-work issues (e.g., family situation and goals).

Kinlaw (1996) outlined critical coaching behaviors:

- *Attending*—facing the other person, keeping comfortable eye contact, nodding in agreement, avoiding distractions, not being too quick to reject ideas, thinking less about what one wants to say rather than what the executive is saying, not being too quick to use one's own beliefs and values to interpret the executive's ideas.
- *Inquiring*—asking how executives perceive the situation and interpret problems and how they think they should be resolved.
- *Reflecting*—coaches communicate that they are listening, understand what the executive is saying and feeling, and suspend judgment.

- *Affirming*—teaching what the executive wants or needs to know, resolving problems, supporting performance, and adjusting performance.
- *Being disciplined*—assuming responsibility for one's own behavior, shaping the conversation.

Using 360-Degree Feedback as a Jumping Off Point for Coaching

Graddick and Lane (1998) described several organizations where external coaches were made available to help the manager interpret 360-degree feedback and other data, prepare to discuss the feedback with others, absorb the feedback in a constructive manner, and develop an action plan for enhancing performance.

Goodstone and Diamante (1998) argued that 360-degree feedback, in and of itself, is insufficient to bring about managerial change. Rather, it is part of a springboard for a developmental process that often involves ongoing coaching or counseling. Indeed, counseling and 360-degree feedback have overlapping goals, such as increasing appropriate assertion, decreasing counterproductive aggression, and improving interpersonal skills (i.e., empathy, listening ability, communication style, and interpersonal effectiveness).

Goodstone and Diamante (1998) noted that one assumption underlying the presumed effectiveness of 360-degree feedback is that it increases self-awareness. The idea is that managers receiving 360 feedback compare the results to their self-perceptions and thereby develop a more objective view of their behavior. However, Goodstone and Diamante pointed out that another view (Rogers, 1980) posits that self-awareness is not enhanced by managers receiving information about how others perceive them, but by exploration of their own perceptions and experiences.

The Rogerian model holds that positive change results primarily from the reduction of the gap between the way individuals see themselves and the way they experience the world. So 360- degree feedback will help if managers receiving the information process it meaningfully and if change is supported by, and is consistent with, organizational goals and culture. Coaching establishes a process that provides components needed for individual change (i.e., empathic understanding, unconditional positive regard, and genuineness) and in line with organizational goals. This feedback can be a starting point for initiating the coaching discussion. Coaching helps to overcome resistance to feedback and helps focus the feedback on organizational objectives.

Coaching goes way beyond traditional performance appraisal discussion to do much more than deliver the news. The coach integrates business issues with the knowledge and art of counseling. Effective coaching strategies involve establishing a secure relationship with the manager built on trust and honesty, explaining the need for change in relation to organization objectives (i.e., strategic change), being unbiased and nonjudgmental, recognizing power bases and po-litical strategies in which the manager operates, and helping the manager be-have in ways that help accomplish organizational goals.

Hollenbeck and McCall (1999) also noted that coaching is a follow-on to 360-degree feedback. Hall et al. (1999) described a program at one company where external coaches were provided with a half-day training session to pre-pare them to provide 12 hours of coaching to executives receiving 360-degree feedback. In the first meeting, the coach and the executive opened the feedback data and explored how to read it. In subsequent meetings, the feedback was re-viewed, and developmental actions were planned and implemented. After 12 hours of coaching (paid for by the corporate client), coaching could continue at the discretion and on the department budget of the executive.

Coaching Responsibilities and Roles

This section outlines how a number of authors have viewed the coaching rela-tionship. The coach and executive have mutual responsibilities in the relation-ship to gather information and monitor progress.

Table 8.1 outlines elements of the coach's and executive's roles. Table 8.2 lists characteristics that describe the coaching relationship. As a reciprocal rela-tionship, the coach and executive jointly establish how often to have formal meetings, schedule the meetings and keep them, periodically discuss how well the relationship is working and how it can be improved, and evaluate the execu-tive's progress and the value of the coaching relationship.

The coach and executive must prepare for each meeting, and meet their obli-gations to each other. They establish a time frame for periodically reviewing the relationship and deciding whether or not to continue.

The coach's role may be as expert, trainer, consultant, and/or counselor (Witherspoon & White, 1997). The coach is not a psychologist. Also, the coach is not necessarily a mentor (role model and guide who tries to advance the exec-utive's career), although mentors are likely to do some coaching.

Mentoring and coaching are not the same thing, although the roles may be blurred (Foster & Seeker, 1997). A mentor is "a trusted tutor or guide who plays an active role in the development of an individual" (p. 9). A coach can be a mentor, but not necessarily. The coach can identify appropriate mentoring op-portunities and facilitate the creation of a mentor–mentee relationship.

Also, the coach is not a counselor. The role of counselor is more appropriate for professionals (e.g., psychologists, therapists, lawyers, doctors, and the clergy) who are able to deal with psychological needs.

Hall et al. (1999) noted that costs can be high if a coach becomes some-thing of a personal trainer or therapist. As one in-house coach said, "A coach is not a life-long mentor. Ending is important so that closure is reached and ac-tion is taken."

TABLE 8.1

Roles of the Coach and Executive

The coach's role is to ...

(a) Clarify the relationship and its purpose

(b) Observe the executive and/or gather data from multiple sources

(c) Help to integrate and summarize the data and determine its meaning

(d) Help to analyze situations

(e) Act as a sounding board for the executive to test ideas without risk

(f) Suggest new or different ways of behaving

(g) Evaluate progress

The executive's role is to ...

(a) Take the coaching seriously

(b) Keep appointments with the coach

(c) Hold self accountable for meeting agreed-upon objectives and trying new behaviors

(d) Thank the coach for ideas and help

Note. Based on Witherspoon and White (1997).

Coaching focuses on behaviors. Coaches focus specifically on monitoring and improving the individual's job behaviors and resulting performance.

Steps in the Coaching Process

There are five major steps to the coaching process (after Weinberger, 1995, and cited in Kilburg, 1996):

1. Develop an intervention agreement. This includes establishing the focus and goals, time commitment, resource commitment, methods, confidentiality constraints, and payments (in the case of external coaches). The goals may include increased behavioral flexibility; increased capacity to manage; improved psychological and social competencies (increased self-awareness, increased tolerance of ambiguity, decreased acting out of emotions and unconscious conflicts, improved capacity to learn and grow); increased ability to manage turbulence, crisis, and conflict; career development; improved ability to manage tensions between work, family, community, and profession; and improved team and organization effectiveness.

2. Build a coaching relationship, which encompasses establishing the alliance, managing transferences, preserving containment.

3. Creating and managing expectations of success.

TABLE 8.2
Characteristics of the Coaching Relationships

- honesty
- trust
- usefulness
- enjoyment
- creative ideas
- amicable—friendly
- value added
- serious
- accountability for change
- recognized responsibilities in the relationship
- mutual respect
- measurements and goals established jointly
- discussions targeted to behaviors and performance
- mutually rewarding
- rewards for improvement
- improvements happen
- deals directly with emotions, defenses, and resistance
- inspirational
- insightful
- resources available
- motivating
- commitment
- organizational standards and expectations recognized

Note. Suggested by Witherspoon and White (1997).

4. Provide an experience of behavioral mastery or cognitive control over the problems and issues. This is the heart of coaching. The coach and executive address performance problems, deal with emotions, manage resistance and defenses, resolve conflicts between themselves, analyze conflicts and help resolve them between the executive and others, use methods flexibly, get the issues on the table, use feedback and disclosure, emphasize what will work most effectively with the best long-term outcomes, confront acting out and ethical lapses in a tactful way, engage in high-level defense operations (e.g., learning and problem solving, communication, curiosity, humor, creativity).

5. Evaluate and attribute coaching success or failure. This includes assessing coaching sessions and periodically looking back over what has been accomplished.

Graddick and Lane (1998) outlined the coaching process a bit differently. They stated that most executive coach interventions include several phases:

Pre-coaching—a meeting with executives, their supervisor, and the coach to discuss specific issues the coaching should address. Often the human resources leader plays a role in these meetings. These meetings are critical to calibrate expectations and set goals.

Data gathering—designed for the coach to gather as much data and information as possible from the executive, as well as others in the organization, to diagnose problems and develop action plans. This can include collecting idiographic information, such as conducting in-depth background interviews; using nomothetic data, such as personality inventories; and 360 assessment either via a survey or interviews with the executive's peers and direct reports.

Coaching—the development of a relation of candor and trust between the executive and coach. The executive and coach meet regularly (often 2–4 times a month) for several months to review the data, develop a plan of action, and monitor progress. Telephone contact is frequent between meetings. Some coaching relationships last up to a year or more.

Saporito (1996) outlined a four stage model of the coaching process. This is provided in Table 8.3.

Ways to Improve Giving Feedback as Part of Coaching

Coaching is more difficult than giving feedback. This is especially the case when dealing with performance problems. Saying what is correct or incorrect about an individual's performance is easier than determining and communicating ways to reverse a performance problem. Here are some steps for an effective coaching discussion (adapted from Hillman, Schwandt, & Bartz, 1990, cited in London, 1997a, pp. 80–81):

1. *State the purpose*: Be direct (e.g., "I want to talk about the report you gave me yesterday.").
2. *State the performance problem*: Have observations or measures. Describe the expected performance, the actual performance, and the effects of the actual performance on the job (e.g., "The Vice President wanted the re-

TABLE 8.3

A Four-Stage Model of the Coaching Process

Stage 1: Setting the Foundation

- What are the organizational imperatives? For example, is the organization in a rapid growth mode, or is it downsizing? Is the business mature, or is it in an earlier stage of development?
- What are the success factors for that particular role with the organization?
- What are the behavioral requirements necessary to achieve these success factors? For example, what are the types of problem-solving requirements individuals will be facing? What are the types of constituencies to whom they must relate, and what is the style of leadership that will be most effective in that context?

Stage 2: Assessment of Individuals

- Semistructured interview covering the experiences that have shaped their managerial philosophy and style.
- Describe the individuals, highlight the key development issues that set the stage for feedback and coaching.

Stage 3: Developmental Planning

- Feedback: In-depth discussions and reviews to help the executive see the developmental issues to be addressed.
- Development planning: Create a development plan.

Stage 4: Implementation

- Moving from determining what the needs are and how to work on them to actually getting it done. The assessment and plan provide continual and reliable points of reference as the coach and client work through the process.

Note. Outline based on Saporito (1996).

port to include demographic data on customers in three key markets, but you didn't do that.").

3. *Get reaction from the subordinate:* Ask for the subordinate's view ("What do you think?", "Do you agree with me?"). Keep the discussion on track. Don't get sidetracked by minor concerns (e.g., a response such as, "Other reports don't include the information and I recall that their authors were given a chance to present the results in person to the Vice President. I hope you'll let me have that chance.").

4. *Analyze why the performance is unsatisfactory:* Talk to the subordinate about possible causes of the performance problem. Ask subordinates to identify factors they have control over that may be causing the problem (e.g., "Maybe you don't know enough about the database or software to get what we need here."). Consider external factors that may have caused the performance problem (e.g., "The computer systems were down.").

5. *Seek a collaborative solution if possible*: Ask the subordinate for ideas about how to solve the problem (e.g., "How can we fix this?"). Be patient, and consider all ideas. Offer your own course of action if the staff member is uncertain about what to do. Summarize the agreed-to course of action (e.g., "Okay, so we agree. You'll ask Herman for help in analyzing the data, and you will revise the report this weekend.").

6. *Provide assistance and follow-up*: Establish assistance that the subordinate will need in the future. Determine what each of you will do for follow-up and subsequent performance review (e.g., "Let me have the revised report on Monday morning. I'll read it right away, and we can discuss it right after lunch.").

Similarly, Whetten and Cameron (1998) described steps for feedback in coaching, such as describing the event, behavior, or circumstance as objectively as possible, avoiding accusations, presenting clear and objective data or evidence, when possible, and outlining the objective consequences that have or will likely result. Also, coaches should describe their own reactions to or feelings about the event, behavior, or circumstance. The coach should focus on the executive's behavior, not on the executive's personal attributes (a recommendation that is consistent with DeNisi and Kluger's, 2000, approach to effective feedback described in chap. 6, this volume). Moreover, the coach should focus on alternative solutions, not on who is right or wrong. Whetten and Cameron (1998) outlined an approach to coaching called a *personal management interview* (PMI) program. This is outlined in Table 8.4. A PMI is a regularly scheduled (biweekly or monthly) one-on-one meeting (30–60 minutes) between the manager/coach and the person being coached (e.g., direct report).

Mone (1988) suggested that managers as coaches should do the following:

1. Ask themselves whether their direct reports (i.e., the people being coached) are achieving their goals and developing the skills that will be required for strong performance.
2. Find out if there is a performance concern, and, if so, whether it is due to ability, motivation, or both.
3. Share concerns with the person being coached and jointly discuss the issues.
4. Mutually decide on an approach that most effectively deals with the concern or issue.
5. Create an action plan based on the approach selected.
6. Later, evaluate the action plan.

According to Kilburg (1996), rigorous coaching has a focus on personality styles, jobs, roles, tasks, and individual knowledge, skills, and abilities. Also, information and issues dealing with systems, relationships, and organizational entities (e.g., groups, departments, subunits, divisions, and the whole organization) help in understanding this focus.

TABLE 8.4

Steps in Conducting a Personal Management Interview (PMI) Program

1. A role negotiation session to discuss each person's expectations of the other
2. A written record of agreements resulting from this and other meetings serves as an informal contract
3. Preparation on the part of both parties for each meeting (e.g., each develops an agenda—list of items to be discussed)
4. Regular (not only when a problem arises), private meetings that focus on
   - Organizational problems or issues
   - Information sharing
   - Interpersonal issues
   - Obstacles to improvement
   - Training in management and related skills
   - Feedback on job performance
   - Personal concerns or problems
5. Each meeting closes with agreement on action items to be completed by both parties before the next meeting
6. Each subsequent meeting begins by reviewing action items from the previous meeting
7. An emphasis on supportive communication, joint problem solving, and continuous improvement
8. Praise and encouragement intermingled with problem solving

Note. Developed by Whetten and Cameron (1998).

COACHING STRATEGIES AND METHODS

Peterson (1996) outlined *coaching strategies* derived from cognitive-behavioral psychology and pragmatic research on change. Coaching strategies include the following:

1. *Forge a Partnership*—build trust and understanding so people want to work with you.
2. *Inspire Commitment*—build insight and motivation so people focus their energy on goals that matter. Cultivate insight by helping people obtain information that is personally relevant to achieving their goals. Categories of information include (a) goals, or what the person wants to do (from personal reflection, personal mission statement, career counseling, etc.); (b) abilities, or what the person can do (from performance evaluations, professional assessments, expert observation and feedback, personal obser-

vation over time); (c) perceptions, or how others see the person (information about others' perceptions—peers, bosses, senior management, clients, customers, friends); and (d) standards, or what others expect of the person (from conversations with the organization's leaders).

3. *Grow Skills*—find the best way for the client to learn. Follow learning principles, such as space the practice and engage in active experimentation.

4. *Promote Persistence*—build stamina and discipline to make sure learning lasts on the job. Do this by being a talent agent to help the client find opportunities to apply new skills; manage the mundane by helping the client with routine aspects of development, such as staying motivated; fight fear of failure by supporting clients so they feel comfortable with risk; and break the habit cycle by helping clients identify and anticipate specific situations in which old, ineffective habits crop up and helping clients to learn and practice new, more effective behaviors.

5. *Shape the Environment*—build organization support to reward learning and remove barriers. Identify and reduce barriers to the client's development.

Table 8.5 lists a number of other methods and techniques for coaching.

Landsberg (1997) stressed the need to diagnose the executive's motivation and skill and recognize the implications for different coaching styles. Coaches *guide* when the executive is high in motivation and low in skill, *direct* when the executive is low in motivation and low in skill, *delegate* when the executive is high in motivation and high in skill, and *excite* when the executive is low in motivation and high in skill.

Determining the Executive's Motivation to Change

Waldroop and Butler (1996) recommended that the coach test to determine whether a problem behavior is based on character, and hence hard to change: (a) The behavior is part of a pattern used in different situations; (b) the behavior is observable over a long period of time; and (c) the behavior is part of a complex array of behaviors, such that changing one or two of these behaviors will not make much of a difference because too many other negative behaviors will still be there. If these characteristics apply, then constant effort may be needed to change character-driven behaviors and then success is likely to be limited. If the behavior is unchangeable, Waldroop and Butler then suggested that the coach ask the following: Can we live with the behavior? Does the behavior occur too frequently to be ignored? Does it occur infrequently and when it does, does it occur with such severe impact that the individual cannot succeed in the organization? Do the negatives outweigh the positives of the individual's contri-

TABLE 8.5
Commonly Used Methods and Strategies for Coaching

Methods for Coaching[a]

- assessment and feedback
- education and training; skill development
- simulations
- role playing
- organization assessment
- brainstorming
- conflict and crisis management
- communications (active-empathic listening)
- clarifications
- reconstructions
- empathy and encouragement
- tact
- helping to set limits
- helping to maintain boundaries
- depreciating and devaluing maladaptive behaviors
- establishing consequences for behaviors
- group process interventions
- working relationships interventions
- journaling, reading assignments
- project or process focus (structure, process, content issues or on input, throughput, and output problems)

Behavioral/Psychological Coaching Techniques for Coaching[b]

- *Stimulus control*: imposing limits on where and when to do the activity, increasing cues for desired behavior, reducing the visibility of problem-related cues
- *Problem-solving strategies*: problem definition, brainstorming solutions, selecting the best solution, and evaluating success
- *Social assertion*: role playing interpersonal situations reflective of the problem, learning to ask for help and support
- *Short-term goal setting and techniques for enhancing motivation*
- *Cognitive strategies for altering self-defeating thoughts* (e.g., pessimism, perfectionism, and self-doubt)
- *Relapse prevention*: learning ways to recognize precursors and consequences of change; planning for how to deal with high risk issues
- *Social support*: techniques for involving spouse and others outside of work

[a]Identified by Kilberg (1996).
[b]Based on Jeffrey, Wing, Thorson, and Burton (1998).

bution? If the negatives outweigh the positives, then the individual should move to a job where the character trait is not a liability.

Whetten and Cameron (1998) described a simple, logical process that the coach can use to determine whether motivation is an important factor in limiting behavior change. They recommended that the coach should not automatically presume that the absence of behavior change is due to poor motivation on the part of the person being coached. Instead they suggested a sequence of steps. First, coaches should ask themselves whether the coach and the person being coached agree that behavior needs to be changed. (If they do not, then there is a perception problem that needs to be addressed—perhaps by clarifying expectations or providing concrete data concerning performance gaps or unmet expectations—before taking other steps). Then the coach should consider whether the problem may stem from inadequate resources (thereby suggesting the need for additional support or cooperation from others). If resources are adequate, then the coach should consider whether the problem may stem from inadequate training (thereby pointing to the need for formal or informal learning, training, or education). Next, the coach can consider whether the problem is due to limited aptitude (which might suggest the need to redesign the current job to match the person's aptitude or to reassign the person to a job that is a better fit). Next, the coach should consider whether the problem arises due to unrealistic expectations or poor communication concerning job goals or requirements (which may point to the need for involving the employee more in the goal setting process). Then the coach can consider whether the lack of behavior change or performance improvement is due to the fact that rewards are not linked to performance (thereby pointing to the need to discuss or create performance–reward linkages). Finally, the coach can consider whether available rewards are simply not salient to or valued by the person being coached (thereby pointing to the need to discuss what rewards the person would find valuable or allowing the person being coached to choose among several rewards).

Landsberg (1997) emphasized the importance of diagnosing the executive's resistance to coaching. Reasons for resistance and ways to overcome them include an unwillingness to admit room for improvement: emphasize factual evidence for the need to improve; mistrust the organization: build the trust over time; temporary lack of available time: agree to a later session; poor prior relationship with the executive: apologize, try to bury the hatchet; major differences in style: discuss style differences explicitly and accept these differences if possible; and perceived nature of your role in the organization as highly evaluative: be explicit about your role (e.g., you determine the executive's pay) and emphasize that coaching is nonevaluative.

Landsberg (1997) indicated that the coach should diagnose where the executive is in motivation. There are positive and negative cycles of motivation. Negative cycles consist of lack of confidence, hesitant attempts, poor results, and unsatisfying feedback. Positive cycles consist of confidence, aspiring to high stan-

dards, strong results, and praise. If they are high in the cycle, then enhance confidence. Develop a vision for being even better at completing a specific task. If low
in the cycle, then work on praise. Identify their need for support and/or training.
Know what motivates the executive: "Encouragement, praise, and suggestion
may not amount to anything without an engaging vision" (p. 127).

Mone (1988) pointed out that managers often are resistant to accept a role as
a coach because they believe they are already developing their people (although
their efforts may be sporadic, infrequent, frustrating, or incomplete).

CHARACTERISTICS OF THE EFFECTIVE COACH

Hollenbeck and McCall (1999) described a firm where executive coaches were
used for each of its 25 senior executives. There were six sessions over 6 months
for each executive. The authors noted that when there is coaching for everyone, coaching is not a secret and can provide a natural reason for discussing in
the hallways the "undiscussable" with other executives. A disadvantage may be
that some executives are more receptive to coaching than others.

Hall et al. (1999) encouraged each organization to develop its own code of
ethics to govern decisions about how coaches are assigned to executives and
how coaches are to use information from coaching conversations. Prospective
coaches can be asked to complete a skills and experience questionnaire and an
instrumentation and certification inventory (to identify assessment instruments they are qualified to use). An ethical issue could also develop if there is
coaching with no follow-up, thereby causing damage to individuals involved
(e.g., areas of weakness are identified and exposed but not addressed).

Hall et al. (1999) stated that, for executives, the two primary factors in good
coaching are honest, reliable feedback and good action ideas or "pointers." Table 8.6 lists other behaviors and characteristics of an effective coach.

Whetten and Cameron (1998) emphasized the importance of distinguishing
between two types of problems. One type of problem is caused by lack of ability,
insufficient information, or misunderstanding on the part of the person being
coached. This type of problem calls for the coach/manager to pass along advice
or information (or sometimes for the coach/manager to set performance standards). The second type of problem stems from attitudes, personality clashes,
defensiveness, or related factors. This type of problem calls for the coach/man-
ager to help the person being coached to recognize that a problem exists and
that change is required. Diagnosing the type of problem has implications for the
approach the coach should take to solve it. In the first situation, the coach can
offer advice. However, merely offering advice in the second situation may increase defensiveness and resistance to change. In general, the second type of situation requires the coach to use reflection and probing responses—for
example, reflecting the message in different words, thereby allowing the person

TABLE 8.6
Characteristics of Effective Coaches

Essential Behaviors and Attitudes[a]

- Use every interaction as an opportunity to coach.
- Be willing to initiate interactions.
- View coaching as a set of competencies that can be learned and tested.
- Be balanced—coaching is not one-sided.
- Focus on the concrete—what can be improved.
- Emphasize the shared responsibility between coach and executive.
- Consist of conversations with clearly stated goals and a flow that expands information and then focuses on how the executive can move toward the goal.
- Demonstrate mutual respect.

Values of a Successful Coach[b]

- Clarity (sense of direction and purpose)
- Supportiveness (commitment to executive and team)
- Confidence-building (personal commitment to build and sustain the executive's self-image)
- Mutuality (true partnership)
- Perspective (on entire business enterprise)
- Risk (reduce punishment for mistakes and encourage learning)
- Patience (view of time and performance that balances learning and business demands)
- Involvement (executives control their work)
- Confidentiality (ability to protect information)
- Respect (valuing people)

[a]Based on Kinlaw (1996).
[b]Based on Hendricks (1996).

being coached to feel listened to and understood, or using elaboration (e.g., Can you tell me more about that?) or clarification probes (e.g., What do you mean by that?).

Hollenbeck and McCall (1999) noted the importance of the coach's credibility, that is, being trustworthy (a sine qua non of coaching), having expertise (in coaching and business), and being dynamic (the personality to engage and convince the person being coached). In this sense, credibility is defined by the context and would be different for someone being asked to teach an executive to use the internet than for a coach dealing with sensitive interpersonal issues.

Waldroop and Butler (1996) indicated that coaching someone else may require that the coach change as much as the person being coached. Coaches cannot be pressed for time, competitive, and quick to think, judge, act, and speak, even though these may be effective business behaviors in some situations. Effective coaches adopt the approach of teacher, not competitor. They try to avoid being judgmental. They observe and think before giving criticism. They focus less on the immediate task and improving business performance now, with more attention to the long term. They give positive encouragement, provide support, and suggest ways to secure resources. They arrange for regular meetings with their executive clients to develop a collaborative relationship. They give coaching subordinates the same priority as other business activities. They arrange to meet regularly and frequently with those they coach, perhaps meeting for an hour every other week. They put these meetings on their calendars and guard the time. They do not get caught up in the immediacy of the coaching relationship but recognize its value for the long term.

Harris (1999) noted that industrial and organizational (I-O) psychologists are usually trained for and focus on assessing and giving feedback, the first two phases of coaching. They are less frequently trained for planning, implementation, and follow-up. Coaches need to think in developmental phases, not static terms.

Evaluating the Effectiveness of the Coaching Relationship

Hollenbeck and McCall (1999) noted that coaching is too often evaluated by anecdotes rather than by research (although separating coaching from other elements of leadership development makes evaluation difficult). They described a follow-up study of a coaching-based executive development process where participants rated the process as very valuable (3.95 out of 5.00) and reported that they changed (4.07 out of 5.00). Hall et al. (1999) asked executives to rate the overall effectiveness of their experiences with coaching; the most frequent rating was 4 (very satisfactory) on a 5-point scale. They concluded that "the positive image of coaching that is presented in the business media is supported by the experiences of the people we interviewed." Another outcome can be learning for the coach. Internal coaches sometimes report that executive coaching was an excellent way for them to learn more about the businesses they were serving.

Hall et al. (1999) noted that organizations implementing coaching on a large scale are becoming very concerned about cost, suggesting that resource constraints will affect the future availability of this approach to management development.

Kilburg (1996) emphasized the importance of evaluating the effectiveness of the coaching relationship. The client and coach evaluate the process to assess success or failure. Perceived attributions of success by clients generally concentrate on the degree to which the coach provided a supportive relationship, stimulated clients to think, feel, and explore new ideas and behaviors, assisted clients in working through resistance to change, forced clients to take time to reflect on aspects of their performance and the performance of the organization, and pushed busy clients to be more reflective on a regular basis.

Witherspoon and White (1997) recommended that the coach develop a "balanced scorecard" to measure the executive's progress on a regular basis covering client service, cost effectiveness, improved teamwork, and related performance ratings.

INEFFECTIVE AND DYSFUNCTIONAL COACHING AND MENTORING

Reasons for Negative Outcomes

Negative coaching outcomes may be the fault of the client and/or the coach. For clients, factors contributing to negative outcomes may include severe psychopathology, severe interpersonal problems, lack of motivation, and lack of follow-through on homework or intervention suggestions (Mohr, 1995). For coaches, factors contributing to negative outcomes may include insufficient empathy, lack of expertise or interest, underestimating the severity of the client's problems, significant or negative countertransference (coach overreacts to the client emotionally), poor techniques (inaccurate assessment, lack of clarity of contract), and prolonged disagreements with the client about the coaching process (Mohr, 1995).

Dysfunctional Mentoring

Research on assigned mentoring shows how the experience can fail. Although mentoring is not the same as coaching, as pointed out earlier, the research suggests ways both coaching and mentoring can fail, just as supervision, in general, does not always go smoothly. Employees may be assigned to mentors who do not provide the expert, social, or career support that the protégé needs. Even in informal mentoring, which happens when senior people promise junior people that they will take them under their wing, show them the ropes, and/or groom them for promotion, the relationship may not pan out as expected. Table 8.7 lists dysfunctional coaching behaviors.

Simon and Eby (2000) found that individuals involved in dysfunctional mentoring experiences organized their attitudes along three dimensions: the severity of the outcome (e.g., were the negative experiences serious and meant to do harm to the protégé vs. minor, passive, and unintentional?), the specificity of the mentor's actions (targeted vs. diffuse), and the potential function of the mentoring (psychosocial vs. career related). This suggests that mentoring rela-

TABLE 8.7
Dysfunctional Coaching Behaviors

1. Manipulating behavior
   - Delegating work the mentors should have done themselves
   - Belittling the protégés
   - Taking credit for protégés' work
   - Sabotaging protégés' work—giving them impossible tasks that essentially set them up for failure.
   - Deceiving protégés—lying to them or not delivering on promises
2. Distancing behavior
   - Showing disinterest in protégés
   - Being unavailable (hard to make an appointment; giving protégés little time)
   - Being self-absorbed (talking only about their own problems, not those of their protégés)
3. No experience being a mentor
   - Not reinforcing or valuing protégés' expertise
   - Not recognizing protégés' technical competencies and abilities
   - Not communicating clearly
   - Seeming unfriendly
4. Mismatch with the protégé
   - Holding different values (e.g., prejudices)
   - Letting differences in cultural backgrounds get in the way
   - Conflicting because of personality differences (e.g., aggressive vs. Complacent) and work style (e.g., detail-oriented vs. Big picture oriented)
5. General dysfunction
   - Having a bad attitude (e.g., being critical, feeling time is being wasted)
   - Experiencing personal problems (e.g., drinking interferes with work)

Note. Based on Eby, McManus, Simon, and Russell (2000).

tionships exist on a continuum from highly positive to neutral to possibly damaging. Some negative mentoring behavioral patterns are diffuse, for instance, generally overdelegating or underdelegating. Others are specific in intentionally excluding, ridiculing, or even sabotaging the protégé. Some negative experiences are viewed as career barriers, whereas others are viewed as lack of interpersonal support and never forming a meaningful bond with the protégé, perhaps because mentors have personal problems that affect their work relationships.

The Effects of Cultural Issues on Coaching

Some cultural issues include eye contact, speaking up, problem-solving orientation, and energy level. Avoiding eye contact in Anglo cultures is interpreted as lying, whereas looking down in the presence of authority in Latin or Asian cultures is seen as a sign of respect. Asian managers may receive coaching on how to make eye contact to "look tougher" and be seen as "hard hitting." Latins are counseled to be less "emotional" and more factual in their communication. For managers who diverge from the dominant culture in U.S. firms, executive coaching can help them understand the social, political, and cultural environments, as well as develop behavioral skills to help them fit and thrive in the dominant culture (Hall et al., 1999).

EXAMPLES OF CORPORATE COACHING INITIATIVES

By way of understanding why and how organizations establish an external coaching process for their top leadership, here are two cases. Both cases involve fast-paced, fast growing companies that saw the potential value of coaches to attract, retain, and enhance leadership talent. Each of the firms are start-ups stemming from stable, successful firms. Now with a new direction in a highly competitive marketplace, the firms' executives face new challenges.

Capital One Financial Services

Capital One is an information-based marketing company in the credit card, telecommunications, and auto financing businesses (Hawes, 2000). In spring 2000, the firm employed 17,0000 "associates," up 11,000 from 2 years earlier. The company entered the Fortune 5000 in early 2000, and was named by Fortune as one of the 100 best places to work. It had a very young management team, and needed to build leadership talent to continue to grow in the fast-paced economic environment. As a result, it needed an accelerated development program that would bring in outside perspectives and focus on real-time solutions to tough situations.

To speed up leadership development, the company's human resources department hired 17 outside coaches to work with the firm's top 150 people (representing 70% of top executives and 40% of the top management team) (Hawes, 2000). Each coach was asked to work with from 7 to 10 executives. The consulting contract defined a time frame (6 months to 1 year) and cost from $10,000 to $15,000 per executive for the year. The coaching effort was coordinated centrally by the company's headquarters so that quality could be maintained and focus would remain on development.

In making this consulting arrangement with outside contractors, Capital One faced several challenges. In particular, the CEO and human resources department asked the following open questions relevant to any coaching effort (Hawes, 2000):

> How can we determine the quality of coaching when every coach seemed to use a different technique? How can we implement a systematic, ongoing evaluation of coaching?

> Since the sessions were private, of course, how can Capital One evaluate the content of the coaching?

> How can Capital One determine the return on investment (ROI) on coaching?

> Is coaching a substitute for closer, more personal management relations between top executives and their direct supervisors?

> What other development opportunities can the firm use in conjunction with executive coaching?

> How can we encourage executives to act as coaches to the people they supervise so that coaching cascades throughout the organization?

Freddie Mac

Freddie Mac, a firm spun off from the government, became a for-profit enterprise in the competitive secondary mortgage market. Executives faced more uncertainty than ever, and a need to adapt to a continuously changing environment. The firm wanted to accelerate leadership development, build dynamic teams, achieve and support a diverse workplace (move away form the pattern of white male executives), and enrich executives' career opportunities. It wanted a coaching process that would optimize executive's strengths, leverage their energy and enthusiasm to benefit the firm and their career opportunities, and speed up learning (Beizer, 2000). It wanted to build an environment of mutual success and trust. It wanted executives who could "play well with others" in a diverse working environment. It wanted to enhance executive's self-awareness, ability to communicate, and contribute to a positive, team-oriented organizational culture. Moreover, it wanted executives who could get up to speed quickly with the firm's goals and adaptive, relationship-building leadership style. The company turned to coaching because the method offered the potential to accelerate leadership development.

To establish the coaching program, the human resources department contracted with external coaches for 6 1-hour sessions costing from $2,000 to $3,000 per executive. As a side benefit, the company felt that offering coaches to newly hired executives was a powerful recruitment tool. The executives felt they would not be left alone as they learned the business, but would have an impartial sounding board and advisor.

THE FUTURE OF EXECUTIVE COACHING

Harris (1999) suggested that whereas executive coaching is popular today, there has been an influx of relatively untrained coaches, decreasing standardization of services and increasing confusion as to what coaching is all about. This could hurt the reputation of executive coaches. Companies will continue to use executive coaching for the foreseeable future, but perhaps more selectively than currently is done. Also, firms may use coaching more strategically, linking it with other human resources techniques, rather than as a panacea for all organizational problems.

THE LEADER AS COACH

Leaders should view coaching as one of their principal responsibilities. Stated another way, being a coach and developer is integral to the role of manager and executive. Ellinger and Bostrom (1999) conducted a qualitative, critical incident study to investigate the different ways that exemplify how managers facilitate their employees' learning. In particular, they wanted to determine the types of activities that contribute to a learning organization—an organization in which one learns continuously and transforms itself in the process to respond to marketplace changes, new technologies, and emerging opportunities (cf. Watkins & Marsick, 1996). The study asked managers to describe at least four effective and/or ineffective critical incidents when they saw themselves to be facilitating their employees' learning. An incident was defined as critical if it was typical, reflected managers' best practices as facilitators of learning, and seemed to make a meaningful difference for their employees.

Ellinger and Bostrom (1999) identified empowering behaviors and facilitating behaviors. Empowering behaviors were those that appeared to encourage employees to assume more personal responsibility and accountability and power and authority for their actions and decisions (e.g., encouraging employees to think through issues, being a resource and removing barriers, and holding back solutions, letting employees come up with their own ideas). Facilitating behaviors were those that appeared to promote new levels of understanding and new perspectives and offered guidance and support to their employees to bring about learning and development (e.g., providing feedback to employees, asking them for feedback, and working together to understand the feedback; also, broadening employee's perspectives by encouraging them to take others' viewpoints).

Smither and S. P. Reilly (2001) considered the cognitive processing that employees go through at each stage of the coaching process as their supervisor initiates the role of coach. As the role is established, if the employee does not know what to expect from coaching and is initially suspicious, especially if the supervisor has not tried coaching before, the employee may block informa-tion, postpone meetings, and generally avoid getting down to business. The supervisor as coach needs to understand the employee's initial frame of refer-ence, and attempt to create a positive frame of reference by explaining at the outset how coaching can work and benefit the employee. During the assess-ment phase, as the supervisor as coach collects and analyzes information about the employee, the employee has to be open to providing information or suggesting sources of information. The employee needs to understand why the information is needed and how it will be used. Otherwise, the employee may try to manage the supervisor's impressions by suggesting only positive sources or providing inaccurate or partial information. During the joint process of an-alyzing and interpreting the information, the employee needs to be helped in dealing with negative or unfavorable results. The employee may be embar-rassed to deal with such information with the supervisor and may argue why the results are invalid or not meaningful under the circumstances (e.g., "You can't believe anything that guy says …"). This stage is especially sensitive as employees consider how their own behavior led to the feedback results. The supervisor as coach can help the employee see this not as a reflection on the employee's character and not as a basis for making unfavorable administrative decisions about the employee (e.g., a lower pay raise), but as suggestions for changing behavior to improve.

Mentoring

In professional partnerships—such as law, accounting, and management con-sulting firms—securing and retaining talent is critical in a tight labor market. The "up or out," "survival of the fittest" model is out. Ibarra (2000) recom-mended that partners take an active role in mentoring their junior profession-als. In particular, she recommended three steps for senior colleagues to follow in encouraging protégés:

1. Take a collage approach to observing role models by selecting a broad range of personalities to accumulate a large repertoire of possible styles and approaches to work. Mentors can help by pointing out different styles and telling which ones work well for them and why.
2. Work with a number of different senior people who can be role models. This also helps expand the protégé's repertoires of work styles. In addi-tion, it helps the junior person find several different mentors who can be the right mix of role models and advisors.
3. Find supportive senior professionals, especially during difficult times (e.g., in managing difficult clients or assignments).

Eddy, Tannenbaum, and Lorenzet (2000) argued that peer mentoring can be fostered by a strong learning environment that recognizes organizational learning as a sustainable competitive advantage. In a continuous learning environment, individuals engage in peer mentoring. Peer mentoring may focus more on giving feedback than mentoring in the true sense of the word (meaning a strong, personal bond between mentor and protégé psychosocial support and smoothing the way for advancement). However, peer mentoring does foster developmental relationships on the job, encouraging team members to help each other, and in the process enhancing the team's capabilities as well as each member's skills.

Smith-Jentsch, Milanovich, Reynolds, Merket, and Eddy (2000) distinguished between supervisor (or hierarchical) mentoring and peer mentoring. Working in the Naval Air Warfare Center's group for Organizational Effectiveness, their goal was to improve on-the-job training and mentoring practice, using mentors as coaches in job skills to improve current performance. Job skill coaching focuses on skill development through sharing expertise and experiences, providing feedback, and offering advice. Mentoring goes beyond coaching to include psychosocial support and directions and opportunities for career advancement.

Smith-Jentsch et al. (2000) distinguished between peer mentoring and hierarchical mentoring from supervisors. Given the prevalence of work teams and flatter organizational structures, peers represent an important source of mentoring. Although hierarchical mentors may be in a better position to help mentees, particularly in advancing their careers because of the higher level officer's position of power, peers may be more similar to mentees in experience and goals. More advanced peers can provide on-the-job coaching that not only improves their colleague's skill and knowledge base, but prepares them for more advanced assignments. Also, peers can learn to reciprocate in assisting each other. Smith-Jentsch et al. recommended including peer mentoring in performance management programs. Peers can be nominated for awards in mentoring to reinforce collaborative development of expertise in the organization.

Pliske, Crandall, Green, and Zsambok (2000) outlined a training program for mentors that builds collaborative development of expertise. Their goal was to help navy subject matter experts become more effective mentors. Working with naval air defense coordinators, a training program was developed to help trainees take responsibility for helping each other, learning how and when to intervene with coaching. Training focused on a wide variety of learning strategies, recognizing that different approaches may work at different times depending on the experience of the trainee and the demands of the situation. Simulations were used in the training environment. Peers learned knowledge strategies (answering questions), thinking strategies (development of good situational awareness), and doing strategies (encouraging trainees to practice skills and gain mastery).

Milanovich, Smith-Jentsch, Buff, and Campbell (2000) devised the concept of "guided team self-correction" as a strategy for structured peer mentoring within a team. In a typical team debriefing session to review the team's work, the leader generally did most of the talking. The goal of this project was to develop a strategy to increase peer mentoring. The idea was to encourage the team, not just the leader, to review their performance, identify performance weaknesses, provide one another with feedback and job skills coaching, and generate possible solutions to problems. As such, the method combined the use of mental models of teamwork and behavior modeling. In training personnel to apply guided team self-correction, participants were asked to focus not just on the technical aspects of their performance but on team process itself. They were asked to consider what they would do to teach skills to overcome team weaknesses. The method valued multiple sources of feedback from different team members, and reciprocal mentoring, as team members teach each other. The team leader's role was to facilitate the process, encouraging all the team members to participate in the performance review process. This method not only promoted team mastery and skill development, but also built a positive work climate and members' sense of collective efficacy: together, the members worked effectively as a team to accomplish team goals. Over a 5-year period, the navy trained more than 13,000 instructors to facilitate intrateam mentoring. Debriefing teams were used after training exercises to apply the method. This became a guide for self-directed reviews of actual team performance on the job.

CONCLUSIONS

Ideas for Enhancing Coaching

Organizations need a way to help both executives and managers coach and be coached. The coaching needs to happen in real time, on the job as well as apart from the job during time slots especially reserved for coaching. Coaching will help executives and managers obtain and use feedback (not just from a 360 survey) and apply the results to immediate business needs, relationship and team development, career and life planning, and meeting the company's bottom-line objectives. Toward that end, consider the following ideas that coaches raised in discussions of the process.

Consider Different Reasons for Coaching.   Coaching should be tied to the executive's or manager's sense of identity, as discussed in chapter 4 of this volume. One way to do this is to link the coaching to helping the executive deal with immediate business needs. This gets the executive's attention and relates to the executive's desire to be successful. More broadly, coaching can focus on the executive's life plan. This is especially relevant for seasoned executives who may be considering alternatives to working. This is often the first time executives ask themselves, "Where am I in the business and in my personal life?"

Focus on Tough Issues that Hit Home.   Coaching should deal with the pain executives are feeling in coping with the demands of the job. The first step in coaching is diagnosing where the executive "is" and the executive's readiness to receive feedback. This requires identifying barriers that may get in the way. The coach could use a set of diagnostic questions to get the coaching process started.

Assess Readiness to Change.   The executives' and managers' receptivity to coaching depends on their readiness to change. Readiness for coaching is likely to be higher when executives are facing a major issue or problem, such as conflict with senior management. Coaching can help the executive overcome barriers and maintain self-regulation (see chap. 3, this volume). Indeed, unless executives can cope with stresses and goal barriers, they are not likely to be able to concentrate on career and life planning.

Consider Involving the Coach in Team Development.   An area for coaching beyond the executive's personal and professional development is team development. As stated in the first chapter, many organizations are relying increasingly on teams for special projects as well as daily operations. The coach's responsibility could be defined in terms of the development of both the executive/manager and the team of the senior executive and direct reports. A strategy for the coach could be to start with the higher level boss about what is happening in the organization and what messages are important to communicate to the executive's or manager's subordinates. In such a case, the coach would be assigned to the team, not to a single executive. This type of organization development coaching would be an iterative process. The coach would work with the senior executive and the human resources person and then move to the senior executive's direct reports and then back to the senior executive and human resources person.

Define Coaching Clearly.   The definition and components of coaching should be clear. For instance, coaching includes giving feedback concisely, directly, and actively (through demonstration, involvement of the recipient, and follow-up) and enhancing the executive's self-insight (see chap. 2, this volume). Coaching is not just helping executives look to the next position. Everyone should be clear about how coaching differs from mentoring and role modeling. (Mentors can be coaches and role models, and coaches can be role models too. But coaches are not necessarily mentors.)

Assure Confidentiality and Build Trust.   A critical component of coaching is confidentiality and trust. As noted in chapter 6 of this volume, this is important in any relationship in which feedback is given and discussed. The coach should be up-front about confidentiality issues right at the start of the coaching process. The coach should discover the executive's or manager's concerns about the process (e.g., "I'm not sure I can handle this."). The coach needs to negotiate the process, essentially saying, "Here's the process, expectations, and intended outcomes (development plan), and here's how we will spend our time together. The trade off is that we will focus on what's important to you." Basically, the coach needs to help the executives and managers recognize what is in it for them. The coach should ask what the executive or manager's expectations and goals are for the coaching. This may seem obvious, but it is worthwhile to emphasize that the coach needs to be respectful of the executive or manager's expectations and feelings. For instance, if the coach thinks that collecting additional information from coworkers or the human resources person would be useful, the coach should ask the executive or manager for permission to do so. The coach can help the executive or manager deal with feedback quickly (whether it comes in the form of a 360 report or in more informal forms) to identify patterns and determine whether the patterns make sense. This can be the basis for more in-depth exploration of feedback after the coach leaves.

Clarify the Executive's Accountability.   Accountability for follow-up and change rests with the executive and manager, not the coach. Coaches should give the executives homework after a coaching session. The coach and the executive/manager can agree on explicit steps that are needed as a result of the coaching. The coach should help the executive to discover the important things and then relate the follow-up "assignment" to the issues the executive perceives to be important to the business or the executive's life. An assignment may be to practice new behaviors outside the job (e.g., with one's family) to reduce the risk of experimenting with new leadership strategies in the workplace and also help build nonwork relationships.

Work Toward Creating an Organizational Culture that Supports Coaching.   Chapter 6 in this volume discussed the value of creating a feedback culture in the organization. This is an environment in which feedback is frequent and welcomed. Coaching is an important element of helping executives and managers use feedback. Coaching across the organization helps create a developmentally oriented culture. Conversely, a feedback culture helps facilitate the value of coaching.

Coach Executives on How to Coach.   The coach should create opportunities to discuss the value of coaching. More generally, the coach can help the executive or manager be a coach. This should be integral to the coaching framework. This will be easier after the coach recognizes what matters most to the executive and manager. Once the link is established between coaching and this need, the coach can expand the conversation to what it means to be an effective coach. Coaches can help executives and managers think about how to role model coaching so that their subordinates can be effective coaches.

Involve the Company's Human Resources Department Executives and Professional Staff in the Coaching Effort. Coaching can be part of a comprehensive human resource development system. (Chap. 5, this volume, described such systematic approaches to development.) The role of the human resources professional in the coaching process should be clarified. The human resources department can be a partner with operational departments in supporting coaching. The human resources partners (executives, generalists, and development specialists) can facilitate the coaching process. More than likely, they want to be in the game, and they can add tremendous value. However, they can create unnecessary administrative busywork, at least in working with the external coaches. The human resources person can become a true partner with the external coach and with the executives and managers in their role as internal coach. To do this, the human resources people must learn what partnership is and how they can add value to the coaching process. In some cases, they may need to work on acquiring and fine tuning their coaching skills. The human resources person can help the coach interpret the situation in general terms (e.g., understand the prevalent themes, work demands, or politics of the situation without divulging the confidentiality of the coach–executive relationship). Also, the coach can facilitate the relationship between the human resources person and the executive being coached.

Involve Top Executives. As coaching is introduced as a corporate policy or program, priority can be put on helping the executive's boss be a coach. That is, start at the top of the house. The executives who have already been through some coaching can help make it easier for these top managers. For instance, the executives can prepare their bosses for meetings about their developmental plans. They should avoid hitting the top executives cold and putting them on the spot, but should send them material in advance along with an outline for the purpose and expectations for the meeting.

Encourage Upward Coaching. Another direction for coaching is to create a role for subordinates to coach their supervisors. That is, coaching is potentially a two-way street. When 360 feedback does not exist, upward feedback is likely to occur in a very informal, nondirect way—if it occurs at all. Subordinates are naturally cautious in providing their supervisors with feedback and giving them ideas for how to be more effective. Subordinates may have keen insights into the ways their supervisors can be better coaches, as well as the ways they can be more effective in achieving goals and relating to others. When executives and managers coach their subordinates, they can encourage their subordinates to coach them. For instance, they can ask for feedback and discuss their own performance and/or interpersonal style. This may enhance subordinates' receptivity to coaching and create a climate where it is okay to discuss performance management issues upward and downward. A similar argument can be made for peers, and a guide may be developed to encourage peer coaching.

Select Competent Executive Coaches.   Coaches vary in how they approach the task, depending on their training and experience. They differ in how much time they spend on the feedback, the implications of the feedback for immediate business needs, building a relationship with the executive, focusing on long-term career development perspective, and/or life planning perspective. They also vary in the amount of time they spend with executives and the extent to which they follow-up to encourage the executives to carry out their career plans.

Questions to help in selecting a coach should focus on who the coach has worked with in the past (i.e., types of organizations, positions, and levels), the results they like to see, the processes they use to ensure the results, and the assessments they use to collect information (Tyler, 2000). Information should be sought from the coaches about their different approaches, including how they prepare for and plan the initial meetings, what they try to accomplish in these meetings, how they learn about the executive's situation, and how they contact the executive. Also, prospective coaches should indicate whether they schedule a series of meetings in advance; how they explain the confidentiality of the process and establish trust; how they maintain contact and encourage the executives to create, take ownership for, and follow-through on their development plans; and when and how they evolve the focus of coaching from the executive's immediate business needs, to the executive's career plan, and eventually to the executive's life plan.

Coaching is an exciting new direction for leadership development. More traditional methods of development, such as the workshop or classroom experience, are also evolving, as technology offers ways to deliver practical training online. The next chapter talks about these advances in leadership development programs.

9

Development Programs

The changing nature of leadership development parallels the changing nature of leadership in the face of rapid evolution in technology, competition, and the international economy. As pointed out in chapter 1 of this volume, leaders need to be strategists, attuned to multiple aspects of organizational performance, flexible, team facilitators, and continuous learners. Development programs increasingly use new technology to gather and provide feedback and deliver training. Workshops and simulations need to mirror reality and provide hands-on experience in dealing with real issues, often in a group setting.

Examples of trends in leadership development programs include:

- The availability of online 360-degree feedback surveys that can be formulated by the manager when the manager wants, not when the corporate human resources department dictates. Internet technology delivers, collects, codes, and feeds back the survey results.
- Distance learning in the form of online delivery of courses and career information and resources. Companies provide this to their people, sometimes subscribing to a service shared by different companies, other times developing their own resources in a Web site. Considerable career information, not to mention job search announcements, are readily accessible on the Web.
- Off-site training programs that ask managers to work in groups on real business problems. The workshop setting provides a nonthreatening environment that may open the participants to more risk taking than would occur on the job. Nevertheless, they have a chance to focus on real strategic problems and invent solutions that may actually be applied.
- Temporary job assignments that are structured for fast track learning in order to build a cohort of experienced leaders ready for promotion. These positions reflect the changing nature of the business.

195

This chapter builds on these trends by exploring how organizations design development programs to create the cadre of leaders they need for the business in the future. Types of leadership development programs are examined, including workshops and self-paced, online career resources and training.

HIGH POTENTIAL MANAGEMENT DEVELOPMENT PROGRAMS

Organizations often look outside for executive talent as a way of bringing in new ideas, viewpoints, and experiences. However, they also like to promote managers from within to leadership positions. This has several advantages: Internal experienced people know the organization well, and they can hit the ground running when they acquire new responsibilities. Internal promotions are motivating in that they show managers that getting ahead is possible in the organization. This promotes loyalty and discourages talented managers from looking elsewhere. Whereas organizations would like to fill as many as 80% of their top leadership positions from within the organization, they have trouble doing so. Byham (2000) suggested that this is because the organizations do not have a pool of qualified people with the characteristics and experiences needed for advancement.

Traditional succession-management systems focus on identifying potential replacements for senior management positions, but focus less attention on developing skills of the potential candidates. Byham (2000) recommended that organizations establish high potential management development programs, or what he called "acceleration pools." Instead of targeting one or two people for particular executive jobs, an acceleration pool develops a group of managers for undefined executive positions. These people are identified from within and outside the organization based on job performance, interviews, and assessment center data. (An assessment center is a one, two, or more day experience during which managers are observed and rated on the basis of their participation in individual and group exercises simulating key managerial job situations.) For those individuals chosen for the pool, the assessment information is used to determine development needs. Members of the pool are assigned mentors who provide coaching and help guide them to challenging training and on-the-job developmental experiences. An organization may have one pool or several based on functional department, business unit, region, or organizational level. People may move between pools. Development happens as the managers in the pool participate in a combination of programs, for instance, short, high-impact training programs targeted to specific competencies; short-term learning experiences that help people stay current in their fields, such as attending a professional conference; and challenging, measurable job assignments in areas that are important for the organization's success.

Byham recommended that organizations not limit the number of years an individual can be in a pool before being promoted to executive ranks. This need not be an up-or-out system. Some people may remain in the pool for years as their growth and development proceeds and is tracked by the organization. The pool members continue to add value to the organization as they progress through diverse job experiences (and remain distinct from people who are not pool members and who are likely to stay in the same position for as long as they are with the company). Also, Byham indicated that there should not be age or tenure limits. Young managers can enter the pool if they are identified early in their career—perhaps when they are hired—and start in a rapid advancement development pool. Others may enter the pool after they have been with the organization for a number of years and show their executive potential.

LINKING LEADERSHIP DEVELOPMENT
TO BUSINESS STRATEGY

The following are corporate examples of the need for leadership development programs that meet business demands for today and the future.

Praxair

The human resources management system at Praxair links corporate strategy to leadership development (Harris, Husellid, & Becker, 1999). The firm is a technology pioneer and global leader in the industrial gases industry. It is the largest industrial gases company in North and South America, and the largest carbon dioxide and helium supplier in the world. According to their Web site (http://Praxair.com, April 3, 2000), "Praxair's regional companies worldwide work in concert to serve global and local businesses, ensuring that all customers benefit from our advanced technologies and supply reliability." The firm has developed and introduced a wide range of patented gas applications that have been critical to the growth of many industries, including steel, food and beverage, electronics, and medicine. A subsidiary, Praxair Surface Technologies, serves the aircraft, chemical and plastics, pulp and paper, printing, and metal production industries. Worldwide, the company is expanding by acquiring new firms, forming joint ventures and partnerships, and investing in its business to meet global customer needs. Given this general strategic direction, the company's human resource management infrastructure includes the development of leadership competencies emphasizing team management. Selection, training, and job rotation programs are aimed at building competencies for effective team management across cultures.

Vulcan

Also consider Vulcan Materials Company, headquartered in Birmingham, Alabama. This firm produces construction aggregate, sand, gravel, and chemicals (Houston, 2000). Vulcan, an "old economy" company, has 9,000 employees in 23 states, and a revenue stream of $2.4 billion. The firm has grown through acquisition, because start-ups in this business are too costly given environmental concerns. The small, regional companies it buys tend to have a lower level of managerial effectiveness than the parent company expects for effective competition in the local market. Executive development follows a basic model of understanding the organization context and goals, determining the core competencies needed for success in the business, identifying managers who appear to have these competencies or the potential to acquire them, assessment of managerial skills, development and feedback, and follow-up/progress review. A 3-day "Lead College" builds trust among managers from different parts of the business. The training methods use action learning techniques, meaning that participants work on actual corporate problems within the context of a training program. In particular, participants form teams, and each team is given a strategic project related to immediate business challenges (e.g., "How can we acquire information on our competitors?", "What are the best management practices in our industry or in other industries for marketing distribution, or other facets of our business?", or "How can we share information about best practices across our divisions?"). The teams continue their work after they leave Lead College, corresponding and occasionally meeting to provide advice to executives and follow-up initiatives they began as a result of their "college" experience.

This experience helps the participants develop behavioral patterns for self-regulation. It helps them see the value of information about the company, their department, and their own managerial style to develop self-insight and encourage them to take advantage of corporate resources that provide feedback and additional development opportunities.

Fiat

The Fiat corporation faced a similar dilemma in the international arena. It needed a program to prepare its executives to work in the global marketplace (Anteri & Tesio, 1990; also described in London & Sessa, 1999). They wanted their managers to understand new global strategies and how to do business in other cultures while maintaining their cultural values from Italy, their home country. Their development program focused on international career paths. More specifically, they wanted to inculcate three intercultural competencies:

1. The ability to recognize and interpret correctly the values of one's own company culture, as well as the peculiarities of other cultural and company contexts.

2. The ability to communicate and represent the company's image abroad.
3. The ability to both negotiate effectively and to optimize any professional relations with other cultures.

The development program consisted of several components: Managers based at the company's headquarters in Italy were sent abroad for brief business trips. Non-Italian managers in the company offices throughout the world were sent to an Italian briefing program to help them understand the headquarters' cultural perspective and to gain a better command of the Italian language. Company briefings were held in various countries for managers who operated international markets to promote an understanding of the most salient features of different cultures. In addition, a program was offered on communication and foreign language to develop language skills and international communication models to help Fiat's managers communicate in English.

Colgate-Palmolive

Colgate-Palmolive established a new fast track program for high potential managers for two reasons: (a) The company wanted to reduce, if not stop altogether, turnover of its talented young managers with international experience who were being lured away by higher salaries and faster advancement. (b) The company was desperate for talent to fill an increasing number of international executive positions as the business expands globally (Conner & Smith, 1998; also described in London & Sessa, 1999). Colgate's human resources executives worked with the company's senior leadership to identify desired qualities of high potential managers, design developmental experiences with global job rotation, identify young managers for the program, and carefully monitor their progress. Next, the human resources department designed a series of self-paced materials to help the managers plan their development. These focused around six key attributes of successful executives in their growth-oriented corporate environment:

1. Business savvy—a thorough understanding of all important aspects of the business.
2. The ability to use corporate resources through formal and informal networks.
3. A global perspective and cultural sensitivity that comes from living in foreign countries and a working knowledge of one or more other languages.
4. Strong character, meaning vision, purpose, and values with clarity (people who can be counted on to do what is right and are not reluctant to resist doing something they oppose).
5. Strong people management skills to engage and motivate people, get their best performance, build teams, and develop alliances with people outside Colgate.

6. Entrepreneurship skills, including risk taking, maintaining vision while overcoming barriers, and a sense of inspired urgency to set and accomplish goals.

The company expected managers to understand these competencies and take responsibility for their own development while the firm provided supporting resources. Methods were established to help managers assess their own competencies and chart a course of action to enhance their development. These tools included the following:

- A competency assessment to help them determine how effectively they demonstrate leadership and management skills.
- A personal values survey to help them gain a better understanding of their deepest values.
- A development activities chart that helps them determine the on-the-job learning and development opportunities that come from particular job assignments and activities.
- A global training curriculum grid that links the company's courses to needed skills.
- An individual development plan worksheet that helps the high potential managers to transform their awareness of needed skills and developmental opportunities into a course of action.
- A concise, dictionarylike reference guide for defining and understanding global competencies.

In addition, managers were offered special compensation packages if they would accept temporary job assignments in less developed areas of the world. These included a post allowance plus a mobility premium, recreation breaks, and a retention bonus paid after a specified time on the job. Family members were offered cross-cultural orientation programs and language training, and managers' spouses were offered $7,500 to help with their career (e.g., to purchase a new computer, start a new business, or maintain contact with the current employer).

Foreign Assignments as a Leadership Development Experience

Foreign assignments are a key developmental opportunity in global corporations. They can by life-transforming experiences for the managers and their families. However, they have their drawbacks. A survey conducted by the Center for Global Assignments reported in the *New York Times* (Abueva, 2000) indicated that whereas businesses in the United States say they want managers to have global experiences, the firms do not always know what to do with them when they return. Eighty percent of midsize and large companies sent their professionals abroad, and 45% plan to increase the number they have on foreign assignments. However, reactions of these expatriates were not positive. Sixty percent of those returning from abroad stated that their firms did not communicate clearly about what they would face at home. One third were still in temporary jobs 3 months after returning to work in the United States. And 75% believed their permanent position after returning home was a demotion. About two thirds said that they did not have a chance to put their foreign experience to work. Finally, 25% actually resigned from the company within 1 year after returning.

The major problem is that returning expatriates are moving from a position of major responsibility in a dynamic environment to a cubicle, a project, and ample time to make single decisions (Abueva, 2000). Often these individuals wind up looking for other opportunities that are more welcoming and exciting. As a result, the firm loses its investment. These managers can help avoid such a problem by planning for the return in advance of leaving.

Sylvia Dickinson, a spouse of a manager who had a 2-year assignment in Tokyo for a small semiconductor company, returned home with her spouse to find that people were not interested in hearing about their experiences. She started a consulting firm to counsel outbound and returning executives and their families. She recommended that those considering an overseas assignment do the following (adapted from Abueva, 2000, p. C8):

- Examine both your technical qualifications and temperament. Do you have the patience and flexibility to live and work in another nation with a different culture?
- Review the possibility of relocating with your family as soon as you know about the job opportunity. Are they enthusiastic and supportive?
- Contact fellow executives who currently work abroad or who have already returned from international assignments. What is their view of the pros and cons?
- Obtain information from your management or company's human resources department about how they handle returning executives. Is there a repatriation policy?
- Talk to your boss about the company's objectives and expectations for you. What do they anticipate will be the length of the assignment?
- Talk to your boss and perhaps your boss' boss or others in the organization (e.g., human resources department or manager of the firm's management development program) about assignments once you return. Do they have some firm ideas?
- Put together a list of people in the company with whom you want to stay in touch about job opportunities and events and changes in the company. These may be people in your current department, peers in other departments, your boss, people who have mentored or coached you in the past,

and/or the human resource staff. Plan to stay in touch with them through e-mail, telephone, and home office visits. Do you feel comfortable staying in touch with these people? Will they be responsive?

Moving to a foreign job assignment requires a "profound personal transformation" (Sanchez, Spector, & Cooper, 2000, p. 96). Expatriate executives find that the coping responses that were effective at home may not work in a another culture. Executives on foreign assignments must find a way to identify with both the host and the parent culture. The executive must realize that these cultural identities are mutually exclusive, and there is a way to move between them, rather than face the frustration of giving one up. Organizations help executives cope with the stressors of conflicting expectations and cultural identities with cross-cultural competence training and a sensible repatriation plan.

Sanchez et al. (2000) outlined the developmental stages faced by expatriate executives in adjusting to a foreign assignment:

1. *Selection, acceptance of assignment, and preparation*—may be accompanied by unrealistic expectations, a hurried time frame, and ignorance of cultural differences. This preparatory period can be facilitated by helping the executive and the family evaluate their readiness, recognize their unwarranted assumptions about cultural differences, and initial cultural awareness training.

2. *Arrival and first experiences*—may be accompanied by cultural shock, feelings of lack of fit, and cultural blunders. Organizations can facilitate this indoctrination period by providing social support, advice from locals and expatriates, and the development of a network of contacts. This is the time to realize that behaviors that worked at home may not work in the new environment. Observing how locals behave and respond to business conditions can be a valuable learning experience.

3. *Transition*—may be accompanied by rejection of the host or parent culture, believing they are not compatible. Instead, the executive can be helped to form attachments with the new culture and maintain attachments with the home culture. Constant communication back home can be reassuring and a way to maintain one identity while developing another.

4. *Mastery and comfort*—may be accompanied by frustration with spanning the boundaries of the host and home countries. Eventually, this dual identity is accepted and becomes comfortable. For some executives who span more than two boundaries, this may mean recognizing and identifying with more than two different cultures.

5. *Repatriation*— may be accompanied by disappointment with unfulfilled expectations and loss of autonomy. Repatriation should be handled as carefully and purposefully as expatriation, with support meetings, networking, and frequent communication within the old host contacts and new contacts in the home country.

Need for Intercultural Sensitivity

The first chapter pointed to the need for leaders to develop intercultural sensitivity. This is certainly important in global corporations for leaders whose responsibilities cross countries and cultures. Consider the acquisition of Seagram by Vivendi (a French company), which created a global telecommunications giant. The combined company faced the challenge of cultural diversity. This was evident at the Paris news conference announcing the merger (Sorkin, 2000). Edgar Bronfman Jr., Seagram's chief executive, does not speak French, could not understand Jean-Marie Messier, the Vivendi chairman, when he spoke at the press conference. The goal of the merger was to pull together multiple modes of communication technology (internet, wireless, cable) and entertainment (movies, music). Of course, differences in mother tongue were just the tip of the cultural iceberg that the many component organizations of the new firm faced.

Executives within the United States (and, increasingly, many other Western countries as well) also need cultural sensitivity given heterogeneous employee populations. A diverse employee body is valuable for many reasons: It reflects the population in which the company operates, and as such, the firm will have better sensitivity to customers and suppliers. Cultural diversity within the organization helps generate a diversity of ideas and perspectives, keeping the organization fresh and responsive.

Dunbar (1996) defined intercultural sensitivity as the ability to interpret events in the same way as those from other cultures. This necessitates recognizing cultural patterns of behavior, perceptions, and cognitions that are natural to natives of the culture (Albert, 1996). Individuals who are interculturally sensitive are aware of these cultural patterns and their difference from their own culture. This helps them interact effectively with people from the other culture, avoiding misunderstandings or conflicts. Intercultural sensitivity is a multidimensional concept consisting of eight dimensions (Albert, 1996; London & Sessa, 1999): comfort with other cultures, positively evaluating other cultures, understanding cultural differences, feeling empathy for people in other cultures (being able to put oneself in their place) and valuing cultural differences, being open-minded, sharing cultural differences with others, seeking feedback about how one is received in other cultures, and adaptability.

A lack of intercultural sensitivity can be a significant barrier to taking advantage of the opportunities diversity presents. It can also be a career barrier for executives who are expected to lead multicultural enterprises. Leaders should assess their own cultural diversity by asking themselves questions such as, What cultural differences do you perceive in your organization? What cultural differences do you perceive in your interactions outside your organization (e.g., with customers or suppliers)? How do you feel about cultural differences? Are you and other executives in your company sensitive to cultural differences in values and behavior? Do you perceive cultural conflicts? To what extent do you place yourself in, and take advantage of, a multicultural environment? Or, do you dislike and avoid multicultural situations? What experiences contribute to your learning to work effectively in a multicultural environment?

There are many ways that organizations can enhance executives' intercultural sensitivity. Fiat Corporation, described earlier, is one example. Companies may use cultural assimilators and workshops that give employees a chance to hear about cultural differences, discuss them, and experiment with new cultural behaviors using role playing and simulations (Fiedler, Mitchell, & Triandis, 1971). Some intercultural training uses shock learning. Simulations may be used to give participants a chance to experience what it is like to be a member of a minority group who is subject to ridicule and embarrassment. A classic method is to randomly assign some participants in a class to a minority group (London & Wueste, 1992). These participants are kept standing in a crowded hallway while the majority group members are briefed and enjoy refreshments. The minority group members are then labeled by giving each of them a collar, pin, or hat to wear. They sit on the floor while the majority group sits around them on chairs. The workshop leader then derides the minority group, addressing the majority group members about how terrible people with collars are, and speaking to the minority members as if they were children. An hour or more of this discomfort gets the point across. Issues are raised during a debriefing discussion, including what it felt like to be a member of either group and how this relates to the way people are treated in the organizations.

Managing Intercultural Management Development in a Joint Venture

Consider an example of one such leadership development challenge: the learning needed to manage an international joint venture. Berrell, Wright, and Hoa (1999) examined the challenges facing Australian and Vietnamese managers working in joint ventures in Ho Chi Minh City and Hanoi. Interviews with 10 Australian and 26 Vietnamese managers showed differences in collectivism/individualism, attitudes toward work, and attitudes toward causality. For instance, Vietnamese managers were predisposed to accept the unequal distribution of power in their organizations. They were more accepting of hierarchical management styles and authority, and they cultivated relationships with those above them while regarding those at their own level as benevolent decision-makers. Australian managers were less tolerant of unequal distributions of power and viewed overbearing leadership styles as unacceptable. They valued individual behavior, achievement, and competition and recognized the need for flexible organizational structures. They were open about their criticism of management decisions they disliked, whereas the Vietnamese managers rarely openly questioned the reasoning behind management decisions. Vietnamese managers relied on personal relationships and implicit understandings in conducting business, whereas Australian managers were more inclusive and open in their business relationships and tended to view the relationship network as unimportant. The Australian managers were action oriented, whereas the Vietnamese managers were "being" oriented, and experienced work in a detached way. They found more gratification in family and community activity than Australian managers, whose lives and sources of satisfaction revolved around work. The Vietnamese managers allowed things to happen, whereas the Australians made things happen. Australians viewed time as finite and linear, and Vietnamese viewed time as infinite and intermittent, which frustrated the Australians by giving less importance to meeting deadlines and schedules.

This study demonstrated the classic dichotomy between Western individualism and Eastern collectivism that results in potential conflicts. The situation would be even more complicated if more than two cultures were involved. As it is, intercultural learning experiences need to be shared by members of the different cultures (Berrell et al., 1999). This is a process that needs to be tracked continuously in a joint venture. Refresher learning experiences need to be scheduled periodically. Cross-cultural training should not occur in isolation from the other culture, and should not be one-time events that cover obvious differences, but do not get at the subtleties that take experience in the culture to recognize and assimilate. The first step should be gaining top management recognition of cultural issues. This can be the preparation of a management briefing paper based on in-depth research and knowledge. Cultural groups should then go through training together. This training may be group discussions of cultural differences, role plays and simulations, business games, and other activities that demonstrate cultural differences in attitudes and behaviors. The members of the different cultures need to go through these experiences together. These experiences should be constantly renewed. "One cannot be 'trained' to live in or with another culture. One has to experience the challenges first hand; one then revisits one's reaction, fear and frustration as part of the management development process" (Berrell et al., 1999, p. 587).

Need to Manage Within-Culture Diversity

Leaders need to understand the many things they can do to manage diversity and support women and people of color (London & Wueste, 1992). Regarding gender, they can institute child-care support, encourage support groups, encourage supervisors to discuss work and family conflicts and job stress with their teams, offer alternative work schedules, hire and promote more women, and ensure that women have opportunities for continuing education and valuable job assignments. They can provide women with information about career opportunities, measure women's satisfaction with development, and track their advancement progress in the organization. They can hire, develop, and promote people of color; reward managers for their affirmative action initiatives and success; and train all employees to be interculturally sensitive. They can ensure that harassment of any kind is not tolerated.

Learning from Tough Experiences

People remember and learn from tough learning experiences. Hardships early in life can transfer to enhance leadership later. Sunny Vanderbeck, 27-year-old chief executive of Data Return (a firm that runs web software), recalled the "constant, incessant physical, mental and emotional harassment" of his Army Rangers indoctrination program (Vanderbeck, 2000, p. C6). He believed that Ranger school prepared him more than anything else for managing in the controlled chaos of the internet. "If you can execute a mission under stress and motivate people who are worn down, then getting a group of people—who did eat today and did sleep last night—aligned around a common vision is not that difficult" (p. C6). The next chapter describes more broadly how leaders learn from career hardships and failure later in life.

LEADERSHIP SKILLS TRAINING

There is a wide range of training experiences. A search on a self-improvement Web site, Selfgrowth.com, unearthed the following programs:

- Seminars offered by the Center for Executive Renewal based on a synthesis of Western knowledge and Eastern wisdom for visioning, mastering change, and self-management.
- A "powerful, life-enhancing" workshop called "THE EXPERIENCE." It is "designed to support participants in living lives that are more fully loving, passionate and truthful, grounded in integrity and freedom of choice."
- Adventure workshops for growth and healing of the mind and spirit offered by a firm called Outdoor Leadership Training Seminars.

These are examples of programs with diverse titles and subject matter all claiming to be valuable executive development experiences. Locating such programs on the internet is easy. Investigating their value is another matter. Let the buyer beware!

Experiential Instruction Methods

Leadership training programs use a wide variety of instructional methods to engage participants. One approach is simple didactic learning—that is, the lecture or "talking head" (on video). This may include demonstrations and case scenarios (often on video). Other approaches try to involve participants in active, experiential learning. This behavioral approach usually begins by providing theory and then examples. Next people have a chance to practice the new concepts, along with feedback from the trainer or fellow participants. The final stage is transfer to the job, meaning having a chance to apply and adapt the new skills and knowledge to actual job situations, determine if the behavior change is successful based on feedback from coworkers, and fine-tune the behaviors over time. Experiential instructional methods include the following:

- *Group discussions*—a chance to interact with others while discussing the topic of the course or a case study. This might also include processing (i.e., discussing) the interaction based on the trainer's report as observer.
- *Role plays*—taking on a role in a relationship to understand the position and experience an interaction with others who are also role playing.
- *Simulations*—these are elaborate role plays, which may last several hours, during which participants assume a role in a fictional organization and work with fellow participants on business issues. The Center for Creative Leadership's "Looking Glass" simulation lasts 6 hours. Participants are assigned offices and telephones, and they interact to resolve a variety of problems initially presented in the participants' in-baskets. Simulations can also be done via computer. Sometimes, the simulation uses mixed media. For instance, the Center for Creative Leadership's "Leadership at the Peak" program asks participants to assume they are on an executive search committee finding a new general manager. A CD-ROM presents candidates via video clips, audio interviews, as well as written information.
- *Peer and trainer feedback*—feedback is often an important aspect of training, and it is often built into leadership development programs. Sometimes 360-degree feedback survey results are available from the participant's coworkers. Other times, the simulations and group discussions are a source of information on leadership behavior. The training setting can be a chance for the leader to experiment with new behaviors without the risk that would occur in applying them on the job.

Readers interested in designing experiential learning can refer to Kaagan (2000) for 25 inexpensive leadership training activities. The primary focus of the exercises is on leadership skills and functions that are of concern to managers today, such as team leadership, risking innovation, fostering collaboration, managing conflict, and promoting diversity.

Training Leaders in Transformational Leadership

Consider a study of two types of training: one aimed at instilling transformational leadership (see chap. 1's, this volume, discussion of this style of leadership), and the other aimed at instilling a more transactional or general approach to leadership. Dvir (2000) conducted a field experiment to test the effects of transformational leadership on follower development and performance. Leaders in the experimental group received training in transformational leadership while leaders in the control group received eclectic leadership training.

Specifically, 54 squad leaders in the Israel Defense Forces were randomly assigned to either the transformational or eclectic leadership training conditions. This 3-day workshop took place during a 6-month infantry officer course. The transformational training was designed to show that transformational and transactional leadership are distinct perspectives, demonstrate the behaviors and actions that reflect the transformational style, indicate that transformational leadership produces higher levels of development and performance than transactional leadership, and suggest that development is a continuous process and transformational leaders continuously develop their followers to higher levels of motivation, morality, and empowerment. The eclectic leadership workshop focused on the "here and now" and how various psychological and sociological concepts operate. Both workshops used similar instructional techniques. Both types of training used similar methods, such as role plays, group discussions, simulations, trainer presentations, case discussions, and trainer and peer feedback.

Two months after the course, after the leaders had been in field assignments for at least a month, questionnaires were administered to the leaders, their 90 direct reports, and the 724 recruits under them. The results showed that those trained in transformational leadership had a more positive effect on direct followers' development. They also had a more positive effect on indirect followers' performance (i.e., the performance of those further down in the organizational hierarchy who report to their direct subordinates). Transformational leadership increased at least one measure of motivation, morality, and empowerment among direct reports. However, it did not affect all aspects of development. For instance, followers' active engagement in the task, internalization of moral values, and self-actualization needs were not significantly higher in the experimental group compared to the control group, although the means were in the positive direction for the group trained in transformational leadership. Dvir (2000) suggested that transformational leadership may prevent decline in some developmental attitudes during stressful work conditions (e.g., averting demoralization and negative feelings about oneself in tough times, such as mergers, takeovers, or restructuring of organizations or work flows). The results also showed stronger correlations between direct and indirect subordinates' development compared to the control group. Thus, transformational leadership training seems to strengthen development throughout an organization, perhaps by creating strong bonds among people at all levels—ties that encourage and reinforce a development ethic. This, in turn, seems to have a positive effect on the actual performance of indirect subordinates.

Off-Site Workshops that Focus on Real Business Problems

As already noted, a trend in leadership training is to send representatives from the same organization to a program that provides focused attention on real business issues, often issues dealing with long-term strategy or direction or issues that are pervasive business problems that can only be solved by concentrated attention and cross-functional perspectives. This is in contrast to workshops or classes that are open to managers from any company or industry. The idea of the off-site, business-focused program is to provide a retreat for participants to focus on key issues without having to deal with daily problems. Also, it is a way for managers from different departments to get together to focus on interdependencies between their departments. The hope is that the workshop will result in some creative, "out-of-the-box" thinking in an open environment that fosters an "anything is possible" mind-set.

Table 9.1 outlines such an off-site workshop. The half-day session follows steps that are typical of a total quality management group process. The topics

TABLE 9.1
Agenda for Off-Site Interdepartmental Meeting That Focuses on Real Problems

8:30–9:00 Coffee and networking

9:00–9:30 Introduction—purpose for the meeting

9:30–9:45 Review of format (facilitated quality improvement groups focusing on work processes)

9:45–10:45 Groups begin work. Facilitators appoint a recording secretary and lead the groups in addressing a series of questions that follow a quality improvement process:

(1) Brainstorm the specific problems that need to be addressed (facilitator boards on flipchart).

(2) Prioritize the problems (facilitator leads group through multivoting).

(3) Select top one or two problems for further discussion and action; define each problem more specifically.

10:45–11:00 Break

11:00–12:00 Continuation of group work session

For each of the problems:

(4) Brainstorm reasons for the problem/barriers to the work process.

(5) Determine actions to overcome the problems/barriers.

(6) Discuss the components of a proactive implementation plan and method for tracking success (indicators and goals for improvement that will result from the change).

12:00–1:00 Lunch

1:00–2:00 Read out results from each group

for discussion were generated and defined beforehand by the planning team. Also, the planning team chose one person for each group to lead and facilitate the group process. These individuals attended a 2-hour training session to be sure they understood the purpose of the meeting and what was intended by each stage in the process. Participants were preassigned to each group in advance, so there would be little confusion after the introductions, even though this meant that people would not have a choice.

The postmeeting reactions were extremely positive. In a follow-up survey, of the 76 participants, 53% indicated the program was very useful and 36% said it was moderately useful. And 92% indicated that the activity benefited the organization as a whole, and when asked to explain how, wrote down responses like, "increased awareness," "creative problem solving," "interaction," "different groups brought together," and "shared information." Overall, this was a *collective* learning experience that not only improved communication, interpersonal relationships, and mutual understanding, but also resulted in many excellent ideas. Several groups had follow-up meetings to flesh out and implement the ideas. Ideas from some other groups were sent to the organization's long-range planning committee.

Open Training Courses

Numerous organizations, including universities, professional associations, for-profit training companies, and consulting firms offer leadership skills courses. These are available to most any registrant with the tuition. Here are some examples from not-for-profit associations and centers.

The American Management Association offers courses such as, "Strategies for Developing Effective Presentation Skills," "Interpersonal Skills," "Negotiating to Win," and "Building Better Work Relationships." One course, "Leadership Skills and Techniques for Professionals," was specifically designed for African American managers, directors, CEOs, and entrepreneurs who want to enhance their leadership skills. The course provides a chance to explore common workplace experiences and network with peers.

The Center for Creative Leadership's weeklong "Leadership Development Program" offers middle and upper level managers a chance to start a process of professional growth that will help them become more successful and productive in their work and personal lives and more effective in leading others to do the same. It includes 360-degree feedback, role-playing simulations, a variety of tests and interviews, group discussions among fellow participants, and ample feedback in one-on-one sessions with coaches. The week leads to a plan for performance improvement and career advancement.

The Center for Creative Leadership also offers a leadership program exclusively for women managers in middle to executive-level leadership positions. The program offers a deeper understanding of the forces that influence their careers and shape strategies for their development as individuals, professionals, and leaders. Participants acquire an improved understanding of themselves and their possible roles, and an understanding of power dynamics in organizations. The workshop attempts to broaden participants' perspectives as women and as leaders by focusing on issues they face as women. The participants focus on strategic leadership skills needed to influence decisions and build coalitions.

Consortia Training Programs

Sometimes companies ban together to offer programs that each company could not afford alone. Noncompeting companies may join a consortium with an educational provider, such as a university, to share in the cost and experience of developing their high potential senior managers (Lawler, 2000). This is a hybrid of public offerings, which is why any firm can send anyone to learn, and customer programs, which are designed specifically for the executives of one firm to participate in the program together. Consortia training programs add richness by broadening the participants who can share experiences from different situations. The programs also provide focus in understanding the needs of those present. Also, they encourage some people from the same firm who may be working together one day (or who are doing so now) to participate together. As such, the program helps develop a network of high potential people within the company. Lawler (2000) specified that the optimum conditions for a consortium program are when the firm sends from 2 to 10 participants per year, when the firm can benefit from outside viewpoints, and when the topics covered require thought and discussion, not just listening.

Online Training

The World Wide Web provides access to a host of information that can be valuable for leadership development. This includes online education/distance learning courses of all sorts, many run by for-profit arms of universities and training companies. New information and educational services are blossoming all the time, presenting a wealth of creative opportunities that can be incorporated into a leader's development plan and that leaders can engage in on their own as their interest and felt need for information emerge. One recent example is Fathom.com, a new for-profit consortium web venture led by Columbia University in partnership with other venerable institutions, including the New York Public Library, the British Library, the Smithsonian Institution's National Museum of Natural History, the London School of Economics and Political Science, and Cambridge University Press (Arenson, 2000). The firm's goal is to offer a broad set of knowledge, with classes taught by renowned academics from universities and think tanks around the world. Users will have to pay for some offerings, and other offerings will be free. This differs from other online courses and training in that they provide a range of materials, rather than just degree programs or courses. The Web site will also be a clearing house for courses provided by other universities, providing ease of access. The value of such a site is that it brings together highly authoritative information and knowledge, and provides ready access to a wide variety of intellectual capital that can be leveraged by a creative leader as needed.

In support of online leadership training, the Forum Corp., a for-profit global leader in workplace learning, announced in a press release on February 8, 2000, that it was supporting the first commercial implementation of eLearning standards. They felt this would accelerate corporate adoption of online learning. This was a joint effort with Microsoft's Learning Resource Interchange (LRN), a software toolkit that provides content and technology partners with the resources to quickly create LRN-compatible content and applications, increasing the viability of online learning for knowledge workers.

Talent Alliance is a nonprofit network of firms such as AT&T, Ceridian, DuPont, Johnson & Johnson, TRW, and Unisys. The alliance provides managers in its member companies with online career services. The current release offers 12 comprehensive career centers and 57 interactive workshops with information and support on job search, self-assessment, career coaching and mentoring, career planning, and stress management, to name a few topics. Companies use this as a resource for professional staff to take responsibility for their own development. They also use it as a resource for managers who have been downsized and are looking for new employment. A powerful feature of the site is the "Career Life Line," which offers a path to the resources that best fit the user's situation. The following are examples of life-line situations:

- A new job requires you to develop a new skill.
- You want to find a new job opportunity in your company.
- You are assigned to be team leader and you want confidential feedback about how you are doing.
- Your company restructures and you gain new responsibilities and new co-workers.
- You have several career options and must decide which fits you best.
- You want to find a career mentor.

The site's Career Centers provide self-assessments, job skill information by industry and discipline, interactive tools, and resource guides, in addition to links to numerous other career-related sites. For example, the "Business Growth Center" provides information on business trends and forecasts of emerging and declining occupations. The Career Coaching Center helps the participant learn how to give and receive career coaching. The Career Decision Center helps make smart decisions about career moves, including changing functions, telecommuting, relocation, or accepting a promotion. The Personal Development Center helps build knowledge and skills in the manager's field of work, and gathers feedback from others to help pinpoint the more effective development actions. (For a preview of the methods, see the Web site: www.talentalliance.org.)

University Curriculum: Preparing for Entrepreneurial Modes of Doing Business

Large companies, such as IBM and Merck, are changing the way they do business to respond to new kinds of competition. They are becoming more entrepreneurial, for example, by allowing new small units to operate as independent businesses unrestrained by corporate bureaucracy. Recognizing this, the Harvard Business School reorganized its curriculum around the study of entrepreneurial ventures, including dot-com start-ups or units of large corporations trying to act like small businesses (Leonhardt, 2000a). Although Stanford is thought to be the more forward-thinking business school, Harvard opened a branch in the Silicon Valley for executive education and a base of operation for MBA students who want to work with West Coast firms.

As an example of the hands-on MBA learning experience, consider two recent students, Tania Yannas and Benjamin Gordon. They began at Harvard in January 1999, and developed a business plan for a business-to-business Web site that would allow shipping agents to communicate better with shippers and truckers (Leonhardt, 2000b). By the time the company, called 3Plex, took second place in the school's annual business plan competition 1½ years later, the operation had 18 employees, including several who had been recruited from large transportation companies like Penske. Gordon and Yannas readily admitted that their company's initial success was supported by advisors, venture capitalists, and customers from the Harvard Business School's network of faculty, alumni, and fellow students. Such linkages are important elements of business success and continued opportunities for individual development. Harvard Business School graduates receive lifetime e-mail addresses. Harvard reports that 20% of the partners of major venture capital firms hold MBAs from the school (Leonhardt, 2000b).

CONCLUSIONS

The complexity of management requires using a variety of leadership tactics (Dalton, 2000). Overusing one style can be just as bad as underutilizing another. Leadership training therefore puts executives and managers into a variety of assignments, and simulated learning situations, using the complexity of managerial assignments and actual business problems for leadership development. As people recognize how they learn best and what they are learning, they will be better self-learners. Self-learning implies knowing how to learn, being able to recognize one's own skill and knowledge gaps and grasp what is learned as experiences arise and evolve.

To grasp and communicate the diversity and complexity of leadership, development programs draw on multiple media. They combine CD-ROMS, internet-driven survey delivery and feedback, web-accessed information, and problem-focused off-site workshops with standard lectures. They concatenate events in time and space that may not normally fit together. They manufacture reality, and help the leader synthesize and abstract relevant yet compressed data to make it understandable and systematic. They localize the training to account for situational effects so that the leader understands cultural differences and effects. They combine multiple sources of input and multiple perspectives, and provide a lens or framework to clarify the inputs and perspectives. In short, they offer a richness that reflects the environment and demands of leadership.

Feedback is the heart of development. It stems from observations and evaluations from others and oneself. One leadership development program begins by giving participants a report of their 360 survey data collected in preparation for coming to the session. The executives then participate in an in-depth simulation and complete a variety of personality, psychological, and ability measures—data that are then fed back to the executives in one-on-one coaching sessions during the training. One might wonder, is this feedback overkill? What kinds of people can benefit most from this process? How much self-esteem does it take to benefit? What are the risks for those who start with low self-confidence? Is there a difference in acceptance and use of the feedback between people who self-selected versus those who were told to attend because of a problem on the job? Similar questions probably arise in therapy situations. The leadership development program may create more positive demand effects than a clinical setting in that the participants realize that they are there to focus on themselves. That is, they approach the program wanting it to be successful, wanting to acquire information and direction from which they can benefit. Still, the program and coaches need to recognize individual developmental and learning style differences. Also, the program should provide the support and encouragement to enhance the benefits and ensure a continued positive outlook after it is over.

The next section of the book turns to challenges and opportunities in leadership development. Chapter 10 in this volume examines career barriers as chances for learning and growth, as well as ways to apply resilience and insight and revise career identity in the process. Chapter 11 in this volume considers the need for leaders to become continuous learners.

Challenges and Opportunities

10

Overcoming Career Barriers

This chapter is about how and what leaders learn from career barriers. A major, unexpected career upset is a frame-breaking experience that causes the leader to reflect on what went wrong. It places the leader in a new situation filled with uncertainty but ripe for experimentation and risk taking. This chapter discusses types of career barriers, how they arise, and what and how a leader learns from these experiences. Leaders can make the most of these barriers by adopting coping strategies that will bring new opportunities and help them manage other barriers that may arise in the future.

TYPES OF CAREER BARRIERS

Most people think of a career barrier as a job loss. However, there are other types. Table 10.1 lists other career barriers. These barriers may occur together, making them more complex and troublesome. For instance, a change in job assignment may involve relocation abroad and considerable job stress. This may come late in life, and could result in unfavorable performance feedback from an unsympathetic boss. Also, nonwork losses can become career barriers, as when a divorce affects the leader's ability to focus on work.

How the career barrier arises and other characteristics of the barrier will affect its impact on the leader's emotions, thoughts, and actions. Career barriers can vary on the following characteristics, each of which can exacerbate the strength of the barrier. Barriers may be sudden, involuntary, visible to others, and traumatic in terms of emotion, disruption, and alternation of one's career and life. They vary in the degree of clarity and certainty, and the number and roles of other people affected (one's spouse, other family members, colleagues, customers, and friends). Also, they vary in their effects on other aspects of life, such as one's health and leisure. In addition, they differ in the degree of control a person has to alter or escape from the situation.

217

TABLE 10.1

Types of Career Barriers

- Discrimination
- Sexual harassment
- Lack of confidence
- Role conflict (e.g., being a boss and colleague)
- Inadequate experience/training for a key assignment
- Disapproval by others, especially public criticism
- Uncertainty about the future, for instance, because of a sudden change
- Lack of information
- Indecision
- Career or job dissatisfaction from a series of small setbacks
- Relocation to another city or nation
- Job transfer
- Overqualified for the job—underutilization
- Physical disability
- Close monitoring of activities
- Early career ceiling
- Job loss
- Demotion
- Passed over for promotion
- Business failure
- Changing business environment
- Job stress
- Unfavorable performance feedback
- Career transition late in life

Note. Based on London (1998).

REACTIONS TO CAREER BARRIERS

Elsewhere, a model was developed to explain how people react to career barriers (London, 1997b, 1998). It was noted that some barriers creep up slowly so that the person affected has time to adjust, as well as time to avoid or deny the increasing problem. Other barriers arise more suddenly and have immediate, dramatic affects on the individual's life and career. Such frame-breaking barriers result in stronger emotions and more mindful cognitive processing to evaluate the situation (e.g., determine why the barrier arose, how much control the individual has, and alternative coping responses). Leaders who have resilient personalities (a strong sense of self-efficacy and self-control) and have external support from their organization, family, and friends are able to develop constructive coping strategies. Leaders who are vulnerable psychologically and lack support from the environment are likely to develop defensive explanations for the barrier and ineffective or possibly destructive coping strategies.

Leana and Feldman's (1992) integrative model of reactions to job loss can be applied to career barriers in general. Reactions depend on the context (e.g., whether job loss is permanent or temporary), the individual's cognitive appraisal (e.g., attributions about severity and degree of reversibility), and the individual's emotional and physical reactions, as variables that predict problem-focused (e.g., finding another job) and symptom-focused strategies (e.g., complaining to garner sympathy).

Reactions to job loss stem from a multistage process (Latack, Kinicki, & Prussia, 1995). Beginning with the initial job loss announcement, individuals do the following:

1. Appraise the situation by comparing their status with a goal or standard.
2. Appraise the gap, or the extent to which the loss is perceived as harmful or threatening (e.g., how long it will take to get another job?). This begins with a primary appraisal ("How bad is it?") and is followed by a secondary appraisal ("What can I do about it?").
3. Set a goal that coping should achieve (the overall desired end result, such as another job).
4. Consider resources available for coping (e.g., outplacement help paid for by the company).
5. Judge whether a coping strategy (or strategies) will work.
6. Adopt one or more of three types of coping strategies: control (proactive strategies aimed at resolving the situation), escape, and/or seeking social support

Coping strategies may be behaviors in direct response to a career barrier or they may be merely thought—essentially interpretation and rationalization of the event and possible reactions. Constructive coping strategies are direct behavioral actions. Consider ways to react to negative performance feedback. Constructive responses may be exerting extra effort, influencing expectations, and explaining one's actions. Other constructive strategies include persisting, establishing new alliances, searching for new goals and alternative behaviors, searching for a rationale, generating and testing hypotheses, seeking disconfirming evidence, and seeking counseling (from a professional or significant other). Other strategies that are more mindless but may be constructive in the long run are copying others who are successful, hitting on the right reason for events and/or a reasonable response by chance, or simply letting things happen without taking deliberate action (e.g., job loss leads to unemployment insurance and being sent on job interviews that results in re-employment) (London, 1998). Dysfunctional responses may be rationalizing that losing one's job does not matter or that the rater's evaluation is not credible or does not count for anything meaningful (Tsui, Ashford, St. Clair, & Xin, 1995). Additional possibly dysfunctional strategies are continuing negative behavior, continuing commitment to a lost cause or dead end, quitting, increasing dependence on others, or feeling apprehensive about being evaluated.

DERAILED EXECUTIVES:
HOW LEADERS GET OFF TRACK

Job loss is often a surprise, even for the savvy executive. Consider the following case: G. Richard Thoman, chief executive of Xerox Corporation, was stunned when he was relieved of his duties in May 2000 after 13 months at the helm (Deutsch, 2000). Besieged by competition and a battered stock price, the Xerox board felt an immediate change was needed. Just several days before his ouster, he indicated to the press that he expected to remain chief executive for some time. Thomas was recruited from IBM in 1997. This was the first time that Xerox had appointed an outsider to the top position. His goal was to develop new products and technologies and invigorate the company's stodgy culture. However, the company faced a number of problems: weak sales overseas, competition (which held down prices for printers and lower end copiers), and new entrants to the high speed digital copier business. One consultant stated to the press that he was convinced that Thoman would not survive the year, "If they're going to get aggressive, flexible and fast enough to compete with the Japanese, they'll need a new management team." They also need to overcome internal upheaval aimed at major cost cutting (e.g., eliminating 14,000 jobs since Thoman was hired). The firm's consolidation of back office operations caused backlogs in accounts receivable and billing. More chaos resulted when the company reorganized long-established sales territories. In addition, the company was slow to increase sales on the internet. But Thoman was surprised by the board's sudden action, despite his role as an outsider in what he recognized as a company with a proud heritage and a long culture.

    In considering such a case, it is natural to wonder how this could have been avoided. Isn't this a loss of a talented individual to the firm? Are there some situations that are just too hard for an executive to anticipate and overcome? These are certainly regrettable situations from the standpoint of both the executive and the company. Do some situations seem to provoke trouble? The next section considers the situation of global assignments. These are especially difficult for leaders who seem to generate regrettable losses. Consider what managers can learn from these situations. Moreover, the cases suggest how they may be avoided.

Regrettable Losses:
The Trials of Global Assignments

Hofmeister (2000) identified factors that cause a manager to derail in Shell Oil. They include mobility without accountability (reassigning managers to new jobs before they are able to live with the consequences of their decisions), management lapses (poor decisions), and classic factors, such as lack of self-awareness and arrogance. Hofmeister suggested several precautions that can avoid low self-awareness. These include feedback early in the manager's career, accurate feedback, and good bosses (supervisors who coach, not just pass on problems). Managers need to learn from setbacks. They should have a variety of experiences, including good and bad bosses. They should also have regular performance appraisals and work with their supervisors to develop, track, and periodically revise a career plan.

Hofmeister (2000) noted that derailed executives often do better if they move to a simpler company. Transferring back to their home department is likely to carry the stigma of failure despite the learning experience. Hofmeister pointed to the importance of linking expatriate managers back home from the start of the assignment. It is important for them to frequently meet with top people in the company. Corporate meetings bringing managers and executives together from all parts of the business are important to help them share and learn from each other and to avoid failed experiences, or at least to understand them better when they occur. Another factor that supports expatriate managers and helps prevent their derailment is a network of spouses. The spouses can meet frequently and provide support for each other, thereby helping to make the executive's home life an easier adjustment.

Mobley (2000) stated that sometimes companies are glad when a manager leaves, often because the manager has failed in some way. Other times, however, companies regret the loss of high potential managers who left because they thought they failed, but really they were put into untenable situations by the firm—jobs that were tough situations or that simply did not match their areas of expertise or their interests. Often, these managers say they did not know the company regarded them so highly until their last day, by which time it was too late. McCall (1998) pointed out that although failure may be due largely to the executive, usually the companies themselves can be implicated in some way.

Mobley (2000) provided some examples of regrettable losses. In particular, he studied high potential managers who left their organization before the company could let them know how much they were appreciated, and before the company was able to correct a negative situation.

Case 1. An executive with a worldwide telecommunications company with headquarters in the United States was assigned to the position of Vice President for Human Resources for the new Asia Pacific unit based in Hong Kong. The role necessitated defining human resource strategy for this high growth, high competition region, encompassing China and southeast Asia. Although an exciting and important position, the individual had been a career human resource professional in the company's headquarters. He had never had another assignment elsewhere in the business, let alone abroad. Moreover, he had no experience traveling abroad. He did not even have a passport prior to the assignment. Once he reached Hong Kong, he tried to transfer standard human resources practices to the unit. He rarely left his Hong Kong office, and even took most of his meals at the American Club. His family lasted 4 weeks, and then went home. He was transferred back to headquarters after only 9 months.

Case 2. A general manager with a well-known, high-end hotel chain headquartered in the United States was an American Caucasian who had been with the company for 20 years. All of his general management experience had been in Asia starting up new hotels or rejuvenating older, floundering properties. He had excellent cultural awareness; he spoke several Asian languages and was married to an Asian. His last assignment was as a general manager of a mature, five-star hotel in Australia. He stayed for 1 year and then quit to join another luxury hotel chain in charge of a major start-up in Indonesia. His former firm regretted the loss deeply. However, neither the executive nor the firm realized the folly of putting this entrepreneurial style manager used to an Asian environment into a mature, well-functioning property in an English-speaking culture.

Cases 3. A Canadian with extensive international experience, but not in Asia, was promoted to the position of president of the business unit in China. The parent company was a multinational energy firm headquartered in Europe. The company's goal was to penetrate the China market in exploration, retailing, and chemicals. In established parts of the company, each business unit operated independently. This was the case in China as well. However, the new Asian unit was supposed to bring together all the firm's business operations in China, with headquarters in Hong Kong. The idea was to put a single face on the company as it established business in China. Although the executive had ample operations experience, he had little experience building relations between business units. He had good interpersonal skills, but he had trouble exerting influence on the different business units within China to get them to work together effectively. This was especially a problem because he lacked the authority to insist on certain working relationships. The heads of the separate business units undercut him time and again. Also, he did not establish high-level relationships with the government in Bejing. After 1 year in the job, he and the company mutually agreed on his departure from the firm.

When Strengths Become Flaws

Derailment is the "nonvoluntary cessation of career progress" (McCall, 1998, p. 23). Derailment may occur to executives and managers who had done well in the past. Their modus operandi was successful after all. Executives may fail because what worked well in the past did not work in a new environment (McCall, 1998). When under the stress of change and uncertainty, executives may rely more heavily on what worked in the past, however, these styles may be the opposite of what is needed now. Executives who continue to rely on their strengths regardless of the environment may find that their strengths turn into liabilities. For instance, a decisive/action orientation may be perceived as not listening. Having a vision for the future may be seen as aloof and arrogant. An authoritarian style that worked well in Europe may backfire in the United States. The excellent track record may narrow the executive's vision to a specific technical or functional area, blinding the executive to a broader context. Alternatively, success may have been achieved in destructive ways, and the executive may not have been in the position long enough to realize the dysfunctional long-range results (e.g., low morale that may have come from exhausting employees to complete a project). Their brilliance may be perceived as intimidating. Their commitment may be viewed as overwork as they seem to be defining their entire lives by their careers. Their charm may be viewed as manipulative. Their ambition may be perceived as willingness to do whatever is necessary to attain personal success regardless of the expense to others. The team play may be perceived as indecisive and lacking in independent judgment and willingness to take a risk. A bias to action may be seen as reckless and dictatorial. (See McCall, 1998, for these and other such examples.)

Personal Fears Can Create Career Barriers

Downs (2000) suggested that executives are their own worst enemy in creating barriers to success. He argued that executives' fear that they must always do more than what they are capable of doing. This cripples them into inaction and causes them to abandon their core strengths. He outlined seven universal fears that plague executives:

1. *Fear of failure.* Instead of acknowledging their weaknesses and accentuating their strengths executives may try to hide their weaknesses and be the best at everything.
2. *Fear of rejection.* Some executives avoid contradicting those at higher organizational levels because they are so eager to fit in and gain approval. They are threatened by evaluations, and so abandon their commitment to excellence in order to conform to what they believe their boss wants.

3. *Fear of scarcity.* Executives who fear scarcity believe that there will not be enough resources for them and others to be successful. So they avoid risks and miss opportunities for growth.
4. *Fear of reality.* Executives look for the quick fix, sometimes hiring a consultant to provide off—the-shelf answers because they fear they or others in the organization have the talent to learn and grow from their mistakes.
5. *Fear of the unknown.* Some executives resist change, even though staying the same makes them obsolete.
6. *Fear of authority.* Executives who fear that those in authority will sacrifice others to serve their own purposes believe that the only way to succeed is to please those above them in the organizational hierarchy.
7. *Fear of aging.* Executives may be concerned that as they grow older, they will become obsolete. They fear that they are too old to start another career or learn major new strategies. So they spend time looking busy rather than learning.

Downs (2000) recommended that executives recognize that they do not possess unlimited talent. Instead, they should realize that they possess, and should exploit, a belief in the talents they do possess.

An earlier section described problems that executives face in global assignments. These situations require the leader to deal with often difficult business situations in unfamiliar surroundings. In addition to the business demands, they face the stress of adapting to a new and possibly very different culture. The next section considers the acculturation stress experienced by immigrants. Unlike expatriates, who are on temporary assignment, immigrants have made a commitment to change their residence and citizenship for the rest of their lives. Whereas they may return home on occasion, this is often a no-return situation.

The Immigrant Experience

The immigrant might be the émigré from the United States working in another country (e.g., the executive expatriate on a developmental assignment or permanent move to another country). Or this might be the immigrant to the United States (e.g., the computer technician from India who remained in the United States after graduating from a U.S. university). These individuals and their families face the stress of acculturating, made all the more difficult by possible bias that affects how they are treated within and outside the company. They need to understand, if not acquire, the values of the dominant culture. They may experience feelings of alienation and marginality, as well as various types of psychosomatic symptoms.

Bhagat and London (1999) outlined three variants of acculturative stress:

1. *Demand stresses.* These derive from the expectations and constraints imposed by their organization and social environment over which they have little to no control. Examples are stereotyping and ethnocentric tendencies in the workplace. These are made worse by differences in physical appearances, skin color, and accent in the language of the host country. Other problems are managing the relations between work and life outside of work. For instance, the norms of a work-oriented society may differ from those in the home country, which may emphasize strong values in familism and collectivism. Another difficulty may be developing a positive relationship with supervisors, and finding colleagues who can be supportive coaches and mentors.

2. *Opportunity stresses.* These emerge in relation to the new opportunities available in the adopted/host country. The individual may have immigrated just to have these educational and career opportunities. Nevertheless, making the most of them creates new stresses in terms of self- and family-imposed expectations, and the need to meet tough, competitive standards.

3. *Constraint stresses.* These are the pressures that the immigrant encounters in dealing with the pace of society and corporate life in the new environment. Immigrants to the United States often face time and behavioral expectations to which they want to adapt but that are difficult even for natives of the country and become all the more stressful when they conflict with home country behaviors and mores.

The way immigrants perceive these conditions determines the stress they feel. If they believe they can manage these conditions, then the stress will be much less than if they do not have effective coping strategies. Similarly, stress will be less if the immigrant has sources of strong social support. Ultimately, the degree and duration of the felt stress will influence immigrants' career success and satisfaction, occupational self-esteem, and commitment to (vs. the tendency to withdraw from) their career. Immigrants are interculturally competent when they are able to communicate effectively, establish effective interpersonal relationships, and deal with the various pressures of acculturation by using their understanding of the host society (Bhagat & London, 1999).

RESILIENCE AND HARDINESS

Chapter 4 described the relations between resilience, insight, and identity (the components of career motivation). Resilience is the ability to overcome career barriers. It is the ability to adapt to changing circumstances, even when the circumstances are discouraging or disruptive (London, 1983, 1985; London & Mone, 1987). Resilience consists of personality characteristics that help maintain motivation during tough times, when a person's self-image is threatened. Resilience includes such personality characteristics as self-esteem, internal control, the desire to achieve, and the willingness to take reasonable risks. Individuals who are high in resilience are able to confront disappointments as challenges.

People acquire adaptive styles that serve them well under stress. However, when stress is unpredictable, unexpected, and new, people are not prepared, and previously adaptive styles may not work (Fine, 1991). An individual's resilience may be the saving grace in such situations: "Resilience is not a miraculous rescue. It can be a mere thread that wrestles itself to the surface in an otherwise despairing existence" (Fine, 1991, p. 499). As people get older and confront more experiences, they focus less energy on behaviors and psychological processes that contribute to personal and professional growth and more energy on ways to remain functional given daily life stresses as well as emerging tough conditions. They develop coping skills over time. These skills allow them to compensate for loss of competence, protect against perceptions of harm, and view career barriers as challenges rather than hardships (Fine, 1991).

Hardiness is a similar concept to resilience. It consists of three personality dispositions: commitment (the tendency to get involved in tough situations rather than isolate oneself), control (the tendency to feel and act influential in the face of tough situations rather than helpless), and challenge (the belief that change rather than stability is normal in life) (Kobasa, 1979; Kobasa, Maddi, & Kahn, 1982). Hardiness makes difficult situations seem less stressful. Individuals who are not hardy are vulnerable to stress and are not optimistic in the face of adversity. They feel hopeless and helpless, out of control, hostile, and/or simply unenthusiastic when it comes to facing life's challenges.

Overall, resilience (and its companion construct, hardiness) fosters positive frames of reference and positive emotions, such as optimism and hope. It promotes mindful cognitive processing that contributes to new self-insights from dealing with the career barrier using constructive coping strategies. Vulnerability generates negative frames of reference (e.g., dependence and depression), which contribute to dysfunctional problem solving (London, 1997b).

Sources of Situational Support

Organizational support can affect the extent to which a career barrier damages an individual's psyche. Negative events can be put in a positive light by the right support. For instance, a job loss can be viewed as a chance for new opportunities. This is made easier if there is career counseling and help in finding another position, as well as a generous severance package. Managers of individuals facing a career barrier can help in providing support in the form of goal setting, feedback, role modeling, listening, two-way communication, reinforcement, and negotiation. The manager can help the subordinate understand the reasons for the career barrier and can suggest ways to overcome it, perhaps even facilitating or altering organizational resources to make the barrier easier to confront directly. In general, organizational support helps the person affected create positive frames of reference, positive emotions, mindful appraisal of the situation, and constructive coping strategies (London, 1997b). Conversely, the absence of support produces negative frames of reference, problem-solving deficits, and dysfunctional or destructive coping strategies.

Emotional Intelligence

Emotional intelligence is a further extension of the concepts of resilience and hardiness. Goleman (1997), a science writer for the *New York Times*, argued that human intelligence is much more than rational, cognitive ability, for instance, math and verbal skills. How people do in life is more a function of "emotional intelligence," which includes self-awareness, impulse control, persistence, zeal, self-motivation, empathy, and social deftness. Additional social and emotional competencies could be included, such as communication, sensitivity, initiative, trust, respect, and other interpersonal skills. Summarizing a wide range of ideas and experiences from psychological and neurobiological literature, Goleman concluded that rational and emotional abilities work jointly to shape intelligence and predict a person's likelihood of success in life. Learning how to regulate emotional responses, understand oneself and others, and deal with conflicts peacefully are ways to enhance success in all aspects, work and nonwork. Whereas Goleman's initial work was based on anecdotes and less rigorous, quantitative study, he later organized a research consortium on emotional intelligence to prove its importance to effectiveness in a variety of life's pursuits.

Emotionally intelligent leaders reflect such social competencies to build effective working relationships with many different people, act as mentors and coaches to subordinates and others in their organization, and demonstrate self-confidence and the ability to control their emotions (Cherniss, 1998). Leaders with emotional intelligence are able to recognize and cope with their inner feelings and thoughts. Moreover, they are able to understand the effect they have on others (L. Johnson, 1999). That is, they have the self- and interpersonal insight (discussed in chap. 2, this volume) and they are able to regulate their own behavior effectively in relation to changing situational demands, including unexpected negative situations (see chap. 3, this volume).

Goleman (2000) studied 3,000 executives to identify effective leadership behaviors. He distinguished between six leadership styles, each a different element of emotional intelligence, and each having a different effect on the culture of the leader's organizational unit. The six styles are (a) *Coercive*, demanding immediate compliance; (b) *Authoritative*, mobilizing people toward a vision; (c) *Affiliative*, creating emotional bonds and harmony; (d) *Democratic*, building consensus through participation; (e) *Pacesetting*, expecting excellence and self-direction; and (f) *Coaching*, developing people for the future.

The most effective leaders are those who do not rely on just one of these styles but use all of them as appropriate. That is, the leader who obtains the best results chooses a style that is best suited for the situation. Other leaders are not able to do this, perhaps because they lack one or more of these styles (e.g., they feel uncomfortable with it or have never had a chance to observe or use it). Such leaders need to expand their repertoires and practice diagnosing the situation and switching styles to fit the demands of the situation.

Reviewing research that shows the value of emotional intelligence, Cherniss (2000) concluded that emotional intelligence predicts important work-related outcomes beyond the effects of cognitive intelligence. Social and emotional variables are often measured in assessments of managerial talent (Thornton & Byham, 1982). Key dimensions of leadership include consideration for others, along with knowing how to structure work (Fleishman & Harris, 1962; Hemphill, 1959). Longitudinal studies have found that traditional IQ makes less of a difference to how someone does in life than the ability to handle frustration, control emotions, and get along with other people (cf. Snarey & Vaillant, 1985). In one study, social and emotional abilities were four times more important than IQ in determining professional success and prestige of scientists who were studies over a 40-year period (Feist & Barron, 1996).

Cherniss (2000) noted that this does not mean emotional intelligence is all that is necessary for success and cognitive ability assessed by IQ does not matter. On the contrary, IQ may be necessary, particularly in complex disciplines and professions. However, it is not sufficient for success. This is where emotional IQ comes in. Also, emotional intelligence needs to be developed into emotional competencies, that is, the personal and social skills that lead to excellent work performance. Emotional intelligence is needed for emotional competencies to develop. For example, being able to recognize accurately what other people are feeling (the emotional characteristics of empathy) is important for being able to develop the competence to influence others. People who are able to regulate their emotions will be able to more easily develop competencies such as initiative and achievement drive (Cherniss, 2000).

Leaders high in emotional intelligence listen to and hear others. They are able to mobilize others around a shared vision, publicly recognize and celebrate others' accomplishments, show interest and concern for others, ask for others' opinions and involve them in decision making, and relate effectively to different levels of employees (based on skills from the 360 feedback survey developed by Wilkes, Nellen, & DelCarmen, 2000). People who are high in emotional intelligence are able to analyze their emotions and cope with them, evaluate the situation realistically (make accurate attributions and forecast likely consequences), and identify viable coping strategies that deal with their emotions and affect the situation directly. Also, they are able to assess what they have learned about themselves and the career environment (their employer, job opportunities), devise tracking mechanisms and a readiness to revise or change strategies to deal

TABLE 10.2

Rate Your Own Emotional Intelligence

Consider the following items. How would you evaluate yourself (high, medium, low) on each of the following characteristics? How do you think others would evaluate you? If you want some actual feedback, ask a few people to rate you on these characteristics and compare the results to your self-evaluations.

_____ self-awareness

_____ objectivity in evaluating your self

_____ impulse control

_____ persistence

_____ zeal

_____ self-motivation

_____ empathy

_____ ability to predict others' emotions accurately

_____ social deftness

_____ sensitivity

_____ initiative

_____ trust in others

_____ respect for others

_____ sociability (desire to be with others)

_____ influence

_____ conflict resolution

_____ negotiation skills

_____ communication ability

_____ tact

_____ honesty

_____ integrity

_____ trustworthiness

_____ antagonizes other (inverse)

_____ gets into arguments (inverse)

_____ is overly evaluative and critical of others (inverse)

_____ must win an argument (inverse)

_____ gets angry easily (inverse)

_____ impatience (inverse)

_____ is arrogant (inverse)

Note. Adapted from Cherniss and Adler (2000).

with the career barrier more effectively, and strengthen their career resilience, insight, and identity. Ways organizations support emotional competencies are provided in Table 10.3.

CONCLUSIONS

There are all types of career barriers, and, indeed, what is a career barrier to one person may be an opportunity to another. However, some leaders feel vulnerable, perhaps only because they lack support from the organization, friends, and family. Leaders' reactions to career barriers depend on the situations, attributions for their cause, and emotional and physical responses. Leaders who focus on their symptoms and feelings are likely to be less successful in dealing with the barrier than those who are problem focused. Some problem-focused responses include trying harder, influencing others' expectations, justifying one's actions, persisting in the face of rejection, becoming part of a new network, and establishing new goals.

Executives may derail in their careers for several reasons. They may make poor decisions, perhaps based on insufficient or inaccurate information. They may have been transferred so often that they have never had to live with, and fix, problems they created. So they do not know how to deal with real problems

TABLE 10.3

Training for Emotional Competencies

- Assess leader's emotional intelligence and demonstrate that the more effective leaders (e.g., those with the better record of performance) are higher in emotional intelligence than the less effective leaders.

- Help leaders evaluate their personal strengths and limitations in dealing with negative emotions. Do so by seeking input from multiple sources.

- Provide leaders with feedback on their emotional intelligence as perceived by their coworkers (e.g., the extent to which they are perceived as caring and respectful of others).

- Help leaders understand what they can do to improve.

- Offer leaders chances to practice new behaviors. Give them frequent feedback on their results.

- Encourage team building by forming small groups where leaders can support and encourage each other as they change. This will have the spin-off benefit of building closer collegial relationships.

- Encourage leaders to think about how they have applied the competencies they are learning. Have them consider how they are using the new competencies to face barriers. Ask them to consider what affected their successful learning, in order to help them learn on their own in the future.

Note. Adapted from Cherniss and Goleman (1999).

when they arise. Ways to counteract career barriers are to get feedback early in one's career, test the accuracy of feedback, and find a coach or mentor, particularly people who have had to face a setback themselves.

One type of career barrier occurs when strengths become flaws—that is, ingredients to successful management at one time may not work in other situations. Immigrants face other career barriers. They experience discrimination, cultural differences, poor access to education, and low-level jobs. Even professionals who immigrate to other countries, in part because of better job prospects in the adopted country, not to mention political and religious freedom, may find they are not readily accepted in the workforce or the workplace.

In general, individuals need to develop resilience to cope with uncertainty and disappointing results. A component of resilience, emotional intelligence, suggests that competence is much more than knowledge and skill. Emotional intelligence involves self-awareness, impulse control, persistence, zeal, self-motivation, empathy, and sociability. These competencies can be learned over time, although some are more difficult to acquire.

This chapter has shown that career barriers can be learning opportunities. However, learning should be a continuous process. Major life and career changes (good and bad) prompt learning (as do everyday activities). The next chapter explores the idea of becoming a continuous learner to make the most from all circumstances and seek opportunities for learning.

11

Becoming a Continuous Learner

This chapter is about the need for leaders to become continuous learners. The chapter defines what this means, outlines elements of continuous learning, describes informal learning opportunities, and examines how the organizational environment supports and encourages continuous learning. Moreover, it shows how work groups and organizations, as well as leaders, evolve and grow continuously, and in the process, support a development-oriented organizational culture.

THE NEED FOR CONTINUOUS LEARNING

Consider how organizational change demands continuous learning and how continuous learning is integral to operating a business. A good example is the case of Cisco Systems and its CEO, John Chambers. (See chap. 5, this volume, for a description of Chambers' leadership development strategy.) The company's prime focus is customer satisfaction ("Cisco—From 3,000 employees to 30,000 employees in 5 years," 2000). Chambers spends 70% of his time with customers and his own employees in order to stay in touch with front line issues. In frequent meetings, he queries employees for ways the firm can improve. He learns about what is not working and what can be done about it. He uses a Web-based data collection and analysis process to track customer satisfaction. He studies customer satisfaction data regularly, examining the data by country, city, key customer, and individual sales representative. Once a month, Chambers attends a breakfast for employees with birthdays that month. He quizzes them for 1½ hours about anything and everything, searching for ideas for improvement. This is a continuous quest for knowledge about what is happening in the firm and the industry, what new products and services are needed, and ways the company can do better. Continuous learning does not happen apart from the operations of the business but is

233

integral to it, and at Cisco, the CEO models this learning process as a hallmark of his management style. Continuous learning is not a training course. Also, it is modeled right from the top of the organization.

WHAT IS CONTINUOUS LEARNING?

At first blush, the concept of continuous learning sounds obvious and trivial. Good leaders recognize that they are learning all the time. This does not happen in a formal classroom or workshop setting, but everyday in the course of daily business, especially in solving problems and dealing with thorny (often interpersonal) issues. However, how often do these leaders stop to think about what they have learned and try out new leadership strategies? If the leaders are not mindful about what they have learned, and maybe more importantly, what they need to learn, then they may miss opportunities for being more effective when business conditions change.

On a deeper level, the idea of continuous learning is daunting. It implies that a person is always learning; it is as if the individual is always in school, never fully graduated and ready to commence life and be fully productive. More accurately, it implies that learning is a personal responsibility that never ends. It must continue because the environment is always changing, and leaders cannot be effective unless they recognize and understand these changes and learn how to respond to them and, indeed, create them. This is a product of experience. Learning accelerates this experience, providing a foundation that must be constantly strengthened to support the weight of new challenges and initiatives. Some leaders need to learn more than others, and they need to learn more quickly, because their environments are changing more rapidly. Others have less to worry about because they are in industries that do not change much over time.

Continuous learning is important to leadership development for several reasons. As discussed in the first chapter, the rapid pace of technological and economic change, along with the expansion of the global economy, have increased the demands of the leadership role. There is more to learn, and there is a need to learn it faster than ever before. Organizations expect their leaders (and increasingly all managers) to diagnose their own development needs and take responsibility for meeting these learning needs.

London and Smither (1999a) defined continuous learning as "a self-initiated, discretionary, planned, and proactive pattern of formal or informal activities that are sustained over time for the purpose of applying or transporting knowledge for career development" (p. 81). They outlined three stages of continuous learning: *PreLearning* is the readiness stage. This occurs as leaders realize that there is a gap between their capabilities and the requirements of their role now or there is likely to be a gap in the future because of the changing nature of the business. *Learning* occurs as leaders gain knowledge, skills, and experience to reduce the gap between their capabilities and current or anticipated role requirements. *Application of learning* occurs as the leader uses newly required knowledge or skills. Continuous learning is not complete until the learning is used.

Continuous learners cumulate and integrate knowledge and skills over time. Consider thefollowing types of continuous learning:

- *Self-Initiated*: Continuous learning is self-regulated and managed. Leaders decide what they need, when they need it, and how to get it. They initiate and maintain their own learning processes. Organizations may provide the enabling resources, and, indeed, leaders are likely to be in a position to allocate resources for their own learning as well as resources to support subordinates' learning.
- *Discretionary*: Leaders recognize the value of continuous learning, and they integrate it into their daily lives. They set aside time for reading, attending workshops, or just thinking about what new ideas, knowledge, skills, and behaviors they have learned.
- *Planned*: There is a deliberate, conscious nature to continuous learning. The continuous learner formulates some objectives and sets out to fill them through one or more means.
- *Proactive*: The continuous learner needs to maintain energy and enthusiasm for learning over time. Although it may be easy to let things ride or rest on one's laurels, continuous learners must go out of their way to take time for learning.
- *Sustained Over Time*: Learning is not a one-time event. It may be incremental, in that it occurs slowly and deliberately over time. Alternatively, it may be episodic in that it occurs at designated times (e.g., attending a workshop or taking time for online, self-paced training) or during a major, sudden change (e.g., a corporate merger or takeover). It may also be frame breaking, in that the learning results in major new insights and directions for behavior change.
- *Cumulative*: Continuous learning means that the knowledge and skills acquired are constantly growing and developing, strengthening the foundation for further new insights. New ideas and knowledge pave the way for refinements and new frames of reference that would not have been possible without the prior learning.
- *Integrated*: Continuous learners do not segment their learning. They link new concepts together to form even newer concepts. In addition, they apply what they learned in one setting to other settings.

Continuous learning may be *instrumental* in that it has a specific goal or immediate purpose (e.g., to handle a particular problem), or it may be *developmental* in that it has a long-term focus with the intention to enhance the leader's ability to cope with whatever challenges may emerge in the future.

The learning may be *formal* and occur over a long time period, as when a senior manager attends an intensive executive MBA program for 2 years. Formal learning may also be short-term, as when an executive attends a week long leadership development course at a training center. Short term learning often focuses on assessment and planning for further development, or it concentrates on specific new techniques or styles of leadership, giving the participants a chance for practice and feedback. Learning may also be *informal*, as when leaders learn by observing others or trying new behaviors on the job, often driven by demanding situations for which old responses and strategies do not work.

Informal learning occurs in the process of conducting daily business. For instance, learning occurs when leaders receive guidance from their coworkers, debate others, listen to what others think of their ideas, observe others, participate on a project team, do something new and different, and/or make decisions. Learning also comes when leaders make mistakes, help their coworkers learn something new, coach their coworkers through the learning process, and become a mentor to others, helping them determine what to learn and how to go about it. Learning may not be the principal purpose of these activities, but it is a valuable outcome. As such, leaders may be able to create situations on the job that enhance opportunities for learning. Consider opportunities that leaders can create that would both help their department and be a learning experience for them: They might form a team to develop a new product or service, method, or procedure, volunteer to work on such a team, ask for a special assignment that will allow them to learn a new skill or apply new knowledge, try out a new skill on the job, experiment with new ways of doing their job, or find someone to teach, coach, or advise them.

Learning occurs as people deal with challenges and problems. Such learning is often unconscious and tacit, meaning that people are not necessarily fully aware of what they are learning while they are learning it or after they have learned it (Marsick, 2000). Mindful learning, on the other hand, can be merely acquiring facts and data. In contrast, *transformational learning* (which parallels the concept of transformational leadership described in the first chapter) entails thinking critically. It means reviewing experiences so that tacitly learned skills, behaviors, and personal characteristics come to the forefront as the individual considers what was learned and how. In considering information acquired, transformational learning means thinking critically not only about the truth of "facts," but also the bias and intentions of those who were involved in "creating the facts" (Marsick, 2000). Transformational learning can occur in the process of problem solving (i.e., seeking and using facts and theories to address an uncertain situation).

Collaborative learning can facilitate the process of transformation in informal settings, that is, situations not designed as structured learning opportunities. Team members bring different perspectives and areas of expertise to bear on a common problem. Each team member critically evaluates others' contributions and learns about the value of their own perspective from others. The danger is that this could lead to unresolved conflict, but the motivation to accomplish a common goal encourages members to learn from each other as they apply their critical analyses to a constructive resolution.

Situational Demands Encourage Learning

Leaders are likely to learn quickly when they encounter unexpected or unusual situations. Their natural tendency may be to do what worked before in tight spots. However, insightful leaders may recognize when formerly tried and true responses are not likely to work. Leaders with less insight, or those facing especially ambiguous situations that are hard to diagnose, are likely to learn the hard way by failing, at least initially. Situations that elicit rapid learning are those that capture the leader's attention and require some action. In particular, learning is most likely to occur when the leader experiences a demanding task, there is an element of surprise, the problem cannot be ignored (some action is necessary), an immediate solution is not evident, and/or the leader feels in control (has the capability to take action) (London & Smither, 1999b; Nonaka, 1994).

Allport (1946) maintained that positive development emerges not just because of what people do, but also because of the effects of their behavior on the environment. Later, White (1959) referred to this as *effectance motivation*, which arises from making a difference to others or to an organization. This is similar to Maslow's (1968) concept of *peak experience* and Csikszentmihalyi's (1993) concept of *flow*. Building on these ideas, Lubinski and Benbow (2000) hypothesized that the way to enhance people's development of effectance motivation is to match their dominant abilities with their interests and focus development toward a corresponding goal.

The implication for leadership development is that organizations should concentrate on developing managers' and executives' behaviors that rely on their most salient talents, and finding areas or niches in the organization within which they are likely to be reinforced for succeeding. The individuals will experience effectance motivation. By the way, effectance motivation is incompatible with feelings of low self-esteem or depression (Lubinski & Benbow, 2000).

Executives need to continuously fine-tune their skills and competencies in areas that match their unique attributes. Instead of being generalists, they need to develop areas that are specific and that they and others can recognize as specific talents and associated achievements. This does not mean setting one main, difficult goal for purposes of skill development, but rather to make incremental learning the goal. Instead, development should concentrate on doing the same thing a little better every day. This is the Japanese concept of *kaizen* (London, 1999a).

Developing true excellence takes time (Lubinski & Benbow, 2000). There is no fast track. It requires constant learning and slow, yet observable, improvement. Moreover, it requires demonstrating that the improved behavior leads to enhanced outcomes. Leaders need to see that they are making a difference.

Changing Organizations and Opportunities for Learning

New organizational structures, team configurations, and organizational alignments and enterprises provide learning opportunities for both leaders and members. These emerging business environments require the ability to create enterprises, transform employees' mind-sets and behaviors, adapt to situational changes, and act in a principled, diplomatic way. Leaders may move from one type of organization or leadership position to another, and learn and refine skills, acquire new knowledge, and establish a track record of successes that leads to further responsibilities and opportunities. Certainly, all successful leaders are not so nimble that they can move easily into very different situations. However, situations do change and leaders need insight into the changing requirements and skill demands. Table 11.1 provides some examples of these changing leadership opportunities and some of the associated challenges and competency requirements.

Note that these opportunities may arise as leaders move between industries (from biotech to computer, health care, transportation, or consumer products, etc.), as Louis Gerstner moved from the head of RJR Nabisco to become the CEO of IBM. This imposes additional challenges to understand industry norms and trends and conduct continuous environmental scanning to keep up with events and developments. Leaders who move between industries need to recognize the challenges and competencies imposed by the nature of the organizational structure, team, and changes, such as those listed in Table 11.1.

Resistance to Continuous Learning: The Authoritarian Mentality

Altemeyer (1999) argued that authoritarians are less likely than most people to exhibit self-awareness. Authoritarians tend to inflate their own strengths and dismiss their failings. As a result, they are not likely to be open to learning new things about themselves. They resist change and are not receptive to keeping up with environmental changes and skill requirements. They know it all now!

Authoritarians are high in submission, aggression, and conventionalism. They tend to trust authorities too much; be punitive and hostile toward persons who attack them in the name of authority; conform to the opinions of others; be prejudiced against people on racial, ethnic, and nationalistic grounds; hold contradictory ideas; uncritically accept insufficient evidence that supports their be-

TABLE 11.1

Learning Opportunities from New Organizational Forms and Structures

Opportunities	Some Key Challenges	Some Key Competencies (Behaviors and Skills) to Learn and Develop
NEW STRUCTURES		
Flat organizational structures (large numbers of direct reports).	Direct reports need autonomy and responsibility. Overall organizational purpose needs to be clear.	Communicate frequently and clearly. Recognize the value of others' ideas. Convey trust and respect for direct reports. Monitor processes and outcomes; don't overcontrol or micromanage.
Matrix arrangements.	Gain cooperation without direct supervisory control, communication is key.	Convey mission and generate commitment. Recognize interdependencies in functions and tasks. Trust others to carry out their assignments. Recognize different vested interests. Make clear assignments and coordinate tasks.
Virtual organizations—loose confederations of associates in different locations and organizations working on joint projects (e.g., a consortium of scientists around the country or globe cooperating to complete a scientific experiment or make an important discovery; the human genome project).	Linkages are needed between independent participants; these need to be established and maintained over time. Frequent communication is needed; different modes of communication will be required. Participants, funding sources, and perhaps the public need regular progress updates. Participants' interest and motivation need to be maintained.	Create flexible structures (roles and responsibilities). Become familiar with multiple communication technologies. Monitor the environment (competitors, related disciplines, funding sources). Lead by persuasion and influence. Assess, and be sensitive to, participants' reactions and feelings; recognize others' accomplishments. Share information and data. Deal with uncertainties. Resolve ambiguities.
Temporary organizations for large-scale infrastructure projects (e.g., building a bridge).	Large numbers of experts from different disciplines must be recruited. Incentives will be needed to attract and retain the best talent. The project should provide training and development so recruits benefit from the experience. Organizational structures should be clear yet flexible to meet needs of different stages of the project.	Inspire commitment to the mission. Establish values and organizational culture (values that affect how people are treated and decisions are made). Value others' inputs. Create a culture that welcomes, trains, and integrates newcomers. Be adaptable and patient—able to respond to unforeseen events and delays. Recognize others' accomplishments and celebrate successes as phases of the project are completed.

Opportunities	Some Key Challenges	Some Key Competencies (Behaviors and Skills) to Learn and Develop
TEAM MANAGEMENT		
Project teams and task forces (e.g., for development of enterprise-wide data systems).	Top-level buy-in must be attained and maintained to ensure that representatives from different departments to the project have the time and motivation to participate. Roles need to be clarified. Participants need to see the big picture (overall purpose for the project) as well as understand their own role.	Communicate frequently and clearly. Build commitment and overcome cynicism. Provide needed resources and support mechanisms. Establish and gain agreement to time lines and due dates. Recognize and help resolve conflicts. Seek feedback.
Process steward (e.g., oversee data quality, corporate-wide marketing coordination, manufacturing and distribution system).	Interest and involvement need to be elicited from representatives of all relevant departments. Representatives' roles and expectations need to be defined. Representatives need to agree on indexes to be used for assessing quality and tracking progress.	Ability to clarify purpose and methods of the process. Recognize and communicate overall corporate goals and individual departmental needs. Understand and use appropriate data gathering and analysis methods to monitor process. Demonstrate personal expertise and role as process leader. Use influence to maintain commitment and involvement.
Enterprise-wide data systems development and implementation (e.g., a new human resource or finance data system for all departments using distributed, PC/intranet-based technology).	Purpose needs to be clear. Buy-in needs to be established across the enterprise, top to bottom. Functional and technical experts need to be identified and involved. Capabilities of the new software must be discovered; fit-gap analyses are needed to determine organizational requirements that will be met by the software and requirements that must be met in other ways. Policies that will be built into the software need to be reviewed and, in some cases, established for the first time. Responsibilities for development and ongoing ownership of data sets and tables need to be assigned. Training needs must be determined and met; users need to understand what they have to do and how their piece of the system fits with the whole. Progress should be communicated and successes should be celebrated.	Maintain enthusiasm. Develop partnerships with external consultants and internal technical support staff and functional users who contribute to system development. Keep development focused and moving. Allocate resources in relation to need and recognize participants' other responsibilities. Be sensitive to individuals' energy, time availability, capabilities, and commitment to the project. Recognize individuals' contributions to the project and accomplishments (goals achieved). Attend to and revise organizational structures and assignments as needed.

Opportunities	Some Key Challenges	Some Key Competencies (Behaviors and Skills) to Learn and Develop
Continuous quality improvement team.	Involvement needs to be elicited from relevant departments. Team needs to stay focused on steps in the organization's quality improvement process (e.g., identifying customers, collecting data about customers, identifying opportunities for improvement, examining process and barriers, selecting improvement areas, making changes, and holding the gains). All representatives must have a chance to participate actively.	Understand customer satisfaction. Understand customer-supplier relationships. Focus on work process across functional departments. Use data collection and analysis skills to assess customer satisfaction. Apply experimental methods to evaluate effects of process changes. Encourage, respect, and reward team members' participation. Welcome and integrate new team members. Know how to facilitate group process.
Geographically dispersed teams (especially global teams).	Multimedia are needed for communication. All team members need to be involved. Methods are needed to evaluate team members contributions.	Communicate frequently using multiple technologies to keep people informed. Be sensitive to resource availability.
Global executive position—expatriate assignment.	Executive may be viewed as a stranger and interloper. Executive needs to deal with the unfamiliar (possibly including a different language).	Be culturally sensitive, respectful of differences in values and behavioral norms. Welcome new experiences. Maintain ethical principles. Practice business diplomacy.
Intercultural domestic team.	Conflicts need to be recognized and managed. Diversity should be taken advantage of for maximum value to the enterprise.	Welcome differences. Be sensitive to differences. Handle conflict patiently.
NEW VENTURES		
Start-ups.	Operations are likely to be fast paced, highly competitive, and financially tight. Employees will need to put in long hours and high energy. The prime reward for key employees may be long-term equity. Employees may have little loyalty and be ready to jump ship to the next promising start-up. Need for shared values. Risk taking should be rewarded. Need to avoid temptation to cut corners in dealings with others.	Monitor the environment. Maintain high energy. Garner resources (e.g., venture capital). Seek feedback. Seek new knowledge. Open to new ideas. Publicly recognize others for their contributions. Be willing to take reasonable risks. Act ethically in making deals and treating employees, customers, and suppliers.
Small entrepreneurial venture within a large company.	Need to transform employees' mind-set from following standards to risk taking. Avoid recreating bureaucracy. Need to reward risk taking.	See the whole and the parts. Overcome and work within bureaucracy of parent company—work through bureaucracy when necessary. Willing to reward creativity and risk taking.

241

Opportunities	Some Key Challenges	Some Key Competencies (Behaviors and Skills) to Learn and Develop
E-commerce.	Venture capital needs to be arranged. The firm needs name recognition, marketing, order and distribution methods, and other procedures that utilize new computer technologies and networks. Staff needs to be current with evolving technologies. Technically sophisticated staff, who are likely to be young, need to work effectively with business-savvy staff who are likely to be older; different contributions need to be appreciated and rewarded.	Think creatively. Take risks. Evaluate the market (competition and market indicators). Data-focused: Establish process measures for continuous calibration of quality and outcome measures to track success.
Joint Ventures.	The venture needs a common mission. Participants need to share values.	Value differences. Recognize others' opinions. Share responsibilities and recognition. Accept feedback. Trust others to do their jobs Is even-tempered in crises and conflicts. Work effectively within and across organizational boundaries.
Mergers.	Existing organizational structures need to be analyzed. Differences in organizational cultures need to be recognized and respected. Financial and market goals need to be established and communicated. Individual goals need to be aligned with business goals. Common set of goals and values need to be clarified.	Manage change. Recognize and resolve conflict. Show sensitivity to different organizational traditions. Foster shared mission and new culture. Focus on new whole organization/break down boundaries or allow components to maintain identities (depending on organizational goals and commitments).

liefs; believe they have no personal failings; and easily erase guilt over their misdeeds (Altemeyer, 1999). They are not inclined to examine ideas, including their own (Altemeyer, 1996). They have no problem using double standards in their thinking. Also, high authoritarians lack self-insight.

Those who are low or moderate on authoritarianism scales usually can predict their own scores. That is, they know they are low or moderate. However, high authoritarians rarely realize they will have a high score (Altemeyer, 1987). They will think they are models of rationality and self-understanding—more so than most people. When asked to write down, anonymously, things they do not like to admit about themselves, they are likely to say that no such thing exists (Altemeyer, 1996).

Authoritarians recognize some things about themselves. They know they are more religious than most other people. They realize that they are fairly hostile toward groups for whom, they believe, there is social support for hostility. When asked to complete a self-description about themselves, their responses are ego-enhancing and filled with socially desirable responses. They want to present a wholesome image of themselves to others, even when they are responding anonymously. So, for instance, they report that they think and act much better than they actually do. For instance, they tend to believe that they reason things out well and seldom make wrong inferences from facts. They believe they have no failings that they are reluctant to think about. In short, they run away from unpleasant truths about themselves. They shy away from feedback, especially if they fear the results will be negative. However, if they are assured the results will be positive, they welcome the feedback (Altemeyer, 1996).

Some Insight About Authoritarians. They do not decipher things for themselves, but rather copy what authorities believe. Critical analysis is necessary for self-understanding, and high authoritarians memorize rather than analyze. They surround themselves with people who have the same viewpoints and who can validate their opinions (Newcomb, 1961, cited in Altemeyer, 1999). By interacting with people who say nothing but good things about them, they are not likely to discover personal failings or recognize they are relatively prejudiced or others in the reference group are prejudiced. Authoritarians are highly defensive. They are afraid to discover unpleasant truths about themselves, in the same way they fear people who are different from them (Altemeyer, 1999).

This is not to say that people who are low in authoritarianism do not have their own blind spots and defenses (Altemeyer, 1996, 1999). They tend to show more integrity, consistency, and fairness. Also, they are more willing to face negative feedback about themselves and to recognize unfavorable aspects of their character. Research is needed to explore what their blind spots may be. Perhaps they have trouble realizing their lack of aggressiveness limits their effectiveness in supervising others or coordinating projects.

A Continuous Learning Mentality

Leaders who have a continuous learning mentality are always seeking out new information about themselves and their environment. They are constantly attuned to evaluating their learning gaps, determining what they do not know, and then are willing to spend the time and money to acquire the knowledge and skills they need to fill these gaps. These leaders want feedback. They seek it and use it to set development goals. Then they actively find ways to learn what they need to know, apply that knowledge, and track their progress.

Leaders who are especially good at doing this are people who have positive self-images but not big egos. They are not threatened by the discovery that there is something they do not know, but rather are challenged by it. They do not have an ego that blinds them to their weaknesses. In addition, they are sensitive to how other people see them and recognize they can learn from this feedback. This feedback may be direct input (perhaps in the form of 360-degree survey results, a performance review, or simply direct discussion with colleague around the question, "How am I doing?"). Alternatively, the feedback may come when leaders keenly observe the way others react to them.

Leaders can learn to be self-developers. They can learn reflective techniques for self-assessment and recognizing what they have learned. They can use self-management strategies to establish and implement plans for their development.

Continuous learners are often missionaries for continuous learning. They contribute to the developmental, feedback-oriented culture in their organizations by providing the resources for others to understand organizational changes, diagnose their own skill and knowledge gaps, and acquire the information and training they need to meet the changing needs of the business and enhance their performance.

EMPOWERED SELF-DEVELOPMENT

London and Smither (1999b) discussed how organizations can encourage self-development by providing nonthreatening performance feedback, ensuring behavioral choices for learning, and rewarding participation in learning activities. Their approach, shown in Fig. 11.1, is a motivational model of self-development. Organizational changes lead to the need for an empowering work environment. An empowered work environment is one that recognizes the problems facing leaders, supports informational and performance feedback, and presents choices with as clear consequences as possible (i.e., so leaders have a good idea of what will happen if they do or do not act in a certain way). The model suggests that a continuous learning organizational culture supports self-development (i.e., feedback seeking, goal setting, and tracking progress), especially for people whose characteristics predispose them to

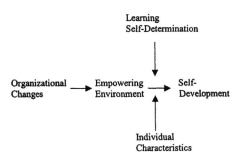

Learning
Self-Determination

Organizational   →   Empowering   →   Self-
Changes   Environment   Development

Individual
Characteristics

Variables in the Model

Organizational Changes

- less controlling and bureaucratic
- individuals ready to make a contribution
- flexible organizational structure
- unstructured career paths
- press for continuous quality improvement
- need for sensitivity to changing customer demands
- continuous technological change
- demanding tasks that require action
- unexpected problems that individuals cannot ignore
- problems with no immediate solutions

Organizational and Managerial
Support for Self-Development

- informational performance feedback
- availability of choices and clarity concerning consequences
- reinforcement that increases resilience and self-efficacy
- empathy
- a demanding task
- reason to act
- core values that inspire employees
- dialogues focus on strategic issues and proactive responses
- clear communication of expectations

Individual Characteristics

- openness to experience
- conscientiousness
- self-efficacy
- education and ability
- public self-consciousness
- self-esteem
- need for control
- uncertainty orientation

Learning Self-Determination

- self-dialogue (self-generated feedback)
- mental imagery, affective states, beliefs
- thought patterns
- increasing self-efficacy

Self-Development Behaviors

- seeking and using feedback
- setting development goals
- engaging in developmental activities
- tracking progress.

FIG. 11.1.   A motivatonal model of self-development

self-determination. Leaders can become more receptive to self-development by teaching them constructive thought processes and by demonstrating that continuous learners are rewarded because they are more likely to be top performers.

Self-Determination

Edward Deci, a social psychologist at the University of Rochester, formulated a theory of self-determination that explains when individuals are likely to take initiative and be self-motivated (see, e.g., Deci & Ryan, 1991; Deci, Egharari, Patrick, & Leone, 1994). A leader is likely to adopt self-control mechanisms and become self-regulated in learning and other behaviors because people are naturally proactive when it comes to their own self-interest for positive outcomes and intrinsically challenging tasks. Self-regulation is about how people take in social values and extrinsic consequences (rewards and punishments) and progressively transform them into personal values and intrinsic motivation (see chap. 3, this volume; Ryan & Deci, 2000). This is encouraged by conditions that foster autonomy and competence and is diminished by conditions that control behavior and hinder feelings of effectiveness. People are more likely to make social values and responsibilities their own when they are in an environment that allows self-control and choice, increases skill building (to make them feel—and actually be—more effective), and builds stronger social bonds to meet relatedness needs. It leads to greater commitment, effort, and ultimately, high quality performance.

Role of the Leader's Manager in Supporting the Leader's Continuous Learning. A leader is more likely to be self-determined as a continuous learner if the leader's manager provides a rationale for learning that the leader finds personally meaningful. As a result, the leader values the possibility of positive outcomes from learning and improved performance, or the leader sees the value of learning to the organization and to being assigned increasingly challenging assignments. The senior manager also supports a subordinate executive's continuous learning by acknowledging the executive's feelings and perspective (recognizing that learning takes time and it is not always easy; and realizing the leader has to have the latitude to try new behaviors and take some risks, even if the initial results are not positive). The senior manager helps support continuous learning by conveying that the executive has choices—that is, several possible courses of action and the discretion to decide which direction to follow in making decisions about which course of action to follow. As a consequence, decisions become learning experiences. In addition, senior managers support continuous learning by providing relevant and timely information about organizational change and conditions, as well as constructive performance feedback (i.e., feedback that is not evaluative, threatening, or compares the leader to others, but simply states the effects of the leader's behaviors, as described in chap. 6, this volume). The senior manager supports continuous learn-ing by minimizing pressures, thereby giving executives freedom to experiment without feeling that they have only one chance to succeed.

Role of the Organization in Supporting Leaders' Continuous Learning. A leader is more likely to be self-determined as a continuous learner if the organization expects managers to be coaches and advocates, espe-cially for new employees (indeed, may assign new employees at all levels to more experienced leaders who can be coaches and mentors). Also, the organizational culture can support continuous learning by allowing and indeed encouraging direct lines of communication between people regardless of function, depart-ment, or level (makes it okay for people at any level to contact anyone else they need to speak to regardless of the individual's level or position). Another way to support continuous learning is to implement a performance management pro-cess that expects leaders who will be responsible for meeting objectives to have a role in setting the objectives (i.e., objectives are set by those who must make them happen). Support also comes when the organization establishes a climate that allows any employee, regardless of position, to assume a leadership role be-cause the employee has special knowledge or experience, is able to coordinate activities, or is talented in other ways and is the best person for the job even if not yet at a high organizational level.

Other sources of organizational support are to expect leaders (and indeed all employees) to make continuous learning a part of their jobs, expect managers to be coaches and developers, hold leaders accountable for their own continuous learning just as they are for other aspects of performance, and measure and re-ward leaders for learning (in addition to the positive effects of learning on their job performance and organizational outcomes). In addition, supportive organi-zations reward leaders who identify areas for future job requirements and impli-cations for needed skill updates, set development goals that reflect needed knowledge and skill structures, participate in learning activities, ask for feed-back to test goal relevance, and track progress (London & Mone, 1999; London & Smither, 1999b).

Table 11.2 offers some questions to help leaders assess the extent to which they feel their organization supports self-development and the extent to which they are open to continuous learning.

LEARNING ORGANIZATIONS

Chapter 6 in this volume explained how an organization can establish a *feedback culture,* or an environment that supports and encourages feedback for learning and development. In the process, the organization itself learns and grows. Orga-nizational learning is a metaphor stemming from an understanding of individual learning. The concept of the learning organization was popularized by Senge

TABLE 11.2
Self-Assessment Questions for Leaders to Evaluate Their Learning Environment and Their Openness to Continuous Learning

Assess Your Self-Development Environment

The following are questions that leaders can ask themselves or that they can ask about their managers to determine the extent to which they feel empowered to be a continuous learner:

1. Do you receive feedback about your job performance? How often? Do you find this helpful or not? Why? Is this typical in your organization?

2. Does your manager suggest ways you can develop? Does your manager provide opportunities for you to participate in developmental experiences?

3. Is learning and development something that happens primarily in training programs off the job? Are you continuously given new assignments and job experiences for purposes of learning and development?

4. Are you evaluated on how much you have learned during the last year?

5. Are there consequences for making a mistake, doing the wrong thing, or not meeting your performance goals? How severe are the consequences?

6. Does your manager ensure that information is available to help you track your job performance and goal accomplishment?

7. In evaluating your performance, does your manager compare your results with preset goals or standards? Does your manager compare you to other managers who are doing similar work to you? Does your manager compare your current performance to your past performance to see areas of improvement, decline, or stability?

8. Does your manager inspire you to do your best? Does your manager communicate a clear sense of mission for you and the department?

9. Does your manager convey to you a strong and clear set of values in how work should be done? Does your manager have a code of proper conduct?

10. Does your manager discuss with you the goals of the organization and how the organization is changing?

11. Does your manager encourage you to get involved in setting work plans and departmental objectives?

12. Does your manager encourage your initiative and creativity?

Are You a Continuous Learner?

Next, here are some self-assessment questions to help leaders determine if their learning is self-directed.

1. When you receive feedback about your performance from your manager, would you just as soon not listen?

2. Do you tend to compare yourself to how others are performing?

3. How often do you think about how well you are doing on the job? Daily? Weekly? Once in a while?

4. How carefully do you look for information about how well you are doing? Do you go out of your way to seek it, or do you take it as it comes?

5. Are you likely to ask you manager or others to critique your performance? Are you inclined to ask your manager or others what you can do to improve on the job?

6. Are you likely to ask your manager for information about the organization?

7. Do you set development goals for yourself, or do you wait for direction from your immediate manager?

8. Are you likely to volunteer for new job assignments, or do you wait for job assignments to come your way?

9. Do you monitor their career progress closely, or don't you spend much time thinking about your career progress?

10. If you become (or are) discontent with your job or career progress, are you likely to take steps to change jobs or career directions or are you likely to wait and see what happens?

(1990). Organizations learn through the learning of the individuals in them, particularly as they develop shared mental models of ways to interact and communicate effectively (Liu & Vince, 1999).

Pfeffer and Sutton (2000) observed that organizations do not excel at learning. Prime examples are companies in which some units are more profitable and efficient than others—for instance, fast food chains that live with large differences in their units' profitability, or oil companies with one refinery that is three times as efficient as another. According to Pfeffer and Sutton, companies cannot sustain a competitive edge simply from what they know. They have to put knowledge into action. Somehow, however, they get lax or fixated on doing things the way they always have—the way that was once successful. Barriers to action include a pervasive atmosphere of fear and distrust. Leaders are so afraid to make mistakes that they are hesitant to voice their concerns or admit to their problems. Ways to overcome this path to mediocrity are to praise and promote people who are willing to deliver bad news and who are willing to talk about, and learn from, their mistakes. Leaders who try new initiatives should be rewarded. Those who humiliate others should be banished. Internal competition is divisive. Instead of encouraging employees to pursue personal gain, they should focus on larger, shared goals. Pfeffer and Sutton went so far as to eliminate employee recognition awards, public rankings of top performers, merit raises from small pools, and contests among departments or individuals. These are all situations in which there are few winners and many losers. Instead, people should focus on higher goals by working cooperatively and identifying and developing opportunities for expanding markets and profits (Andrews, 2000a).

Marsick (2000) explored the core organizational practices that allow the organization, and the individuals within them, to continuously grow and develop. These organizations create opportunities for continuous learning, promote inquiry and dialogue, encourage collaboration and team learning, and/or create systems to communicate and spread the learning. They may also empower people to work on a common vision for the organization, or link the organization to its environment through partnerships, joint projects with other institutions, and simply sensitivity to others' interests outside the organization.

In addition, Marsick (2000) considered the following three ways to enhance organization learning:

1. *Critical reflection.* Because learning often occurs tacitly as a result of experiences, critical reflection draws out the knowledge learned by explicating and then questioning underlying values and assumptions. Group members may be asked to describe how they made a decision and then dissect the process to explore the reasons and assumptions.

2. *Collaboration.* Group learning occurs as team members gather and share new ideas and models of how they operate. In the process, team members recognize new perspectives, particularly those that challenge their original viewpoints. This leads them to reframe the way they process information and draw conclusions. Essentially, this is an iterative cycle of data gathering, sharing, reflection, action, and further reflection. This is facilitated by effective communication about perceptions of changes in the environment. Methods are necessary that provide frequent, accurate feedback about the changing environment and about the skills and contributions of specific people. Frequent and open feedback is especially important in cross-functional, cross-organization level groups that were created explicitly to create new knowledge and innovations (cf. Nonaka & Takeuchi, 1995).

3. *Social Capital.* This is the trust people need to reflect critically, collaborate, and communicate. It is the values and norms that members share for beginning reliably and honestly (Fukuyama, 1999). Mutual trust is likely to be challenged in the normal course of group and organizational process as conflicts arise, differing interests are negotiated, and organizational changes occur that seem to break social promises and contracts.

A target for continuous organizational and individual learning is to foster *learning communities.* These are organizational and group environments in which members share information and ideas, and develop a sense of self-mastery and empowerment from modeling and observing others. The group members (i.e., the leaders, managers, and employees) develop a better sense of their own self-efficacy in the face of difficult problems and conflicts. These coping behaviors are built on mutual understanding, frequent communication, and continuously learning new skills to deal with life's challenges (Bandura, 1977; Marsick, 2000).

Organizational Learning in Joint Ventures

The success of joint ventures requires organizational learning, particularly if they involve different organizational and national cultures. Child (1994), who studied joint ventures in China, identified three types of learning and change: (a) *technical learning*—the acquisition of new techniques, such as Total Quality Management; (b) *systemic learning*—the introduction and operation of new systems and procedures, such as production control and budgeting; and (c) *strategic learning*—senior managers developing common mind-sets about criteria for business success.

Liu and Vince (1999) emphasized the importance of taking into account the cultural context in which learning occurs. This requires being sensitive to the effect of cultural and institutional constraints on learning and identifying the defensive routines and avoidance strategies that inhibit learning and change. They also studied Western–Chinese joint ventures, and discovered that Chinese managers' patterns of behavior in joint ventures tend to demonstrate their dependency on higher authority in decision making, their reluctance to assume responsibility, their avoidance of risk taking, and their poor communication with other departments and organizations. Although these patterns are national in Chinese organizations, Liu and Vince noted that Western managers may see them as problems to be solved. However, Western managers who try to force their Chinese counterparts to change their behavior are likely to meet resistance. They assume the Chinese managers are the ones who need to change. In one case, a joint venture experienced high turnover of Western managers who were brought in by the Western partner. These managers found that their Chinese colleagues did not meet their commitments. In meetings, they would intimate their agreement to proposal, at least by not saying no. However, after the meetings, they would take no action. In general, the Chinese managers did not initiate proposals. Also, they tended to conceal problems until they became really serious. The Western managers were frustrated by how long it took to get things done.

Liu and Vince (1999) pointed out ways that organizational learning can be enhanced by international joint ventures. In particular, organizational learning is an intercultural activity that requires sensitivity to differences in cultural values and the transferability of management theory and practice to the new culture. (It may not transfer!) Learning is a two-way process; both partners need to learn, and it should not be assumed that "knowledge" needs to be imposed on the other. The managers involved need to work through their anxieties and uncertainties rather than avoid them; this requires creating an environment for dialogue. The managers need to face the conflicts that underlie their attempts to work together. Overall, managers from all cultures in the venture need to recognize that they are engaging in mutual or collective learning and this is a part of making the joint venture work.

CONCLUSIONS

Leaders need to be continuous learners. Their jobs demand it, and their careers would be dead without it—at least, their careers would probably have an early demise. Indeed, this is what happens to some executives, as the last chapter showed. Continuous learning is a frame of mind and a set of behaviors that contribute to ongoing professional renewal and creation of opportunities. Self-regulation (the topic of chap. 3, this volume) is important to continuous learning. Continuous learners are self-directed and proactive about assessing the gaps in their knowledge and skills and finding and taking advantage of learning resources. Some leaders do this because they have a specific business or career goal in mind. Others do it as a way to enhance their readiness to achieve success in the future, no matter what challenges emerge. Also, they find the learning experience itself challenging. Unexpected and major changes are an important opportunity for learning. However, this is learning the hard way. A more systematic, ongoing approach to self-development is less stressful and may open unexpected avenues to job and career success.

Despite these obvious advantages to continuous learning, some leaders resist it. These authoritarian-type personalities usually have inflated egos and are not receptive to new ideas. The converse is transformational learners, or critical thinkers, who think about what they learned from their experiences and informal learning opportunities. They take time to digest what they learned, integrate that knowledge with other information, and build on it over time, especially in working in groups.

Organizational leaders, from the CEO on down, can empower themselves and their people to engage in self-development. The organization provides the enabling resources, such as 360-degree feedback results, coaching, training programs, technological access to online self-paced learning, and, of course, new job experiences. Organizations themselves can be continuous learners. The learning organization is one that is constantly evolving in response to changing conditions and requirements, benefiting from technological advances and fresh ideas from newly hired employees at all organizational levels. In the process, learning organizations create opportunities to encourage its leaders and employees to be continuous learners.

12

Conclusion: Becoming a Principled, Diplomatic Leader

This book has been about how leaders develop insight into themselves and their environment and use this knowledge to regulate their behavior and set a course for development. Along the way, they get some help from organizational support systems, such as 360-degree feedback survey results, executive coaches, and training courses and workshops. They muster their inner strength to overcome career barriers and become continuous learners.

The book began by highlighting dimensions of effective leadership behavior and performance that serve as a guide for assessing skills and knowledge in relation to organizational requirements, setting development goals, and seeking developmental experiences and feedback. Leaders need not only leadership skills, but also emotional maturity to be resilient and maintain their motivation. Leadership skills can be learned easily in comparison to emotional maturity, which is harder to grasp and may take years to acquire. This concluding chapter explores more deeply how leaders can be guided by solid values and be effective. In particular, the focus is on how to be a principled leader, especially when problems arise. It also suggests ways leaders can develop their health and creativity and, in the process, gain acclaim for their overall wisdom.

ACTING DIPLOMATICALLY AND MAINTAINING PRINCIPLES IN TOUGH TIMES

Self-interest and profits are not the main motives behind an executive's success. Solomon (1999) argued that business is primarily a social enterprise. Therefore, success requires awareness and promotion of mutual interests and concerns. This requires cooperative effort, trust, and personal integrity. Executives may be pulled between doing what is ethically right and doing what seems expedient for short-term gain. This tension can be resolved by holding to the belief that business activity is consistent with personal value systems of conscientiousness and virtuous behaviors and decisions. The Western world's free enterprise system is driven by the values of fairness, competition, honesty, trust, integrity, and justice (Small & Dickie, 1999). Of course, this list of values is high on social desirability, at least in the West. Also, several of these values may seem mutually contradictory, in particular, competition versus trust. This is part of the dynamic tension of business these days. The challenge is to maintain a balance of being ethical and trustworthy while also being competitive. The press regularly reports examples of people who fail to maintain this balance and engage in unfair, unethical, unscrupulous, and illegal behavior.

Despite the cutthroat stereotype of the competitive business environment, businesses can develop executives' sense of morality by working hard at understanding mutual interests and cooperation through trust and integrity. Ethical leaders are able to apply their personal value systems in a way that maintains their integrity while recognizing the particular conditions of the situation. Leaders become sensitive to analyzing situational conditions and making decisions that help build consensus and trust. Shared values become the foundation for business success and continued leadership development.

Emotionally intelligent leaders are able to adopt constructive coping strategies in difficult situations. They should be effective diplomats, although research is needed to verify this. Also, emotionally intelligent leaders are able to maintain principles of good business and sensitivity to others' interests and concerns. Saner, Yiu, and Sondergaard (2000) applied business diplomacy to global companies, borrowing diplomatic skills from government and public policy. They cited Satow's definition of diplomacy, written in 1917, as "the application of intelligence and tact to the conduct of official relations between the government of independent states, or more briefly the conduct of business between states by peaceful means" (from Gore-Booth, 1979, p. 3). They also cited the qualities of a diplomat developed by the famous British diplomat, Sir Harold Nicolson, consisting of "truth, accuracy, calm, patience, good temper, modesty, loyalty, intelligence, knowledge, discernment, prudence, hospitality, charm, industry, courage, and tact" (Saner et al., 2000, p. 84; adapted from Gore-Booth, 1979, p. 451). Saner et al. (2000) concluded:

> Internationally, competent business diplomats lobby with finesse, are gracious hosts, and know how to comply with protocol according to local customs and practices. They are able to develop local connections and relationships and manage the multiple and sometimes conflict-filled interfaces. They need to be active at important international forums to influence the agenda and public opinion. (p. 85)

Skills of Successful Business Diplomats

According to Saner et al. (2000), skills of successful business diplomats include international business acumen, career development maturity, knowledge of international relations and diplomacy, a multicultural mind-set and tolerance, political competencies such as mastering political negotiations and handling media, role versatility and tolerance for ambiguity, and mastery of analytic tools to anticipate the potential impact of investment in different countries.

The business diplomat needs to understand the interaction between economics, politics, and culture by region or country, and must be able to analyze the risks involved in key decisions. Also, business diplomats should have a link with the strategic planning function of the company as a way to develop a business-related sociopolitical perspective for stakeholder analysis, managing hostile stakeholders, and auditing stakeholder satisfaction.

Diplomacy and Principled Leadership. Corporate culture of the 1980s was marked by downsizing, which was characterized by a loss of job security and a building of employee fear and mistrust. This often generated a corporate culture of cynicism toward management, questioning leaders' motives as out for themselves and the almighty dollar, not the long-run viability of the firm or valuing the contribution of the employees who made the company successful. Dreilinger (1997) suggested specific steps transformational leaders can take to overcome this cynicism. They can discuss and learn from past history rather than hide it under the rug. They can discuss previous change efforts, including what did and did not work. In describing upcoming changes, they can anticipate and address unintended and potentially adverse consequences. Also, they can communicate information to employees—that is, tell them what is known and can be discussed, what cannot be discussed now, and what is not known yet. They can help allay fear by increasing predictability, that is, be sure what is promised actually happens. Also, leaders can clarify expectations, define responsibilities, provide consistent and fair rewards, actively support ethical treatment and decisions, and ensure that outcomes are fair, and the process of the deciding who receives them is equitable.

PRINCIPLED LEADERSHIP
AND BUSINESS DIPLOMACY

Many leaders are less than aboveboard when faced with organizational problems, and indeed sometimes create problems for others, so it is pertinent to explain how leaders can be both principled (i.e., value driven) and successful diplomats. This section explains the main elements of principled leadership and how it can be maintained though diplomatic leadership (based on London, 1999a, 1999b).

Principled leadership is applying ethical business values, including honesty, fairness, mutual respect, kindness, and doing good. Principled leaders are executives and managers who apply these values in their daily business lives. They do not ignore the realities of tough business, but rather make difficult decisions, resolve conflicts, and negotiate deals using business diplomacy.

Business diplomacy is a way to help managers understand each other's point of view and reach common ground without hostility. Business diplomats treat work associates with respect and honesty. They recognize and value differences between people. Business diplomats use tact and understanding to build trust and develop relationships. Principled leadership and business diplomacy work together to enhance interpersonal work relationships. A principled, diplomatic leadership style is particularly valuable in making tough decisions, resolving emotional conflicts and turf battles, and negotiating sensitive issues. It is useful in handling performance problems, managing diversity, improving teamwork, overcoming resistance to change, and gaining cooperation from others. Diplomacy is the best strategy when others' attitudes and behavior are obstacles to getting things done rapidly and effectively. Diplomacy will not necessarily be welcomed and met with in-kind behavior and attitudes. Others may care less about avoiding or resolving conflict. A principled approach to such a situation requires patience, insight, and resilience to persist and not give into anger and frustration. The diplomat's challenge is to maintain diplomacy in the face of criticism, threat, and manipulation.

In developing these ideas further, this chapter outlines principled, diplomatic values, strategies, and behaviors (London, 1999a). These are presented in Table 12.1. Also explored are diplomatic strategies to handle difficult situations (London, 1999a). These vary from conservative to risky. These are listed in Table 12.2.

Next, consider what happens when principled, diplomatic leadership does not work (from London, 1999a, pp. 162–163).

When Principled Leadership and Diplomacy Fail

Principled leadership and diplomacy will not always work out. However, this can be a learning experience. When diplomacy sours, perhaps because other participants are continuously intransigent, uncooperative, or uncommunicative despite best efforts, diplomats can aim for small gains of which they can be proud. In the long run, maintaining a diplomatic stance, being approachable and open to new ideas and maintaining respect for others will pay off. Diplomatic managers will develop a reputation for being trustworthy and honest, yet will not be regarded as someone others can take advantage of. So in future conflicts or negotiations, they may be sought after as a voice of reason or looked to for effective mediation.

However, principled leadership and business diplomacy are likely to fail when the context does not match a diplomatic style. For example, being diplomatic is hard when others with whom diplomats have to interact are powerful

TABLE 12.1
Components of Principled, Diplomatic Leadership

Principled, Diplomatic Values

- Hold honesty and trust as key values.
- Act with prudence and wisdom built on experience.
- Don't put personal needs above others' needs.
- Find and involve those who care about an issue.
- Recognize differences in opinions.
- Appreciate different ways of getting things done.
- Don't try to get what you want no matter what.
- Don't be driven by self-righteousness.
- Don't lash out when frustrated or angry.

Leadership Strategies

- Be an advocate.
- Take time to identify alternative solutions.
- Lobby when you need to.
- Champion ideas.
- Put your foot down when necessary.
- Recognize the political context and work within it.
- Don't believe that kindness and empathy always work.
- Don't get angry; others will know they can control you.
- Emphasize gains when the other party fears loss.
- Voice caution when the other party acts precipitously.

Behavioral and Personal Tendencies

- Put aside your self-serving, Machiavellian tendencies.
- Be willing to change and adapt.
- Recognize and let go of your biases.
- Recognize your and others' ulterior motives.
- Recognize your viewpoint.
- Be willing to give up or try another course of action.
- Be willing to relinquish power.
- Don't go into a situation with preconceived ideas.

Treatment of Others

- Recognize what others want and need.
- Avoid alienating others.
- Show concern for others' feelings.

- Treat others with respect.
- Ask, don't tell people what to do.
- Don't threaten—act in a nonthreatening way.
- Don't go behind others' backs.
- Don't arouse hostility or anger.

Communication

- Disclose useful information.
- Explain issues and ideas to others as fully as you can.
- Be clear.
- Communicate frequently.
- Don't close off dialogue.

Participation

- Get advocates involved.
- Get input from different perspectives and constituencies.
- Ask others to resolve their disagreements themselves.
- Ask others who disagree with you for their opinion.
- Take time to collect all points of view.
- Don't act without asking or informing.
- Don't meet negative behavior with negative behavior.
- Don't manage by fiat.
- Don't be authoritarian.

Interpersonal Relationships

- Invest in the relationship in terms of time.
- Be a team player.
- Be responsive.
- Remain cooperative.
- Be helpful; perform tasks beyond the call of duty.
- Promote organization image to those outside the organization.
- Give encouragement, support, and reinforcement.
- Be considerate.
- Be socially responsible.
- Don't close doors.
- Don't offend.
- Avoid being oppositional.

Note. Adapted from London (1999a , pp. 48–49).

TABLE 12.2

Diplomatic Tactics

Conservative Tactics

- The trial balloon. Businesses often float ideas to see how stakeholders react.
- Systematically collect data and ideas.
- Shuttle diplomacy. Shuttle diplomacy is meeting with each party separately and making the rounds over and over until agreements are achieved.
- Round table discussions. "Coming to the table" is the most common form of negotiation. All parties are present at once so the issues can be hashed out and something can get accomplished.
- Establish decision rules. As the diplomat begins the initiative, whether through shuttle diplomacy or committee work, the first step may be establishing the rules of interaction, i.e., how the diplomatic process will work.
- Wait-and-see. Delaying is another diplomatic strategy. Sometimes problems are best resolved on their own.

Risky Tactics

- Coopt potential dissenters. Cooptation is trying to get others on the diplomat's side, especially those who are, or could be, your opponents.
- Announce a decision, but be ready to back off. Here, diplomatic managers make the decision according to their best judgment and announce it along with a full explanation and rationale. Then they step back and wait for the reaction and adjust accordingly.
- Build a coalition and move forward unilaterally. Find those who agree with them position and take action.
- Make a perspective known and lobby for it. Here diplomats go on the offensive. They let others know where they stand, provide cogent and forceful arguments, and present their position every chance they get. For this to work, diplomats need a good strong argument and the energy and aggressiveness to drive it forward.

Goals for process (how to get work done) and outcomes (what to achieve) are as follows (from London, 1999a, pp. 161–162):

Process Goals

- Working together in the spirit of cooperation, and in the process, avoiding coercion, threat, and other negative interactions.
- Keeping communication open.
- Remaining flexible.
- Suggesting, and being open to, new ideas.

Outcome Goals

- Achieving positive outcomes.
- Being unanimous or at least arriving at a consensus.
- Ensuring some stability, that is, agreements that last.
- Improving interpersonal competencies.
- Establishing a team identity (participants feel part of a relationship and can be relied on to pull together in the future).
- Fostering continued positive relationships to deal with future dilemmas, disagreements, and deals (the development of a new culture of relational empathy).

Note. Summarized from London (1999a, pp. 59–65).   259 and want to have their way. Diplomats can try to change their behavior (give up diplomacy), withdraw, wait and see if the situation changes, wait until the situation is more favorable (can't always do that—may be too risky), try to be diplomatic anyway, and change the environment by bringing in others who have different expectations and sources of power. They can start talking about a superordinate goal—one that all parties think is important. Also, they can let diplomacy evolve. People will get used to it and start to be more diplomatic over time, especially when it is rewarded in the organization. Thus, to a certain extent, diplomatic managers can make the situation conducive to diplomacy over time.

Ways to Make Diplomacy More Effective

The following are recommendations for making diplomacy more effective in an organization (excerpted from London, 1999a, pp. 163–164):

1. Establish a diplomatic organizational culture. Establish a diplomatic climate within the organization and make it clear that the organization's style of operation is diplomacy—as opposed to aggressive, cut throat management, standoffishness, and closed-door/unilateral approach to viewpoints and decisions, to cite a few negative management styles.
2. People in a leadership position, especially, should demonstrate business diplomacy in their dealings with subordinates, peers, supervisors, and customers, and in the process, show others the value of business diplomacy.
3. Diplomatic managers should take time out to think about how well the diplomatic process is going.
4. Learn from mistakes. Don't overuse diplomacy or one diplomatic strategy. Don't get arrogant about being a diplomat. Know when to back off, and don't feel too badly about it.
5. Let diplomacy become a way of life. Be a diplomat off the job as well as on. In this way, diplomacy will become a natural way of interacting with people.
6. Learn to manage crises in a diplomatic fashion. Ways to do this include keeping objectives limited (not expecting too much too quickly), deciding how far to go and stick to that (recognizing that while flexibility is important, diplomacy does not mean giving in to all demands), using power and authority carefully (not resorting to using power when things get the least bit frustrating), and widening the community of those concerned (show that other people care too).

Principled, diplomatic leadership is the goal for executives to work toward. Other developmental goals are good health, creativity, and, perhaps most generally, wisdom. These are considered next.

EXECUTIVE HEALTH RISK FACTORS

Good health sounds basic, but it is often ignored. Good health is partly physical, but also psychological, spiritual, and ethical. J. C. Quick, Garvin, Cooper, and J. D. Quick (2000) presented a comprehensive model of executive health. They distinguished between four components of executive health: physical, psychological, spiritual, and ethical. These components are likely to be higher for executives who maintain their strength by staying physically fit, maintaining a network of colleagues and friends for support and encouragement, applying stress management skills (e.g., relaxation techniques, planning, time management, spiritual discussion, and cognitive/behavioral skills of framing problems positively and dealing with people calmly and objectively), and balancing their investment in life's activities.

Executives need these sources of strength to face the challenges of their role. Quick et al. (2000) described four such health risk factors:

1. *The executive's Achilles Heel*—The individual's inherited or acquired health vulnerabilities. These are predisposing characteristics, not predetermining factors that are inevitable. This suggests that the vulnerabilities can be managed and guarded against (e.g., not smoking and staying trim).
2. *The loneliness of command*—Leaders are prone to social isolation. They want to instill confidence in their workforce by giving the impression that they are secure and confident in their decisions, and they do not depend on others. However, like everyone else, they need reassurance and connections to others.
3. *Work demands and overload*—Executives work hard and long, with work weeks of from 60 to 70 hours and possibly more. Globe hopping, technological changes, and market competition combine with weighty responsibility to stockholders, employees, and customers and the need to pay attention to multiple performance indicators.
4. *Crises and failures*—Industrial accidents, bankruptcies, and personal threats or attacks may be learning experiences in the long run, but they are sources of severe stress and the need for high energy, effort, and aggravation in the short run. Corporate crises become personal failures that affect all aspects of their lives. Executives may get discouraged all the while they are bolstering the morale of their employees.

The goal is to enhance individual vitality and happiness while attaining positive organizational outcomes. Next consider why and how leaders aspire to be more creative.

DEVELOPING CREATIVE LEADERS

Facing challenges, acting diplomatically, and maintaining one's principles and health require a certain amount of creativity. The concept of creative leadership is hardly new (witness the work of the Center for Creative Leadership in Greensboro, North Carolina), and creativity is not an easy concept to understand let alone develop. Simonton (2000) summarized the research on creativity by examining cognitive processes involved in being creative, characteristics of the creative person, the development of creativity during the course of a career, and environments that support creativity.

Cognitive Processes Involved in Being Creative

Creativity is not the magically sudden appearance of unexpected and seemingly unprepared inspiration, but rather the lawful operation of subliminal stimulation and mental processes. As a result, creativity does not require exceptional talent. Almost anyone can be creative with systematic training and practice. "Creative individuals do not produce new ideas de novo, but rather those ideas must arise from a large set of well-developed skills and a rich body of domain-relevant knowledge" (Simonton, 2000, p. 152). This is the purpose for apprenticeships, internships, and management development programs.

Characteristics of the Creative Person

Although research has shown that people identified as highly creative tend to be intelligent (or at least exceed a certain threshold of intelligence), intelligence is not a unidimensional concept. There are multiple intelligences and talents, including music, art, physical, social/interpersonal, mathematical, oral and written communication, and so on (Gardner, 1983; Guilford, 1967; Sternberg, 1985). (For another example, see the discussion of emotional intelligence in chap. 10, this volume.) Creativity can emerge in each of these areas.

Creativity is also associated with personality. Creative individuals are known to be independent, nonconformist, risk taking, and flexible, with wide ranging interests and openness to new experiences (Simonton, 2000). These personality tendencies are likely to be quite adaptive over the course of a career as individuals show resilience in overcoming career barriers and, in some cases, reinventing themselves as situational demands and opportunities emerge.

Development of Creativity During a Career

People who have attained a level of acclaim for their creative efforts have made the most of their potential over a long period of time. That is, they have developed their potential over the course of years if not decades. Creative potential may stem from a number of factors, such as the role of parents, role models, and mentors at formative times in a person's life (e.g., during trauma or major change). The key is not necessarily a nurturing environment, but rather a diversity of experience that weaken constraints imposed by usual socialization and challenging experiences that strengthen the individual's resilience. Creative ideas emerge over time in connection with the individual's ideas and the sociocultural environment. This can occur throughout the life span, and sometimes is manifest in a resurgence of recreativity late in life (good news for the large generation of "baby boomers") (Simonton, 2000).

Environments that Support Creativity

Creativity seems to be enhanced when people engage in creative tasks for the inherent enjoyment rather than for some external reason. However, extrinsic rewards can amplify the creative effort (Amabile, 1996). That is, people who enjoy the work and are paid for it may do better than those who enjoy the work but are frustrated by receiving little appreciation for their efforts. Creativity occurs within a set of rules that guide the discipline. Even though the work is original, it must be close to, if not squarely in, this set of rules, otherwise its value and usefulness may not be recognized in its time. (This is why some products and creators are not lauded until many years later.) Creativity also occurs within a social setting of fellow creators, critics, and users (e.g., customers and subordinates). At any one time, the discipline and those with whom the creator interacts designate products as creative or not creative.

Times of unrest and change make it hard to be creative, whereas times immediately following major unrest or change generate a sense of renewal and a golden age of opportunity. So organizations experiencing trauma and turmoil (e.g., major employee downsizing due to a financial downfall) may produce stresses that prevent creative executive action and create inertia (e.g., "Don't move or you'll be next out the door."). However, organizations that have recently taken new directions or are following exciting opportunities prompt their people to take risks and think out of the box. Cultural diversity (e.g., from a corporate merger) is welcomed and appreciated as enriching the environment. However, the diversity needs to be viewed with a positive, optimistic frame of reference, not a threatening "bunker-down-the-hatches" mind-set.

In the work setting, leaders can be creative in different ways. This is especially so because of the changing nature of work. In the not too distant past, organizations were structured in a few standard ways (i.e., research, production, marketing, finances, administrative services). Also, departmental structures and organizational hierarchies provided similar demands from leaders in managing people regardless of functional area. Today's organizations are increasingly fluid systems, with new organizational structures and forms (see Table 12.2 in the last chapter). There is a vast new array of job niches made possible by computers, the internet, and digital commerce (Reich, 2000). People in all fields are starting web-based businesses and using multimedia outlets for their talents and finding creative ways to create markets and serve customers. There is no one avenue for creative leadership just as there is no one way to develop a leader.

DEVELOPING WISE LEADERS

Principled diplomacy is a value-laden direction for leadership development. It suggests a path for fair, good, and creative leadership. As such, it sets up an ideal goal that leaders can strive to achieve. More generally, this higher level development is a process of self-actualization—making the most of one's potential and being of ever-increasing value to others and the organization. This might be termed *wisdom*.

Ideally, organizations want to develop leaders with wisdom. That is, organizations want the best of what executives can accomplish in terms of the executives' own development and the executives' development of others.

P. B. Baltes and Staudinger (2000) reviewed the concept of wisdom and factors that contribute to it. According to their model, wisdom is the pinnacle of insight. Generally, it refers to excellence in mind and virtue. Pragmatically, it is excellence in the conduct and meaning of work and, more broadly, life. It assumes knowledge about facts and procedures. Factual knowledge covers such topics as human nature, life-long learning, interpersonal relationships, social norms, critical life events and their possible implications, and conditions that contribute to one's own and others' well-being, satisfaction, enjoyment, and fulfillment. Procedural knowledge refers to the fundamental practical aspects of life, such as ways of giving feedback and advice, structuring and weighing goals, handling conflicts and decisions, and being knowledgeable about, and being ready to implement, back-up strategies in case things go wrong or do not go as expected.

Wise leaders understand different life domains (e.g., education, work, leisure, family, co-workers, friends, public appearance, and social welfare), their interrelationships, and the different forms they take in different cultures (P. B. Baltes & Staudinger, 2000). Wise leaders acknowledge and benefit from the different values held by individuals and society. They are tolerant of differences while they maintain their concern for, and demonstration of, virtue and common good. They value others' advice, knowledge, and judgment. They understand that they and others are not omniscient—that their information processing is inherently limited. They recognize that people have access to limited information, and that the future can never be fully predicted. Wise leaders can deal with these uncertainties and ambiguities.

Wise leaders have experience and expertise that is developed over time in dealing with critical work and life issues. They have certain characteristics that help them benefit from these experiences, including a motivational drive for excellence and continuous learning. They are open to new experiences, show creativity, and have a strong sense of self-identity, self-esteem, and resilience. They may have benefited from a supportive environment, including nurturing parents and mentors. They may also have benefited from creating such a supportive environment for others. They engage in work and life review, planning, and management.

Three elements are the foundation for successful life development: selection of meaningful goals, optimizing the means to achieving these goals, and adopting compensatory mechanisms when established means fail to achieve a certain goal (P. B. Baltes, 1997). (Recall that these elements are analogous to the concepts of identity, insight, and resilience as the three domains of career motivation, described earlier in chap. 4, this volume.)

Leaders can acquire wisdom. To put it another way, they can become wiser over time. Indeed, this can be fostered by the right support. They learn strategies and establish goals for the conduct and meaning of work and life. They learn to make sound decisions and give good advice in a way that is welcomed. Their knowledge gains depth, scope, and balance. Also, they balance their own and others' well-being.

Wise leaders are flexible and adaptable in the way they apply their expertise. They are able to process highly complex sets of information about events in life and reduce them rapidly to their essentials without being lost in the unending process of searching for information. This is bounded rationality. That is, wise leaders recognize both the constraints and the need to move ahead despite the constraints. They are able to organize large amounts of complex information and ideas as events unfold. Without wisdom, leaders' judgment and knowledge about business life is fragmented. It lacks integration, practical direction, and optimization of process.

In short, developing leaders are able to achieve more advanced levels of knowledge and judgment over time. Moreover, they become role models—guideposts of excellence for those who may not achieve the height of wisdom, yet demonstrate a level of behavior to which everyone can aspire (P. B. Baltes & Staudinger, 2000).

A LEADERSHIP DEVELOPMENT CONTINUUM

The last chapter provided examples of the leadership requirements and competencies imposed by increases in flexible organizational structures and forms, reliance on teams, and emerging business opportunities. This concluding chapter examined some directions for insightful leadership development, in particular, principled, diplomatic leadership, the leader's health and well-being, creative leadership, and wisdom as the culmination of experience, insight, and continuous learning. Wise leaders understand the needs of the organization, alternative leadership styles, and their own capabilities, interests, and goals. They regulate their behavior as they calibrate their actions in line with environmental changes, demands, and barriers and as they participate in the continuous process of leadership development. They seek and welcome feedback and coaching to support this process.

Table 12.3 summarizes emerging opportunities, leadership challenges, key attitudes and values, and directions for personal and professional growth. Each column represents a continuum from basic levels of task demands, challenges, values, and growth at the bottom of the table to higher levels at the top. This is not an exact formulation, in that the elements in each box could be placed at higher or lower levels depending on the situation. Nevertheless, the concept conveys the idea of an evolutionary leadership development process.

At the lowest level, basic tasks and new initiatives require the development of task-based skills. Leaders need to maintain their own and others' motivation and commitment. Principled leadership is formed at this level. The challenge for leaders is to maintain it as situations become more difficult and complex at higher levels of the continuum. In conducting daily business activities, leaders gain insight, regulate their behavior, and calibrate their career directions and sense of self-identity. This level of the continuum is also the foundation for physical, psychological, spiritual, and ethical health that is developed at higher levels.

In managing teams, the challenge is to apply process leadership skills, value and reward team members' contributions, and learn from team members. Considerable work gets done in teams these days such that leading groups is a critical executive skill. Team members may be diverse in functions, disciplinary knowledge, demographics, cultural background, and organizational level. Also, they may be members of different organizations (as in a joint venture or a customer support team). Moreover, they may be geographically dispersed and may rarely, if ever, actually meet face to face. Also, they vary in the time span required for their work, some working for very short time spans, others over extended periods of time—months and possibly years, with complex goals and systems. Employees may be members of different teams at one time, and team leaders need to direct members who do not report directly to them in the organizational hierarchy. Some teams require a great deal of sensitivity to manage negotiations and work through conflicts.

Teams are used to create new organizational forms. New, large-scale organizational structures and forms impose the next level of demands in the leadership development hierarchy. The leader's challenge is to be sure that all employees understand their role and the purpose for the structure. Department, team, and individual strategies and tasks must be aligned with larger corporate goals. New organizational forms may be flat structures (many people reporting to the same supervisor) that provide employees and teams with newfound autonomy and accountability. Large-scale organizations may be temporary, requiring a strong vision and clear organizational culture to capture employees' commitment to the effort. The leader must be open to new ideas in refining the organizational

TABLE 12.3
A Leadership Development Continuum

Opportunities	Leadership Challenges	Leader's and Organizational Members' Attitudes and Values	Leader's Growth
HIGH DEMANDS			INCREASED DEPTH
Continuous change (e.g., new technology, shifting economic conditions, globalization)	Have insight into changing conditions Manage ambiguity and help others deal with uncertainty	Flexibility Openness to new directions and goals Testing principles and diplomacy	Renewal Self-actualization (Flow)
New ventures (e.g., mergers, start-ups, internet-based commerce)	Apply mix of skills demanded by organization strategy (e.g., finance, customer/marketing, people development) Create new organizational culture	Excitement Creativity Investment Focus on creating value	Development of wisdom and (potentially) wealth
New organization forms (e.g., flexible and flat structures, temporary organizations, coalitions and joint ventures, enterprise-wide systems design and implementation)	Communicate purpose, processes, and roles	Openness to new methods; willing to experiment	Trial-and-error learning New insights Overcoming barriers reinforces resilience
Team structures (e.g., quality improvement teams, project teams, geographically dispersed teams)	Apply process-focused requirements for setting team direction, encouraging member participation, and facilitating group dynamics (e.g., conflict resolution and diplomacy)	Emotional maturity Sociability Valuing differences Recognizing individual contributions	Learning from others Fulfillment from group accomplishments
Basic tasks New initiatives and projects	Apply basic task-focused skills (selecting and developing people, organizing and planning work, delegating assignments, measuring individual performance, project tracking success)	Motivation and commitment Connecting task to larger purpose Linking individual rewards to task accomplishment Maintain stable foundation of principled leadership	Continuous development of insight, self-regulation, and identity The basis for physical, psychological, spiritual, and ethical health
LOW COMPLEXITY AND DIFFICULTY			FOUNDATION

form and experimenting with new structures. The leader learns through trial and error, gaining new insights and overcoming barriers, which in turn reinforce the leader's resilience.

The alternative organizational forms may be used in the creation of new ventures, at the next level of this leadership development hierarchy. Here, organizational strategy dictates leadership skill demands. The leader generates and communicates the vision and maintains the excitement, creativity, recognition of stockholders' and employees' investment, and focus on creating investor value. The experiences make the leader wiser, and if the enterprise is successful, wealthier.

Continuous change is at the top of the continuum. Leaders use task, process, and strategically linked skills and apply their insight as they cope with ambiguities and create new structures and directions. They remain flexible and open to new ideas. The stress and uncertainty tests principled, diplomatic leadership as it provides opportunities for enjoyment, renewal, and self-actualization.

CONCLUSIONS

Principled leadership is a standard for all leaders to achieve. Diplomacy is a practical set of behaviors to implement principled leadership. Most executives are indeed principled and try to be diplomatic. Those who do not bother, or, more radically, behave in opposite ways, make headlines as white-collar criminals. For the vast majority, principled, diplomatic leadership can still be a struggle, especially in tough times and new cultures that have different norms. Principled, diplomatic leadership can be developed and refined through a process of continuous learning. This book began by showing how self-insight, regulation, and identity contributes to the leadership development process. Feedback, coaching, and a variety of developmental programs are support mechanisms that enable leaders to learn from experiences (sometimes demoralizing career barriers) and benefit from ongoing learning opportunities. Ultimately, the goal of leadership development is to promote the leader's physical, psychological, spiritual, and ethical health. Furthermore, leaders have a chance to develop their creativity throughout the course of their careers, and indeed their lives. And, finally, they have a chance to apply their rich experiences in principled, diplomatic ways to demonstrate the wisdom of their years.

REFERENCES

Abueva, J. E. (2000, May 17). Return of the native executive: Many repatriations fail, at huge cost to companies. *New York Times*, pp. C1, C8.

Ajzen, I., & Fishbein, M. (1977). Attitude–behavior relations: A theoretical analysis and review of empirical research. *Psychological Bulletin, 84*, 888–918.

Albano, C. (2000). What is adaptive leadership? Online paper from http://www.selfgrowth.com/articles/calbano.html, accessed April 26.

Albert, R. D. (1996). A framework and model for understanding Latin American and Latino/Hispanic cultural patterns. In D. Landis & R. S. Bhagat (Eds.), *Handbook of intercultural training* (2nd ed., pp. 327–348). Thousand Oaks, CA: Sage.

Allport, G. W. (1946). Effect: A secondary principle of learning. *Psychological Review, 53*, 335–347.

Altemeyer, B. (1987). *Enemies of freedom: Understanding right-wing authoritarianism.* San Francisco: Jossey-Bass.

Altemeyer, B. (1996). *The authoritarian specter.* Cambridge, MA: Harvard University Press.

Altemeyer, B. (1999). To thine own self be untrue: Self-awareness in authoritarians. *North American Journal of Psychology, 1*(2), 157–165.

Amabile, T. M. (1996). *Creativity in context.* Boulder, CO: Westview.

Anderson, L. R. (1987). Self-monitoring and performance nontraditional occupations. *Basic and Applied Social Psychology, 8*, 85–96.

Andrews, F. (2000a, June 25). Separating the talkers from the doers. *New York Times*, p. BU 7.

Andrews, F. (2000b, May 28). Will managers relate to this gripping tale? *New York Times*, sect. 3, p. 6.

Anteri, E., & Tesio, V. (1990). The internationalization of management at Fiat. *The Journal of Management Development, 9*(6), 6–16.

Antonioni, D. (1994). The effects of feedback accountability on upward appraisal ratings. *Personnel Psychology, 47*, 349–356.

Arenson, K. W. (2000, April 3). Columbia in web venture to share learning for profit. *New York Times*, p. A1.

Arkin, R. M., & Oleson, K. C. (1998). Self-handicapping. In E. E. Jones, J. Cooper, & J. M. Darley (Eds.), *Attribution and social interaction: The legacy of Edward E. Jones* (pp. 313–347). Washington, DC: American Psychological Association.

Ashford, S. J. (1989). Self-assessments in organizations: A literature review and integrartive model. In L. L. Cummings & B. M. Staw (Eds.), *Research in organizational behavior* (Vol. 11, pp. 133–174). Greenwich, CT: JAI Press.

Ashford, S. J. (1986). Feedback seeking in individual adaptation: A resource erspective. *Academy of Management Journal, 29*, 465–487.

Ashford, S. J., & Cummings, L. L. (1983). Feedback as an individual resource: Personal strategies of creating information. *Organizational Behavior and Human Performance, 32*, 370–398.

Ashford, S. J., & Tsui, A. S. (1991). The influence of upward feedback on self- and follower ratings of leadership. *Personnel Psychology, 48*, 34–59.

"Assessing and developing top leaders." (2000). *SHL North America Network Newsletter: People, Work, Organizations,* spring, pp. 1, 3.

Atwater, L. E., Ostroff, C., Yammarino, F. J., & Fleenor, J. W. (1998). *Personnel Psychology, 51*, 577–598.

Atwater, L. E., Roush, P., & Fischthal, A. (1995). The influence of upward feedback on self- and follower ratings of leadership. *Personnel Psychology, 48*, 34–59.

269

Atwater, L. E., Waldman, D. A., Atwater, D., & Cartier, P. (2000). An upward feedback field experiment: Supervisors' cynicism, reactions, and commitment to subordinates. *Personnel Psychology, 53,* 275–297.

Atwater, L. E., & Yammarino, F. J. (1997). Self–other rating agreement: A review and model. *Research in Personnel and Human Resources Management, 15,* 121–174.

Avolio, B. J., & Bass, B. M. (1988). Transformational leadership, charisma and beyond. In J. G. Hunt, H. R. Baliga, H. P. Dachler, & C. A. Schriescheim (Eds.), *Emerging leadership vistas* (pp. 29–49). Lexington, MA: Heath.

Baltes, P. B. (1997). On the incomplete architecture of human ontogeny: Selection, optimization, and compensation as foundation of developmental theory. *American Psychologist, 52,* 366–380.

Baltes, P. B., & Staudinger, U. M. (2000). Wisdom: A metaheuristic (pragmatic) to orchestrate mind and virtue toward excellence. *American Psychologist, 55*(1), 122–136.

Bandura, A. (1977). *Social learning theory.* Englewood Cliffs, NJ: Prentice-Hall.

Bandura, A. (1982). Self-efficacy mechanisms in human agency. *American Psychologist, 37,* 122–147.

Bandura, A. (1986). *Social foundations of thought and action.* Englewood Cliffs, NJ: Prentice-Hall.

Bandura, A. (1997). *Self-efficacy: The exercise of control.* New York: Freeman.

Bandura, A. (2000). Exercise of human agency through collective efficacy. *Current Issues in Psychological Science, 9*(3), 75–78.

Bandura, A., & Jourden, F. J. (1991). Self-regulatory mechanisms governing the motivational effects of goal systems. *Journal of Personality and Social Psychology, 60,* 941–951.

Barboza, D. (2000. May 28). Teacher, cheerleader and C.E.O. *New York Times,* sect. 3, p. 2.

Bass, B. M. (1999). *New paradigm of leadership: An inquiry into transformational leadership.* Hillsdale, NJ: Lawrence Erlbaum Associates.

Bass, B. M., & Avolio, B. J. (1994). *Improving organizational effectiveness through transformational leadership.* Thousand Oaks, CA: Sage.

Bassett, G. A., & Meyer, H. H. (1968). Performance appraisals: The impact of ratee competence, rater location and rating correctability on fairness perceptions. *Group and Organizational Management, 20*(1), 39–60.

Baumeister, R. F. (1982). A self-presentational view of social phenomena. *Psychological Bulletin, 91,* 3–26.

Baumeister, R. F., Heatherton, T. F., & Tice, D. M. (1994). *Losing control: How and why people fail at self-regulation.* San Diego: Academic Press.

Baumeister, R. F., & Tice, D. M. (1990. Anxiety and social exclusion. *Journal of Social and Clinical Psychology, 9,* 165–195.

Beach, L. R. (1990). *Image theory: Decision making in personal and organizational contexts.* New York: Wiley.

Beizer, B. (2000, April). *Coaching as an organizational intervention: Practitioner perspectives.* In M. B. Sokol (Chair), Practitioner Forum presented at the 15th annual meeting of the Society for Industrial and Organizational Psychology, New Orleans.

Bem, D. J. (1972). Self-perception theory. In L. Berkowitz (Ed.), *Advances in experimental social psychology* (Vol. 6, pp. 1–62). New York: Academic Press.

Benedict, M. E., & Levine, E. L. (1988). Delay and distortion: Tacit influences on performance appraisal effectiveness. *Journal of Applied Psychology, 73,* 507–514.

Berenson, A. (2000, May 28). In Silicon Valley, loyalty means paying a high price. *New York Times,* sect. 3, pp. 1, 9.

Berke, R. L. (2000, June 9). Gore dots the I's that Bush leaves to others. *New York Times,* pp. A1, A28.

Bernardin, J. H., Hagan, C., Ross, S., Kane, J. S. (1995, May). The effects of a 360-degree appraisal system on managerial performance. In W. W. Tornow (Chair), *Upward feedback: The ups and downs of it*. Paper presented at the 10th annual conference of the Society for Industrial and Organizational Psychology, Orlando, FL.

Berrell, M., Wright, P., & Hoa, T.T.V. (1999). The influence of culture on managerial behavior. *Journal of Management Development, 18*(7), 578–589.

Bhagat, R., & London, M. (1999). Getting started and getting ahead: Career dynamics of immigrants. *Human Resource Management Review, 9*(3), 349–365.

"The boss: Making the best of a mess." (1999, September 29). *New York Times*, p. C8.

Brockner, J., & Wiesenfield, B. M. (1996). An integrative framework for explaining reactions to decisions: Integrative effects of outcomes and procedures. *Psychological Bulletin, 120*, 189–208.

Brunstein, J. C., & Gollwitzer, P. M. (1996). Effects of failure on subsequent performance: The importance of self-defining goals. *Journal of Personality and Social Psychology, 70*, 395–407.

Brutus, S., London, M., & Martineau, J. (1999). The impact of 360-degree feedback on planning for career development. *Journal of Management Development, 18*(8), 676–693.

Byham, W. C. (2000). How to create a reservoir of ready-made leaders. *Training & Development Magazine, 54*(3), 29–33.

Cherniss, C. (1998). Social and emotional learning for leaders. *Educational Leadership, 55*(7), 26–28.

Cherniss, C. (2000, April). *Emotional intelligence: What it is and why it matters*. Paper presented at the 15th annual meeting of the Society for Industrial and Organizational Psychology, New Orleans.

Cherniss, C., & Adler, M. (2000). *Promoting emotional intelligence in organizations*. Alexandria, VA: American Society for Training and Development.

Cherniss, C., & Goleman, D. (1999). *Bringing emotional intelligence to the workplace*. Technical report issued by the Consortium for Research on Emotional Intelligence in Organizations. Piscataway, NJ: Rutgers University.

Cheung, G. (1999). Multifaceted conceptions of self–other ratings disagreement. *Personnel Psychology, 52*, 1–36.

Child, J. (1994). *Management in China during the age of reform*. Cambridge, England: Cambridge University Press.

"Cisco—From 3,000 employees to 30,000 Employees in 5 years." (2000, June 1). *Profile Plus Newsletter*, www.profileplus.com.

Conner, J., & Smith, C. A. (1998). Developing the next generation of leaders: A new strategy for leadership development at Colgate-Palmolive. In E. M. Mone & M. London (Eds.), *HR to the rescue: Case studies of HR solutions to business challenges* (pp. 120–148). Houston, TX: Gulf Press.

Csikszentmihalyi, M. (1993). *The evolving self*. New York: Harper Collins.

Dalessio, A. T. (1998). Using multi-source feedback for employee development and personnel decisions. In J. W. Smither (Ed.), *Performance appraisal: State-of-the-art in practice* (pp. 278–330). San Francisco: Jossey-Bass.

Dalton, M. (2000, April). An exploration of learning versatility within a model of work experience. In C. D. McCauley (Chair), *Developments on development: The process and consequences of continuous learning*. Symposium presented at the 15th annual meeting of the Society for Industrial and Organizational Psychology, New Orleans.

Deci, E. L., Egharari, H., Patrick, B. C., & Leone, D. R. (1994). Facilitating internalization: The self-determination theory perspective. *Journal of Personality, 62*, 119–142.

Deci, E. L., & Ryan, R. M. (1991). A motivational approach to self: Integration in personality. In R. Dienstbier (Ed.), *Nebraska symposium on motivation: Perspectives on motivation* (Vol. 38, pp. 237–288). Lincoln: University of Nebraska Press.

DeNisi, A. S., & Kluger, A. N. (2000). Feedback effectiveness: Can 360-degree appraisals be improved? *Academy of Management Executive, 14*(1), 129–139.

Dewey, J. (1922). *Human nature and conduct.* New York: Holt.

Deutsch, C. H. (2000, May 12). After bad year, Xerox ousts top executive. *New York Times,* pp. C1, C19.

De Waele, M., Morval, J., & Sheitoyan, R. (1993). *Self-management in organizations: The dynamics of interaction.* Toronto: Hogrefe & Huber.

Dowell, B. E (2000, April). Integrating leadership development within Bristol-Myers-Squibb. In D. V. Day (Chair), *Systemic leadership development: Conceptual models and best practices.* Symposium presented at the 15th annual meeting of the Society for Industrial and Organizational Psychology, New Orleans.

Downs, A. (2000). *The fearless executive: Finding the courage to trust your talents and be the leader you are meant to be.* New York: American Management Association.

Dreilinger, C. (1997). Beyond cynicism: Building a culture which supports both ethical business practice and high performance. *Ethics Today, 2*(1), 5.

Dunbar, E. (1996). Sociocultural and contextual challenges of organizational life in Eastern Europe. In D. Landis & R. S. Bhagat (Eds.), *Handbook of intercultural training* (2nd ed., pp. 349–365). Thousand Oaks, CA: Sage.

Dvir, T. (2000, April). *Impact of transformational leadership on follower development and performance: A field experiment.* Paper presented at the 15th annual meeting of the Society for Industrial and Organizational Psychology, New Orleans.

Dweck, C. S. (1998). The development of early self-conceptions: Their relevance for motivational processes. In J. Heckhausen & C. S. Dweck (Eds.), *Motivation and self-regulation across the life span* (pp. 257–280). Cambridge, England: Cambridge University Press.

Eby, L. T., McManus, S., Simon, S. A., & Russell, J.E.A. (2000). The protégé's perspective regarding negative mentoring experiences: The development of a taxonomy. *Journal of Vocational Behavior, 57*(1), 1–21.

Eddy, E. R., Tannenbaum, S. I., & Lorenzet, S. (2000, April). The influence of a continuous learning environment on peer mentoring behaviors. In K. A. Smith-Jentsch (Chair), *Theory-based approaches to improving the practice of mentoring in organizations.* Presented at the 15th annual meeting of the Society for Industrial and Organizational Psychology, New Orleans.

Edmondson, A. (1999). Psychological safety and learning behavior in work teams. *Administrative Science Quarterly, 44*(2), 350–383.

Ellinger, A. D., & Bostrom, R. P. (1999). Managerial coaching behaviors in learning organizations. *Journal of Management Development, 18*(9), 752–771.

Evered, R. D., & Selman, J. C. (1989). Coaching and the art of management. *Organizational Dynamics, 18*(2), 16–32.

Fedor, D. B., Rensvold, R. B., & Adams, S. M. (1992). An investigation of factors expected to affect feedback seeking: A longitudinal field study. *Personnel Psychology, 45,* 779–805.

Feist, G. J., & Barron, F. (1996, June). *Emotional intelligence and academic intelligence in career and life success.* Paper presented at the annual convention of the American Psychological Society, San Francisco.

Ferstl, K. L. (2000, April). Effects of feedback sign and regulatory focus on post-feedback intentions. In J. W. Johnson & K. L. Ferstl (Chairs), *Cognitive reactions to performance feedback.* Symposium presented at the 15th annual meeting of the Society for Industrial and Organizational Psychology, New Orleans.

Ferstl, K. L., & Bruskiewicz, K. T. (2000, April). Self–other agreement and cognitive reactions to multirater feedback. In J. W. Johnson & K. L. Ferstl (Chairs), *Cognitive reactions to performance feedback.* Symposium presented at the 15th annual meeting of the Society for Industrial and Organizational Psychology, New Orleans.

Festinger, L. (1954). A theory of social comparison processes. *Human Relations, 7,* 117–140.

Fiedler, F. E., Mitchell, T., & Triandis, H. C. (1971). The culture assimilator: An approach to cross-cultural training. *Journal of Applied Psychology, 55,* 95–102.

Fine, S. B. (1991). Resilience and human adaptability: Who rises above adversity? *American Journal of Occupational Therapy, 45,* 493–505.

Fiorina, C. (1999, September 29). Making the best of a mess. *New York Times,* Wednesday, p. C8.

Fleishman, E., & Harris, E. F. (1962). Patterns of leadership behavior related to employee grievances and turnover. *Personnel Psychology, 15,* 43–56.

Fletcher, C. (1986). The effects of performance review in appraisal: Evidence and implications. *The Journal of Management Development, 5*(3), 5–6.

Flint, D. H. (1999). The role of organizational justice in multi-source performance appraisal: Theory-based applications and directions for research. *Human Resource Management Review, 9*(1), 1–20.

Folger, R., & Cropanzano, R. (1998). *Organizational justice and human resource management.* Thousand Oaks, CA: Sage.

Foster, B., & Seeker, K. R. (1997). *Coaching for peak employee performance.* Irvine, CA: Richard Chang Associates.

Fukuyama, F. (1999). *The great disruption: Human nature and the reconstitution of the social order.* New York: The Free Press.

Funder, D. C., & Block, J. (1989). The role of ego-centered, ego-resilience, and IQ in delay of gratification in adolescence. *Journal of Personality and Social Psychology, 44,* 1198–1050.

Gardner, H. (1983). *Frames of mind: A theory of multiple intelligences.* New York: Basic Books.

Ghorpade, J. (2000). Managing six paradoxes of 360-degree feedback. *Academy of Management Executive, 14*(1), 140–150.

Goldstein, J. (1994). *Insight meditation: The practice of freedom.* Boston: Shambhala Publications.

Goleman, D. (1997). *Emotional intelligence.* New York: Bantam.

Goleman, D. (2000). Leadership that gets results. *Harvard Business Review, 78*(2).

Gollwitzer, P. M., & Kirchhof, O. (1998). The willful pursuit of identity. In J. Heckhausen & C. S. Dweck (Eds.), *Motivation and self-regulation across the life span* (pp. 389–423). Cambridge, England: Cambridge University Press.

Gollwitzer, P. M., & Wicklund, R. A. (1985). The pursuit of self-defining goals. In J. Kuhl & J. Beckmann (Eds.), *Action control: From cognition to behavior* (pp. 61–85). Heidelberg: Springer.

Goodstone, M. S., & Diamante, T. (1998). Organizational use of therapeutic change: Strengthening multisource feedback systems through interdisciplinary coaching. *Consulting Psychology Journal: Practice and Research, 50*(3), 152–163.

Gore-Booth, L. (Ed.). (1979). *Satow's guide to diplomatic practice* (5th ed.). London: Longman.

Graddick, M. M., & Lane, P. (1998). Evaluating executive performance. In J. W. Smither (Ed.), *Performance appraisal: State-of-the-art in practice* (pp. 370–403). San Francisco: Jossey-Bass.

Greenberg, J., Pyszczynski, T., & Solomon, S. (1986). The causes and consequences of a need for self-esteem: A terror management theory. In R. F. Baumeister (Ed.), *Public self and private self* (pp. 189–212). New York: Springer.

Greenwald, A. G. (1980). The totalitarian ego: Fabrication and revision of personal history. *American Psychologist, 35,* 603–618.

Guilford, J. P. (1967). *The nature of human intelligence.* New York: McGraw-Hill.

Hall, D.T., Otazo, K.L., & Hollenbeck, G.P. (1999). Behind closed doors: What really happens in executive coaching. *Organizational Dynamics, 27*(3), 39–53.

Harris, B. R., Huselid, M. A., & Becker, B. E. (1999). Strategic human resource management at Praxair. *Human Resource Management, 38*(4), 315–520.

Harris, M. (1999). Practice network: Look, it's an I-O psychologist ... No, it's a trainer ... No, it's an executive coach! *Industrial-Organizational Psychologist, 36*(3), 38–42.

Harris, M., & Schaubroeck, J. (1988). A meta-analysis of self–supervisor, self–peer, and peer–supervisor ratings. *Personnel Psychology, 41,* 43–61.

Hawes, S. R. (2000, April). *Coaching as an organizational intervention: Practitioner perspectives.* In M. B. Sokol (Chair), Practitioner Forum presented at the 15th annual meeting of the Society for Industrial and Organizational Psychology, New Orleans.

Hazucha, J. F., Hezlett, S. A., & Schneider, R. J. (1993). The impact of 360-degree feedback on management skills development. *Human Resource Management, 32,* 325–351.

Hegarty, W. H. (1974). Using subordinate ratings to elicit behavioral changes in managers. *Journal of Applied Psychology, 59,* 764–766.

Heifetz, R. A., & Lauder, D. L. (1997). The work of leadership. *Harvard Business Review, 75*(1), 124–134.

Heine, D. (2000, April). Using I-O psychology to turn around a business. In G. J. Curphy (Chair), *The role of I-O psychology in executive assessment and development.* Symposium presented at the 15th annual meeting of the Society for Industrial and Organizational Psychology, New Orleans.

Hemphill, J. K. (1959). Job description for executives. *Harvard Business Review, 37*(5), 55–67.

Hendricks, W. (1996). *Coaching, mentoring and managing.* Franklin Lakes, NJ: Career Press.

Hernez-Broome, G., Beatty, K. M., Nilsen, D., Scott, K., & Steed, J. (2000, April). How top leadership sees top leadership. In G. J. Curphy (Chair), *The role of I-O psychology in executive assessment and development.* Symposium presented at the 15th annual meeting of the Society for Industrial and Organizational Psychology, New Orleans.

Higgins, E. T. (1987). Self-discrepancy: A theory relating self and affect. *Psychological Review, 94,* 319–340.

Higgins, E. T. (1998a). From expectancies to worldviews: Regulatory focus in socialization and cognition. In E. E. Jones, J. Cooper, & J. M. Darley (Eds.), *Attribution and social interaction: The legacy of Edward E. Jones* (pp. 243–269). Washington, DC: American Psychological Association.

Higgins, E. T. (1998b). Promotion and prevention: Regulatory focus as a motivational principle. In M. P. Zanna (Ed.), *Advances in experimental social psychology* (Vol. 30, pp. 1–46). New York: Academic Press.

Hillman, L. W., Schwandt, D. R., & Bartz, D. E. (1990). Enhancing staff members' performance through feedback and coaching. *Journal of Management Development, 9*(3), 20–27.

Hirshhorn, L. (1997). *Reworking authority: Leading and following in the post-modern organization.* Cambridge, MA: MIT Press.

Hitt, M. A. (2000). The new frontier: Transformation of management for the new millennium. *Organization Dynamics, 28*(3), 7–17.

Hofmeister, J. D. (2000, April). Derailment dynamics in Shell International. In G. P. Hollenbeck (Chair), *Yesterday's heroes: The derailment of international executives.* Symposium presented at the 15th annual meeting of the Society for Industrial and Organizational Psychology, New Orleans.

Hogan, R. T., & Hogan, J. C. (2000, April). What they do and why they do it. In G. J. Curphy (Chair), *The role of I-O psychology in executive assessment and development*. Symposium presented at the 15th annual meeting of the Society for Industrial and Organizational Psychology, New Orleans.

Hollenbeck, G.P., & McCall, M.W. (1999). Leadership development: Contemporary practices. In A. I. Kraut & A. K. Korman (Eds.), *Evolving practices in human resource management* (pp. 172–200). San Francisco: Jossey-Bass.

Houston, W. (2000, April). The impact of executive education on Vulcan's culture. In W. Casio (Chair), *Executive education as a vehicle for organizational change*. Symposium presented at the 15th annual meeting of the Society for Industrial and Organizational Psychology, New Orleans.

Ibarra, H. (2000). Making partner: The mentor's guide to the psychological journal. *Harvard Business Review, 78*(2), 146–155.

Ilgen, D. R., Fisher, C. D., & Taylor, M. S. (1979). Consequences of indivudal feedback on behavior in organizations. *Journal of Applied Psychology, 64*, 349–371.

Jeffrey, R.W., Wing, R.R., Thorson, C., & Burton, L.R. (1998). Use of personal trainers and financial incentives to increase exercise in a behavioral weight-loss program. *Journal of Consulting and Clinical Psychology, 66*, 777–783.

"Johnson & Johnson credo" (2000). http://www.j&j.com, accessed April 19.

Johnson, J. W., & Ferstl, K. L. (1999). The effects of interrater and self–other agreement on performance improvement following upward feedback. *Personnel Psychology, 52*, 271–303.

Johnson, J. W., Olson, A. M., & Courtney, C. L. (1996). Implementing multiple perspective feedback: An integrated framework. *Human Resource Management Review, 6*, 253–277.

Johnson, L. (1999). Emotional intelligence. *Executive Excellence, 16*(8), 10.

Jussim, L., Yen, H. J., & Aiello, J. R. (1995). Self-consistency, self-enhancement, and accuracy in reactions to feedback. *Journal of Experimental Social Psychology, 31*, 322–356.

Kaagan, S. S. (2000). *Leadership games: Experiential learning for organizational development*. Thousand Oaks, CA: Sage.

Kagan, J. (1989). *Unstable ideas: Temperament, cognition, and self*. Cambridge, MA: Harvard University Press.

Kaiser, R. B., & Kaplan, R. E. (2000, April). *Getting at leadership versatility: The case of the forceful and enabling polarity*. Paper presented at the 15th annual conference of the Society for Industrial and Organizational Psychology, New Orleans.

Kaplan, R. E. (1998). Getting at character: The simplicity on the other side of complexity. In R. Jeanneret & R. Silzer (Eds.), *Individual assessment: The art and science of personal psychological evaluation in an organizational setting* (pp. 178–227). San Francisco: Jossey-Bass.

Kaplan, R. S., & Norton, D. P. (1996). *The balanced scorecard: Translating strategy into action*. Boston: Harvard Business School.

Kaplan, S., & Smith, C. S. (2000, May 3). Adventure the Chinese way. *New York Times*, Wednesday, p. C8.

Kilburg, R. (2000). *Executive coaching: Developing managerial wisdom in a world of chaos*. Washington, DC: American Psychological Association.

Kilburg, R. R. (1996). Toward a conceptual understanding and definition of executive coaching. *Consulting Psychology Journal: Practice and Research, 48*(2), 134–144.

Kinlaw, D. (1996). *Coaching: The ASTD trainer's sourcebook*. New York: McGraw-Hill.

Kobasa, S. C. (1979). Stressful life events, personality, and health: An inquiry into hardiness. *Journal of Personality and Social Psychology, 37*, 1–11.

Kobasa, S. C., Maddi, S. R., & Kahn, S. (1982). Hardiness and health: A prospective study. *Journal of Personality and Social Psychology, 42*, 168–177.

Kotter, J. P. (1996). *Leading change.* Boston: Harvard Business School.

Kruger, J., & Dunning, D. (1999). Unskilled and unaware of it: How difficulties in recognizing one's own incompetence lead to inflated self-assessment. *Journal of Personality and Social Psychology, 77*(6), 1121–1134.

Kuhl, J., & Fuhrmann, A. (1998). Decomposing self-regulation and self-control: The volitional components inventory. In J. Heckhausen & C. S. Dweck (Eds.), *Motivation and self-regulation across the life span* (pp. 15–49). Cambridge, England: Cambridge University Press.

Landsberg, M. (1997). *The tao of coaching: Boost your effectiveness by inspiring those around you.* Santa Monica, CA: Knowledge Exchange.

Langer, E. J. (1992). Matters of mind: Mindfulness/mindlessness in perspective. *Consciousness & Cognition: An International Journal, 1,* 289–305.

Larson, J. R., Jr. (1984). The performance feedback process: A preliminary model. *Organizational Behavior and Human Performance, 33,* 42–76.

Larson, J. R., Jr. (1986). Supervisors' performance feedback to subordinates: The impact of subordinate performance valence and outcome dependence. *Organizational Behavior and Human Performance, 37,* 391–408.

Larson, J. R., Jr. (1988). The dynamic interplay between employees' feedback-seeking strategies and supervisors' delivery of performance feedback. *Academy of Management Review, 14,* 408–422.

Latack, J. C., Kinicki, A. J., & Prussia, G. E. (1995). An integrative process model fo coping with job loss. *Academy of Management Review, 20,* 311–342.

Latham, G. P., & Wesley, K. N. (1981). *Increasing productivity through performance appraisal.* Reading, MA: Addison-Wesley.

Lawler, W. (2000) The consortium approach to grooming future leaders. *Training & Development Magazine, 54*(3), 53+.

"Leadership development: Present challenges/future opportunities" (2000, June). Third annual Leadership Conference sponsored by the Conference Board and the Center for Creative Leadership, New York, *http://www.ccl.org.*

Leana, C. R., & Feldman, D. C. (1992). *Coping with job loss: How individuals, organizations, and communities respond to layoffs.* Lexington, MA: Lexington Books.

Leonhardt, D. (2000a, June 18). California dreamin': Harvard Business School adds Silicon Valley to its syllabus. *New York Times,* sect. 3, pp. 1, 16.

Leonhardt, D. (2000b, June 18). A little start-up gets a big push. *New York Times,* sect. 3, p. 16.

Lewis, P. (2000, May 22). William Segal, 95, publisher who painted self-portraits. *New York Times,* p. B7.

Lind, E. A., & Tyler, T. R. (1988). *The social psychology of procedural justice.* New York: Plenum.

Liu, S., & Vince, R. (1999). The cultural context of learning in international joint ventures. *Journal of Management Development, 18*(8), 666–675.

Locke, E. A, & Latham, G. P. (1990). *A theory of goal setting and task performance.* Englewood Cliffs, NJ: Prentice-Hall.

Logue, A. W. (1998). Laboratory research on self-control: Applications to administration. *Review of General Psychology, 2*(2), 221–238.

London, M. (1983). Toward a theory of career motivation. *Academy of Management Review, 8*(4), 620–630.

London, M. (1985). *Developing managers: A guide to motivating and preparing people for successful managerial careers.* San Francisco: Jossey-Bass.

London, M. (1988). *Change agents: New roles and innovation strategies for human resource professionals.* San Francisco, CA: Jossey-Bass.

London, M. (1993). Relationships between career motivation, empowerment, and support for career development. *Journal of Occupational and Organizational Psychology, 66,* 55–69.

London, M. (1994). Interpersonal insight in organizations: Cognitive models for human resource development. *Human Resource Management Review, 4,* 311–332.

London, M. (1995). *Self and interpersonal insight: How people learn about themselves and others in organizations.* New York: Oxford University Press.

London, M. (1997a). *Job feedback: Giving, seeking, and using feedback for performance improvement.* Hillsdale, NJ: Lawrence Erlbaum Associates.

London, M. (1997b). Overcoming career barriers: A model of cognitive and emotional processes for realistic appraisal and constructive coping. *Journal of Career Development, 24*(1), 25–38.

London, M. (1998). *Career barriers: How people experience, overcome, and avoid failure.* Hillsdale, NJ: Lawrence Erlbaum Associates.

London, M. (1999a). *Principled leadership and business diplomacy.* Westport, CT: Quorum.

London, M. (1999b). Principled leadership and business diplomacy: A practical, values-based direction for management development. *Journal of Management Development, 18*(2), 170–192.

London, M. (2001). The great debate: Should multisource feedback be used for administration or development only? In D. W. Bracken, C. W. Timmereck, & A. H. Church (Eds.), *The handbook of multisource feedback: The comprehensive resource for designing and implementing MSF processes* (pp. 368–388). San Francisco, CA: Jossey-Bass

London, M., & Mone, E. M. (1999). Continuous learning. In D. R. Ilgen & E. D. Pulakos (Eds.), *The changing nature of performance: Implications for staffing, motivation, and development* (pp. 119–153), San Francisco: Jossey-Bass.

London, M., & Noe, R. A. (1997). London's career motivation theory: An update on measurement and research. *Journal of Career Assessment, 5*(1), 61–80.

London, M., & Sessa, V. (1999). *Selection of international executives: An introduction and annotated bibliography* (Monograph). Greensboro, NC: Center for Creative Leadership.

London, M., & Smither, J. W. (1997, November 26). *Unpublished report to the United States Army—Special Operations Command—Psychological Applications Directorate on the Development and use of the military leader development measures.* Fort Bragg, NC.

London, M., & Smither, J. W. (1999a). Career-related continuous learning: Defining the construct and mapping the process. In G. R. Ferris (Ed.), *Research in Human Resources Management, 17,* 81–121.

London, M., & Smither, J. W. (1999b). Empowered self-development and continuous learning. *Human Resource Management, 38*(1), 3–16.

London, M., & Smither, J. W. (in press). Feedback orientation, feedback culture, and the longitudinal performance management process. *Human Resource Management Review.*

London, M., Smither, J. W., & Adsit, D. J. (1997). Accountability: The Achilles heel of multi-source feedback. *Group and Organization Management, 22,* 162–184.

London, M., Wohlers, A. J., & Gallagher, P. (1990). A feedback approach to management development. *Journal of Management Development, 9*(6), 17–31.

London, M., & Wueste, R. A. (1992). *Human resource development in changing organizations.* Westport, CT: Quorum.

Lubinski, D., & Benbow, C. P. (2000). States of excellence. *American Psychologist, 55*(1), 137–150.

Marsick, V. J. (2000). Learning organizations. In V. J. Marsick, J. Bitterman, & R. Van der Veen (Eds.), *From the learning organization to learning communities toward a learning society*

(Information Series No. 382). Columbus, OH: ERIC Clearinghouse on Adult, Career, and Vocational Education.

Marsiske, M., Lang, F. R., Baltes, P. B., & Baltes, M. M. (1995). Selective optimization with compensation: Life-span perspectives on successful human developmetn. In R. A. Dixon & L. Backman (Eds.), *Compensating for psychological deficits and decline: Managing losses and promoting gains* (pp. 35–79). Hillsdale, NJ: Lawrence Erlbaum Associates.

Maslow, A. H. (1968). *Toward a psychology of being.* Princeton, NJ: Van Nostrand.

Maurer, T. J., & Palmer, J. K. (1999). Management development intentions following feedback: Role of perceived outcomes, social pressures, and controls. *Journal of Management Development, 18*(9), 733–751.

Maxwell, J. C. (1999). *The 21 indispensable qualities of a leader: Becoming the person others will want to follow.* Surrey, England: Thomas Nelson.

McCall, M. W. (2000, April). Discussant remarks. In D. V. Day (Chair), *Systemic leadership development: Conceptual models and best practices.* Symposium presented at the 15th annual meeting of the Society for Industrial and Organizational Psychology, New Orleans.

McCall, M. W., Jr. (1998). *High flyers: Developing the next generation of leaders.* Boston: Harvard Business School Press.

McCauley, C. D. (2000a, April). A systemic approach to leadership development. In D. V. Day (Chair), *Systemic leadership development: Conceptual models and best practices.* Symposium presented at the 15th annual meeting of the Society for Industrial and Organizational Psychology, New Orleans.

McCauley, C. D. (2000b, April). Using 360-degree feedback to enhance self-understanding. In L. E. Atwater (Chair), *Beyond 360-degrees: Contextual considerations in personnel development.* Symposium presented at the 15th annual conference of the Society for Industrial and Organizational Psychology, New Orleans.

McCauley, C. D., Van Velsor, E. V., & Moxley, R. S. (1998). *The Center for Creative leadership handbook of leadership development.* San Francisco: Jossey-Bass.

McHenry, J. J. (2000, April). Leadership 2000: A framework for leadership development at Microsoft. In D. V. Day (Chair), *Systemic leadership development: Conceptual models and best practices.* Symposium presented at the 15th annual meeting of the Society for Industrial and Organizational Psychology, New Orleans.

McMillen, S. (2000, June). *Using web technology to deliver integrated leadership development.* Paper presented at the 3rd annual Leadership Development Conference, "Leadership development: Present challenges/future opportunities" sponsored by the Conference Board and the Center for Creative Leadership, New York.

Meyer, H. H. (1991). A solution to the performance appraisal feedback enigma. *Academy of Management Executive, 5*(1), 68–76.

Milanovich, D., Smith-Jentsch, K. A., Buff, W. L., & Campbell, G. E. (2000, April). Guided team self-correction: A strategy for structured peer mentoring. In K. A. Smith-Jentsch (Chair), *Theory-based approaches to improving the practice of mentoring in organizations.* Presented at the 15th annual meeting of the Society for Industrial and Organizational Psychology, New Orleans.

Miller, D. T. (1999). The norm of self-interest. *American Psychologist, 54*(12), 1053–1060.

Mintzberg, H. (1973). *The nature of managerial work.* New York: Harper & Row.

Mitchell, T. R., & Beach, L. R. (1990). "… Do I love thee? Let me count …" Toward an understanding of intuitive and automatic decision making. *Organizational Behavior and Human Decision Processes, 47,* 1–20.

Mobley, W. H. (2000). Colonials, compasses, competencies along the silk road: Derailment in Asia. In G. P. Hollenbeck (Chair), *Yesterday's heroes: The derailment of international exec-*

utives. Symposium presented at the 15th annual meeting of the Society for Industrial and Organizational Psychology.

Mohr, D. C. (1995). Negative outcomes in psychotherapy: A critical review. *Clinical Psychology: Science and Practice, 2*(1), 1–27.

Mone, E.M. (1988). Training managers to be developers. In M. London & E. Mone (Eds.), *Career growth and human resource strategies* (pp. 207–222). New York: Quorum Books.

Moxley, R. S. (2000). *Leadership & spirit: Breathing new vitality and energy into individuals and organizations*. San Francisco: Jossey-Bass.

Murphy, E. C. (1996). *Leadership IQ: A personal development process based on scientific study of a new generation of leaders*. New York: Wiley.

Nadler, D. A. (1979). The effects of feedback on task group behavior: A review of the experimental research. *Organizational Behavior and Human Performance, 23*, 309–338.

Napolitano, C. S., & Henderson, L. J. (1997). *The leadership odyssey: A self-development guide to new skills for new times*. San Francisco: Jossey-Bass.

Nease, A. A., Mudgett, B. O., & Quinones, M. A. (1999). Relationships among feedback sign, self-efficacy, and acceptance of performance feedback. *Journal of Applied Psychology, 84*(5), 806–814.

Newcomb, T. M. (1961). *The acquaintance process*. New York: Holt, Rinehart & Winston.

Nonaka, I. (1994). A dynamic theory of organizational knowledge creation. *Organization Science, 5*(1), 14–36.

Nonaka, I., & Takeuchi, H. (1995). *The knowledge-creating company*. New York: Oxford University Press.

Pearce, J. L., & Porter, L. W. (1986). Employee responses to formal performance appraisal feedback. *Journal of Applied Psychology, 71*, 211–218.

Perkins, D.N.T., Holtman, M. P., & McCarthy, C. (2000). *Leading at the edge: Leadership lessons from the limits of human endurance. The extraordinary saga of Shackleton's Antarctic expedition*. New York: AMACOM.

Peterson, D. B. (1996). Executive coaching at work: The art of one-on-one change. *Consulting Psychology Journal: Practice and Research, 48*(2), 78–86.

Pfeffer, J., & Sutton, R. I. (2000). *The knowing-doing gap: How smart companies turn knowledge into action*. Boston : Harvard Business School Press.

Pliske, R. M., Crandall, B. W., Green, S. L., & Zsambok, C. E. (2000, April). The collaborative development of expertise (CDE): A training program for mentors. In K. A. Smith-Jentsch (Chair), *Theory-based approaches to improving the practice of mentoring in organizations*. Presented at the 15th annual meeting of the Society for Industrial and Organizational Psychology, New Orleans.

Podsakof, P. M., & Farh, J. L. (1989). Effects of feedback sign and credibility on goal setting and task performance. *Organizational Behavior and Human Decision Processes, 44*, 45–67.

Quick, J. C., Garvin, J. H., Cooper, C. L., & Quick, J. D. (2000). Executive health: Building strength, managing risks. *Academy of Management Executive, 14*(2), 34–43.

Reich, R. B. (2000, July 11). One education does not fit all. *New York Times*, Tuesday, p. A25.

Reilly, R. R., Smither, J. W., & Vasilopoulos, N. L. (1996). A longitudinal study of upward feedback. *Personnel Psychology, 49*, 599–612.

Rhodewalt, F. (1990). Self-handicappers: Individual differences in the preference for anticipatory self-protective acts. In R. L. Higgins, C. R. Snyder, & S. Bergals (Eds.), *Self-handicapping: The paradox that isn't* (pp. 69–106). New York: Plenum.

Rhodewalt, F. (1998). Self-presentation and the phenomenal self: The "carryover effect" revisited. In E. E. Jones, J. Cooper, & J. M. Darley (Eds.), *Attribution and social interaction: The legacy of Edward E. Jones* (pp. 373–398). Washington, DC: American Psychological Association.

Rogers, C. R. (1980). *A way of being.* Boston: Houghton Mifflin.

Ross, A. O. (1992). *The sense of self: Research and theory.* New York: Springer.

Ross, L., Greene, D., & House, P. (1977). The false consensus effect: An egocentric bias in social perception and attributional processes. *Journal of Experimental Social Psychology, 13,* 279–301.

Rothwell, W. J., & Kazanas, H. C. (1999). *Building in-house leadership and management development programs: Their creation, management, and continuous improvement.* Westport, CT: Greenwood.

Ryan, R. M., & Deci, E. L. (2000). Self-determination theory and the facilitation of intrinsic motivation, social development, and well-being. *American Psychologist, 55*(1), 68–78.

Sanchez, J. I., Spector, P. E., & Cooper, C. L. (2000). Adapting to a boundaryless world: A developmental expatriate model. *Academy of Management Executive, 14*(2), 96–106.

Saner, R., Yiu, L., & Sondergaard, M. (2000). Business diplomacy management: A core competency for global companies. *Academy of Management Executive, 14*(1), 80–91.

Saporito, T. J. (1996). Business-linked executive development: Coaching senior executives. *Consulting Psychology Journal: Practice and Research, 48*(2), 96–103.

Schein, E. H. (1978). *Career dynamics: Matching individual and organizational needs.* Reading, MA: Addison-Wesley.

Schlenker, B. R., & Trudeau, J. V. (1990). Impact of self-presentations on private self-beliefs. *Journal of Personality and Social Psychology, 58,* 22–32.

Schön, D. A. (1983). *The reflective practitioner: How professionals think in action.* New York: Basic Books.

Schrauger, J. S. (1975). Responses to evaluation as a function of initial self-perceptions. *Psychological Bulletin, 82*(4), 581–596.

Senge, P. (1990). *The fifth discipline: The art & practice of the learning organization.* New York: Doubleday Currency.

Siegler, R. S. (2000). Unconscious insights. *Current Directions in Psychological Science, 9*(3), 79–82.

Silverman, S. B. (1991). Individual development through performance appraisal. K. N. Wexley (Ed.), *Developing human resources.* Washington, DC: The Bureau of National Affairs, Inc., pp. 120–151.

Simon, S. A., & Eby, L. T. (2000, April). A typology of negative mentoring experiences: A multidimensional scaling study. In T. D. Allen (Chair), *Effective mentoring relationships: From dysfunctional to functional and everything in between.* Symposium presented at the 15th annual meeting of the Society for Industrial and Organizational Psychology, New Orleans.

Simonton, D. K. (2000). Creativity: Cognitive, personal, developmental, and social aspects. *American Psychologist, 55*(1), 151–158.

Siwolop, S. (2000, May 10). Breaking out of the back room: Chief information officers get new respect and power. *New York Times,* Wednesday, p. C6.

Small, M. W., & Dickie, L. (1999). A cinematograph of moral principles: Critical values for contemporary business and society. *Journal of Management Development, 18*(7), 628–638.

Smither, J. W., London, M., Vasilopoulos, N. L., Reilly, R. R., Millsap, R. E., & Salvemini, N. (1995). An examination of the effects of an upward feedback program over time. *Personnel Psychology, 48,* 1–34.

Smither, J. W., & Reilly, S. P. (2001). Coaching in organizations. In M. London (Ed.), *How people evaluate others in organizations: Person perception and interpersonal judgment in I/O psychology* (pp. 221–252). Hillsdale, NJ: Lawrence Erlbaum Associates.

Smith-Jentsch, K. A., Milanovich, D., Reynolds, A. M., Merket, D. C., & Eddy, E. R. (2000, April). An investigation of the unique effects of peer and traditional mentoring. In K. A.

Smith-Jentsch (Chair), *Theory-based approaches to improving the practice of mentoring in organizations.* Presented at the 15th annual meeting of the Society for Industrial and Organizational Psychology, New Orleans.

Snarey, J. R., & Vaillant, G. E. (1985). How lower- and working-class youth become middle-class adults: The association between ego defense mechanisms and upward social mobility. *Child Development, 56*(4), 899–910.

Snyder, M. (1974). Self-monitoring of expressive behavior. *Journal of Personality and Social Psychology, 30,* 526–537.

Snyder, M. (1987). *Public appearances, private realities: The psychology of self-monitoring.* New York: Freeman.

Solomon, R. C. (1999). *A better way to think about business: How personal integrity leads to corporate success.* New York: Oxford University Press.

Sorkin, A. R. (2000, June 21). Melding of cultures the next step in Seagram deal. *New York Times,* pp. C1, C8.

Stajkovic, A. D., & Luthans, F. (1998). Self-efficacy and work-related performance: A meta-analysis. *Journal of Applied Psychology, 124*(2), 240–261.

Staw, B. M. (1976). Knee-deep in the big muddy: A study of excalating commitment to a chosen course of action. *Organizational Behavior and Human Decision Processes, 16*(1), 27–44.

Sternberg, R. J. (1985). *Beyond IQ: A triarchic theory of human intelligence.* New York: Cambridge University Press.

Stone, D., & Stone, E. (1985). The effects of feedback consistency and feedback favorability on self-perceived task competence and perceived feedback accuracy. *Organizational Behavior and Human Decision Processes, 36,* 167–185.

Swann, W. B. (1983). Self-verification: Bringing social reality into harmony with the self. In J. Suls & A. G. Greenwald (Eds.), *Psychological perspectives on the self* (Vol. 2, pp. 33–66). Hillsdale, NJ: Lawrence Erlbaum Associates.

Swann, W. B. (1987). Identity negotiation: Where two roads meet. *Journal of Personality and Social Psychology, 53,* 1038–1051.

Tesser, A. (1988). Toward a self-evaluation maintenance model fo social behavior. In L. Berkowitz (Ed.), *Advances in experimental social psychology* (Vol. 21, pp. 181–227). New York: Academic Press.

Thibaut, J., & Walker, L. (1975). *Procedural justice: A psychological analysis.* Hillsdale, NJ: Lawrence Erlbaum Associates.

Thornton, G.C.I., & Byham, W. C. (1982). *Assessment centers and managerial performance.* New York: Academic Press.

Tice, D. (1991). Esteem protection or enhancement: Self-handicapping motives and attributions differ by trait self-esteem. *Journal of Personality and Social Psychology, 60,* 711–725.

Tichy, N., & Charan, R. (1995, March–April). The CEO as coach: An interview with Allied Signal's Lawrence A. Bossidy. *Harvard Business Review,* pp. 68–78.

Tichy, N. M., & Devanna, M. A. (1997). *The transformational leader: The key to global competitiveness.* New York: Wiley.

Tornow, W., & London, M. (Eds.). (1998). *Maximizing the value of 360-degree feedback: A process for successful individual and organizational development.* San Francisco, CA: Jossey-Bass.

Tsui, A. S., Ashford, S. J., St. Clair, L., & Xin, K. R. (1995). Dealing with discrepant expectations: Response strategies and managerial effectiveness. *Academy of Management Journal, 38,* 1515–1543.

Tyler, K. (2000). Scoring big in the workplace: Corporate coaches help managers produce the right plays on the job. *Human Resource Magazine, 45*(6), 96–109.

Vanderbeck, S. (2000, May 10). The boss: How I cured my boredom. *New York Times*, Wednesday, p. C6.

Van-Dijk, D., & Kluger, A. N. (2000, April). *Positive (negative) feedback: Encouragement or discouragement?* Paper presented at the 15th annual meeting of the Society for Industrial and Organizational Psychology, New Orleans.

Vicere, A. A., & Fulmer, R. M. (1998). *Leadership by design: How benchmark companies sustain success through investment in continuous learning.* Boston: Harvard Business School Press.

Waldroop, J., & Butler, T. (1996, November–December). The executive as coach. *Harvard Business Review*, pp. 111–117.

Walker, A. G., & Smither, J. W. (1999). A five-year study of upward feedback: What managers do with their results matters. *Personnel Psychology, 52*, 393–423.

Wallington, P. M. (2000). Inspiring minds. *CIO On-Line Magazine*, http://www.cio.com, June 9.

Watkins, R. G., & Marsick, V. J. (1996). *In action: Creating the learning organization.* Alexandria, VA: American Society for Training and Development.

Weinberger, J. (1995). Common factors aren't so common: The common factors dilemma. *Clinical Psychology: Science and Practice, 2*(1), 45–69.

Weisband, S., & Atwater, L. E. (1999). Evaluating self and others in electronic and face-to-face groups. *Journal of Applied Psychology, 84*(4), 632–639.

Wheatley, M. (2000). ERP training stinks. *CIO On-Line Magazine*, http://www.cio.com, June 1.

Whetten, D.A., & Cameron, K.S. (1998). *Developing management skills.* New York: Addison-Wesley.

White, R. W. (1959). Motivation reconsidered: The concept of competence. *Psychological Review, 66*, 297–333.

Wilkes, S. B., Nellen, V. C., & DelCarmen, J. D. (2000, April). *From insight to action: Strengthening development after delivery of 360 feedback.* Paper presented at the 15th annual meeting of the Society for Industrial and Organizational Psychology, New Orleans.

Williams, J. R., & Johnson, M. A. (2000). Self–supervisor agreement: The influence of feedback seeking on the relationship between self and supervisor ratings of performance. *Journal of Applied Social Psychology, 30*(2), 275–292.

Williams, J. R., & Lueke, S. B. (1999). 360° Feedback system effectiveness: Test of a model in a field setting. *Journal of Quality Management, 4*(1), 23–49.

Williams, J. R., Miller, C. E., Steelman, L. A., & Levy, P. E. (1999). Increasing feedback seeking in public contexts: It takes two (or more) to tango. *Journal of Applied Psychology, 84*(6), 969–976.

Witherspoon, R., & White, R. P. (1997). *Four essential ways that coaching can help executives.* Greensboro, NC: Center for Creative Leadership.

Wohlers, A. J., & London, M. (1989). Ratings of managerial characteristics: Evaluation difficulty, coworker agreement, and self-awareness. *Personnel Psychology, 42*, 235–249.

Yammarino, F. J., & Atwater, L. E. (1997). Do managers see themselves as others see them? Implications of self-other rating agreement for human resources management. *Organization Dynamics*, Spring, 35–44.

Yearout, S., Miles, G., & Koonce, R. (2000). Wanted: Leader-builders. *Training and Development Magazine, 54*(3), 34–46.

Yukl, G. (1997). *Leadership in organizations.* New York: Simon & Schuster.

Zenger, J., Ulrich, D., & Smallwood, N. (2000). The new leadership development. *Training & Development Magazine, 54*(3), 22–28.

AUTHOR INDEX

A

Abueva, J. E., 200, 201, 269
Adams, S. M., 126, 272
Adler, M., 229, 230, 271
Adsit, D. J., 142, 143, 144, 145, 277
Aiello, J. R., 94, 130, 275
Ajzen, I., 65, 269
Albano, C., 10, 269
Albert, R. D., 203, 269
Allen, T. D., 280
Allport, G. W., 236, 269
Altemeyer, B., 238, 243, 269
Amabile, T. M., 263, 269
Anderson, L. R., 39, 269
Andrews, F., 9. 10, 249, 269
Anteri, E., 198, 169
Antonioni, D., 146, 269
Arenson, K. W., 211, 259
Arkin, R. M., 74, 269
Ashford, S., 47, 75, 126, 147, 220, 269, 281
Atwater, D., 142, 150, 151, 270
Atwater, L. E., 41, 42, 45, 46, 47, 48, 141, 142, 145, 150, 151, 269, 270, 278, 282
Avolio, B. J., 7, 8, 270

B

Backman, L., 278
Baliga, H. R., 270
Baltes, M. M., 89, 278
Baltes, P. B., 89, 264, 265, 270, 278
Bandura, A., 71, 72, 77, 128, 149, 250, 270
Barboza, D., 30, 270
Barron, F., 123, 228, 272
Bartz, D. E., 122, 173, 274
Bass, B. M., 7, 8, 270
Bassett, G. A., 146, 270
Baumeister, R. F., 59, 63, 87, 270, 273

Beach, L. R., 36, 279, 278
Beatty, K. M., 6, 274
Becker, B. E., 197, 274
Beckman, L. 278
Beckmann, J., 273
Beizer, B., 186, 270
Bem, D. J., 87, 270
Benbow, C. P., 237, 277
Benedict, M. E., 122, 270
Berenson, A., 9, 270
Bergals, S., 279
Berke, R. L., 86, 270
Berkowitz, L., 270
Bernardin, J. H., 141, 271
Berrell, M., 204, 205, 271
Bhagat, R. S., 224, 225, 26, 271, 272
Bitterman, J., 277
Block, J., 65, 273
Bostrom, R. P., 187, 272
Brewer, G., 277
Brockner, J., 146, 271
Brunstein, J. C., 88, 271
Bruskiewicz, K. T., 53, 273
Brutus, S., 150, 151, 271
Buff, W. L., 189, 278
Burton, L.R., 178, 275
Butler, T., 165, 177, 181, 282
Byham, W. C., 196, 228, 271, 281

C

Cameron, K.S., 175, 176, 179, 282
Campbell, G. E., 189, 278
Cartier, P., 142, 150, 151, 270
Casio, W., 275
Charan, R., 165, 281
Cherniss, C., 227, 228, 229, 271
Cheung, G., 43, 44, 46, 271
Child, J., 250, 271
Conner, J., 199, 271
Church, A. H., 276
Cooper, C. L., 202, 261, 274, 279, 280

SUBJECT INDEX